Southwestern Gardener

By

Dewey P. Compton

Gulf Coast Press

1967

Library of Congress Catalog Card Number 61-17660

Gulf Coast Press; No. 201; 6800 Main, Houston, Texas

Printed by Capital Printing Co., Inc., Austin, Texas

AUTHOR'S PREFACE TO FIRST EDITION

TO THOSE WHO LOVE AND ENJOY GARDENING

As I end the writing of this book dedicated to people who love and enjoy gardening in the Southwest, please let me beg your indulgence for probable sins of commission and omission. My ultimate endeavor in this venture is to supply you with timely up to date information pertaining to current cultural practices, new and adapted varieties, insect and disease control, shrubs and trees that you wish to grow in your garden. My endeavor is to compile this information in a manner that will be easily assimilated and understood, so written that the average gardener can readily digest any part of it and put it into practice.

I realize that this as well as any book on gardening is never complete. For as a famous man once said, "Nothing is as constant as change." This is especially true with things that deal with nature. There are so many variables involved when contending with problems of different soils, climatic conditions, etc., that it is humanly impossible to make concrete, concise, authoritative statements to all problems. This in a sense is the mystery and intrigue that overwhelms most gardeners—making a plant or shrub to grow, blossom and bring forth its fruit in an unfriendly atmosphere, complicated with numerous problems. Indeed, when we work in the garden we are close to God. "The Kiss of the Sun for Pardon,

> The Song of the Birds for Mirth.
> We are Closer to God's Heart in a Garden
> Than Anywhere Else on Earth."

This book has been laid out in 10 chapters dealing with all phases of gardening. Each chapter is a short book on a specific segment of gardening and can be used as a reference whenever problems arise or knowledge of the subject is sought. The last chapter has no direct relationship to the other nine chapters, but in a sense has questions answered in it that revolve around all nine chapters. These questions are a composite of the thousands of questions asked me each year as a result of the Garden Programs conducted on radio programs. Since they have been posed by a large segment of a rather broad listening audience and represent several years of broadcasting, I felt compelled to include them in this book.

I also realize that all problems are not answered nor is a thorough coverage of all garden subjects included in this book. This is impossible since gardening is a broad subject and libraries have been written about it. Always something is left out.

I hope this book furnishes you with a great deal of assistance in dealing with gardening problems in the Southwest. As Longfellow wrote:

> "In all places, and all Seasons,
> Flowers expand their light and soul-like wings
> Teaching us by most persuasive reasons,
> How akin they are to Human beings."

DEWEY P. COMPTON

September, 1961

iii

PREFACE TO SECOND EDITION

Gardens and gardening continually change. Now that the rewriting is over, I'm amazed at all the new material that had to be included, at all the new developments that have occurred in the six years since the first edition.

You'll find the newest insecticides included and the latest information on how to use the old ones. There's a section on new turf grasses especially adapted to the Southwest. Of course, the fabulous Medina had to be treated at length as well as the exotic plants like aloe vera.

I hope you like it.

DEWEY COMPTON

September, 1967

Table of Contents

Chapter 1

Soils and Problems

Soils are a primary requirement for gardening. An understanding of soils and the problems that they present are of great importance to any gardener. As one soil scientist put it, "Soil is important only from the standpoint that it furnishes support for the growing plant," but, in obtaining this support through root growth, many problems confront the gardener.

"The main part of any soil is usually composed of ground up or broken down rock, and the nature of the soil is directly related to the rock from which it was made. Some soils are made of only one kind of rock, but generally soils consist of several kinds of rock, thus a mixture is most prominent."

Any given soil is made of different size soil particles. Those which make up a clay soil are fine and have a tendency to fuse together. Or, as one might put it, to compact. Sandy soils are open and porous because they are made up of rather large particles. Clay soils and sandy soils represent two distinct different types, and in between the two are many different soil types.

In the Southwest most soils are of a clay or sand nature, being given such names as Lake Charles Clay; Beaumont Clay, etc. Along with the clay, sand and silt particles, other elements are often times found in varying quantities within the soil structure. The elements are essential to plant and animal life, but if present to an extreme they can cause difficulty . . . difficulty, of course, often times results in plants dying. Such elements found in our Southwest soils that interfere with plant growth and normal functioning are: sodium, calcium, soluble salts and other elements.

While the main portion of a soil is usually composed of sand or clay, silt, clay and sand mixed together, it cannot be considered fertile unless the remains of plant and animal residue are present. This part of the soil is commonly referred to as organic matter, and it is generally true that the fertility of any ordinary soil is in direct proportion to the organic matter it contains. Soils that are excessively high in organic matter, though, will not always grow the best plants. These type soils often times are low in mineral materials so vital for plant growth. Unless they are added, production will be disappointing. Potash and Phosphoric acid are most frequently needed and should be added. Manganese, copper, iron and other elements also may be helpful. Basically speaking, organic matter is sorely needed in most soils throughout the Southwest and the addition of it to a soil will pay big dividends.

1

Humus

Organic matter is any plant or animal material that is added to the soil. As the organic material decays in the soil, humus is produced. This is a very complex material, brown or black in color, and light in weight in proportion to its bulk. Humus is extremely valuable in a soil, and the major difference between a poor and a fertile soil usually lies in the humus content and not in the mineral part of it. Humus is very rich in nitrogen. It may contain from three to 10 or 12%, and as it breaks down this is released for use by the plants.

Humus has a distinct benefit on the physical make-up of the soil. It is characteristic of a clay soil—such as those in the Southwest—that they are very close, solid and compact. Water and air, and even roots of plants do not enter readily or easily. The addition of organic matter into such soil will improve such difficult conditions. Its sticky, compact nature broken up and changed, it becomes open and crumbly—making it easier to work and better material in which to grow plants.

As a contrast to this, a sandy soil is porous and unable to hold moisture or plant food solution. It leaches out readily, the soils are generally poor. But, organic matter added to the soil acts as a sponge, thus helping to hold the water and plant food nutrients for the plant to utilize. Regardless of how poor a soil might be, there is a beehive of activity going on all the time. The workmen in the soil are called micro-organisms and they are constantly working over and breaking down various materials in the soil that go to make plant food. The number of these workmen are generally in direct ratio to the organic matter present in the soil. They are constantly working on the cellulose and fibrous material, breaking it down into humus and plant food nutrients. These little workmen must have a high diet of nitrogen, they steal it from the soil solution to the detriment of plant life. They must have an ample supply of it at all times to convert the organic matter into humus. Therefore, it is a wise practice to add nitrogen fertilizer to organic matter—be it plowed or spaded into the soil, unless you have a soil already high in available nitrogen. Thus it will pay to add nitrogen at the time of plowdown or spading in of organic matter.

Humus is made from the remains of plants and animals, and this of course is the tip off as to the source from where the supply can be obtained. Animal manure—cattle, horses and poultry—furnishes an excellent source of organic material. Leaves, twigs, the prunings from trees, the clippings from the lawn, sawdust, shavings—are all excellent sources of organic materials. It is also a good practice never to burn the residue of grass, weeds or plants, but turn them back into the soil also. But, remember, to hasten decomposition the addition of nitrogen will certainly help.

It seems to be a misconception of a lot of people that once the humus content of the soil is increased, and there is ample in the soil, that it remains there indefinitely. In the Southwest, due to high temperatures, heavy rainfall and other factors, the destruction of vegetative matters proceeds very rapidly in the soil, much faster than in northern climates where the earth is frozen several months of the year. The breakdown of organic matters goes on all the time in the Southwest, and unless organic matter is added from time to time, the supply will gradually be exhausted and the soil becomes non-productive. A large percentage of our garden problems can be solved or arrested if a proper level of organic matter is maintained in our soils.

Soil pH or Reaction

Soil reaction has a great deal to do with the way plants thrive, therefore a thorough understanding of this subject is vital and basic to successful gardening.

Based on their chemical reactions, soils are divided into three groups; acid, neutral and alkaline—sometime referred to as basic. In other coloquial terms an acid soil is often times referred to as a "sour soil," while an alkaline soil is referred to as a "sweet soil."

In order to simplify the soil reaction, chemists have made up an arbitrary scale, graduated from zero to fourteen. On this scale, number 7 is the neutral point where acidity and alkalinity are in balance. Below the figure 7 the reaction is called acid, with the lower the number indicating a greater degree of acidity. While those numbers up from 7 on the pH scale, the soil is considered alkaline, and as you go up from 7 toward 10 and 12—the degree of alkalinity increases. The diagram below will illustrate this point.

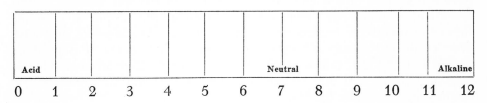

| Acid | | | | | | Neutral | | | | Alkaline |
| 0 | 1 | 2 | 3 | 4 | 5 | 6 | 7 | 8 | 9 | 10 | 11 | 12 |

Although pH does not add plant food to the soil, it nevertheless has a great deal to do with the availability of what is there. Adjustment of the pH to different levels affects the intake of food nutrients that a plant gets, but actually adds nothing to the total of what the soil contains. Adjustment of the pH also aids in the percentage of available nutrients and elements that are essential for profitable plant growth. For example: a high reading on a pH scale generally designates an excessive amount of calcium or lime, and generally with this condition being present there is a tie up of both iron and phosphorus, making

3

them unavailable to the plant. Thus the plant shows definite signs of a deficiency existing for these two compounds. But addition of a specific material to reduce the pH makes the soil more acid; therefore these elements become more available to the plant.

Through research, scientists have established a pH range within which plants grow. Some plants have a broader range on the pH scale in which they will thrive and grow. Others are rather restricted and require a soil reaction that is set and specific, otherwise they will not produce. But every plant, tree and shrub that is grown in the world today has a set range on the pH scale in which it will thrive and perform.

For such crops as alfalfa, clovers, etc., lime is of value and essential. But by far most vegetables and ornamental species in which gardeners in the Southwest are interested, require an acid soil. Excessive lime is distinctly injurious to them.

Plants differ in the amount of soil acidity required. Some, as azaleas and camellias, require a high degree of acidity, while others such as holly, violets, roses and many ferns do best in less acid soils. To some plants the degree of soil reaction, unless in the extremes, show an indifference to the pH. Some plants change the color of their flowers as the soil reaction changes from one range to another. Certain varieties of hydrangeas have blue flowers when grown in an acid soil. The flowers change to pastel shades when grown in soils showing a weak acid reaction, and they are pink when they are grown in soils that show a high alkaline reaction. Therefore, due to the nature of the soil reaction or pH of our Southwestern soils it is practically a mandate that in order to do a good job of gardening, some additives are essential in order to bring the pH into the range needed for maximum production.

The acidity of soils may be increased to a certain degree by securing acid peat or mulch from marshes and working it into the soil. The addition of certain organic materials such as animal waste products will not only make the soil more acid, but the organic material added will also be of utmost benefit. The application of chemical fertilizers, whose manufacturer calls for acid, will also tend to acidify the soils.

Soils may also be made more acid by adding sulfur, aluminum sulfate, iron sulfate, or iron chelates. The best form of sulfur to use is agricultural sulfur. Sulfur is slow reacting in the soil but very effective if given time. As a rule of thumb, it has been found that $1\frac{1}{2}$ pounds of sulfur, or three pounds of aluminum sulfate or iron sulfate—applied to 100 square feet of ground is generally sufficient enough to lower the soil reaction from a pH of 6.5 to 6.0. When treating areas around plants that show definite sign of adverse effect of pH in extreme, the best plan to follow is to apply two to four ounces of sulfur, aluminum or iron sulfate to a square yard of surface about the plants. Repeat this operation about every two to three weeks if necessary until symptoms apparent in the plant disappear. Normally the yellowing of chlorotic conditions of the leaves will disappear, and the leaves will return to a normal green again.

Acids and Acid Soils

Where the underlying rocks are quartz, granite, mica, sandstone shale or slate, the soil above is usually acid, though sometimes shales and sandstones are neutral or moderately alkaline instead.

The soils above limestone, marble or serpentine, on the contrary, is nearly always alkaline. Where drinking water from shallow wells is hard, expect the soil nearby to be alkaline. If this hard water is used in sprinkling it may injure acid soil plants. The soil condition may be roughly guessed at from the kind of plants which grow naturally upon it. Where acid soil plants predominate, look for acid soil; while alkaline plants indicate a soil alkalinity. It is often said that where you find sheep sorrel the soil is acid, but this weed is not a reliable indicator.

Swamps are usually acid unless surrounded by limestone land, and poor sandy soils are often acid, also peat or muck soil.

To decide definitely whether a soil is acid, neutral or alkaline— samples should be tested by a reliable Soil Testing Laboratory, such as the one at Texas A&M and also at the Wharton Junior College, in order to determine the pH of the soil.

It is not known for certain whether the demand of acid soil plants is for acidity or for other soil conditions which go along with this characteristic. Until this important question has been decided, neutral acid materials such as those just specified earlier should be supplied to the soil, rather than a true acid itself.

There are a number of plants that demand and must have an acid soil for maximum production. Lists of plants requiring acid soils have been published from time to time, but are often contradictory. Most plants grow equally well in neutral, mildly alkaline or mildly acid soils—ranging from 6 to 8 on the pH scale, even sometimes spreads as wide as 5 to 9. With these we are not too particularly concerned. Real acid soil plants prefer a soil that tests not over 6.5 and thrive best at a pH of 4 to 6. Acidity below pH 4 is too extreme even for most acid loving plants. Plants which seem to need a decidedly acid soil include:

azalea	flax	leather leaf	radishes
blackberry	hemlock	lupine	raspberry
blueberry	spruce	lily	rhododendron
chrysanthemum	hickory	magnolia	sweet fern
cranberry	huckleberry	oak	spice bush
fir	lady slipper	pine	wintergreen

Most extreme in their demand for an acid soil and most frequently damaged or injured by alkalinity are plants of the Heath family, especially azaleas. Injury often follows their use as a foundation

5

planting material. House builders are likely to throw at the base of the wall and cover with earth pieces of lime, concrete, mortar, stucco and plaster, all of which are poisonous to acid soil plants. Even evergreen of the Pine family, most of which prefer mildly acid soil, are often harmed and sometimes killed by such alkaline material. Consequently, before planting any acid soil plant near the foundation of a home, dig out all filled earth and either reject it or screen it to remove the debris. If the wall is concrete, stucco, brick or stone with mortar joints, the drip from it will cause the soil close by to become gradually alkaline. To prevent this, keep the plant well forward from the wall and use peat moss or leaf mold frequently, and also work into the soil quite often some soil sulfur.

Signs of alkaline poisoning in acid soil plants are drooping, yellowing and falling of the leaves, lack of root development, poor health—otherwise not explainable—and a condition known as chlorosis; whereby there is a deficiency of iron and the color of the leaf actually leaches out.

Remember—always use fertilizers known to contribute to the acidity. Most chemical fertilizers that have been made with a sulfuric acid will certainly contribute to the acidity of the soil, and these should be used on high alkaline soils by all means. Fertilizers that contain great amounts of rock phosphate should never be used because they themselves will never have an opportunity to perform because the alkalinity will neutralize the formation of phosphoric acid and the plant will not only suffer from the lack of acidity, but also will starve from a phosphate deficiency as well.

Alkaline Soil

Alkaline soil is just the opposite of an acid soil and is usually found in limestone country or along the Texas Gulf Coast where deposits of oyster shell and limestone are natural. Extreme alkalinity as found in Western Badlands is injurious to most plants. It follows lack of enough rain to wash away the alkali salts—and long continued irrigation with hard water, evaporation of which leaves a constantly increasing accumulation in the soil. In most instances a mild alkaline soil is to the gardener's advantage, except where certain strongly acid loving plants are to be grown. In fact, it has been a long time custom to add lime to cultivated land in order to obtain better efficiency from the plant food nutrients applied. This is especially true in the acid soils of East Texas. Much of such benefits comes from changes in soil texture and release of mineral foods, but there is also an increase in pH readings as the acid soil is made neutral or alkaline.

Old exhausted soil is usually acid, and here lime is particularly valuable to increase fertility. Sometimes the soil is acid because it is not well drained, in which case ditching or under draining will help to neutralize the acidity. Moderately alkaline soil favors the growth and productiveness of many garden plants, while others prefer acidity or are apparently indifferent. Therefore, it is of great importance that the gardener find out what the pH is of his soil and then to determine what plants will respond best on the type of soil he has and to try to grow these plants.

Clovers and other members of the Pea family usually require an alkaline soil to aid the nitrogen selecting bacteria on their roots to fix nitrogen. The following list of plants may become stunted, sickly yellow, or reddish in highly acid soil:

asparagus	cauliflower	parsnips
beans	celery	peas
beets	cucumber	phlox
cabbage	iris	rhubarb
carnation	lettuce	squash
cantaloup	onions	sweet peas

To neutralize soil, if one has a soil that is extremely high in acidity, the application of lime or gypsum will fulfill this requirement.

Gypsum

A number of gardeners are confused as to the use and the terminology of gypsum. This material, known also as land plaster, is chemically sulfate of lime. It contains some 23% of calcium oxide and was formerly considered a satisfactory source of lime for soil. As a matter of fact, it does serve to liberate unavailable potash and in general improve a soil's texture tilth. But owing to its sulfur content, it tends to make soil acid and therefore has just the opposite effect of limestone or any of the carbonate forms of lime. Where this is not an objection, it can be used preferably in finely ground form. Gypsum forms up to 50% of most commercial acid phosphate fertilizers, but in the case of some of the chemically compounded fertilizers, this material is extracted from fertilizer as it would constitute great bulkiness and a waste economically to the farmer, as he can apply lime much cheaper than he can buy it in the sack of commercial fertilizer.

Lime

Lime is the common name for calcium. Limestone is the carbonate. Quick-lime, oxide, slake or hydrated lime, the hydroxide. All three forms are used to improve soils and reduce acidity or sourness. For most garden purposes—hydrated lime is preferred as it comes highly powdered in convenient paper bags, easy to handle and is not caustic. It usually contains some magnesium, in addition to the calcium, and the analysis printed on the bag should be noticed for lime with more than 25% magnesium is not desirable. Nor should waste lime from chemical factories be used, unless analyzed and found free of injurious impurities. Hydrated lime should not be kept over from year to year for it gradually turns back to limestone.

7

Most vegetables and some flower plants benefit if lime is spread in the winter and mixed thoroughly with the soil as soon as it can be worked. Average soil will take about 100 to 200 pounds a year on a plot 50 feet square. Remember—it should not be used for acid soil plants, as this would be injurious to them. It is valuable in combination with leaf mold and compost, hastening decay, releasing plant food and neutralizing acidity. By liming the soil with agricultural limestone, as used in the field or by hydrated lime in a small garden plot, the soil is changed in chemical nature. Not only is it made less acid, but also the phosphorus and potash salts are altered into forms that make better plant food, while some injurious elements are made harmless. Soil texture is also improved, clay is broken up and sand compacted. Lime also helps the complicated process by which soil bacteria, especially those that live in the roots of legumes put valuable nitrogen in plant food form. In extremely acid soils it is highly beneficial for an application of lime to be made for all previous purposes mentioned.

Sulphur

Sulphur is one of 16 or more chemical elements believed to be essential to the growth of plants. It apparently ranks close to phosphorous in both the amount used by crops and the supply in the soil. Sulphur comes in many different forms in so far as the gardener is concerned. There is dusting sulfur and there is soil sulfur. For soil application, one should use soil sulfur, which is a little heavier granulated than the fine dusting sulfur that is used in insecticidal dusts.

In so far as soil application of sulphur for acidity, one should not use over 3 pounds per 100 square feet of bed area. Work into the soil and keep it well watered.

Magnesium

Magnesium is one of the chemical elements essential for plant growth, but it is also believed to be present in most average soils in sufficient quantities to meet the need of crops. Magnesium compounds, in which it occurs, includes carbonates, nitrates, sulphates, silicates, phosphates and chlorides. Their function in plant life is not completely understood, but magnesium is known to be associated with nitrogen in protoplasm, the content of living cells and a component of chlorophyll, the green coloring matter of plants. Magnesium sulfate and magnesium carbonate have limited use as indirect fertilizers. Most folks who run into a shortage of magnesium generally apply epsom salts, which is the magnesium sulfate compound, around the feeder roots, and this will alleviate all possibilities of a magnesium deficiency.

Iron

Besides being one of the principal commercial minerals, iron is also one of the essential elements for plant growth. However, it is present generally in sufficient quantities in all soils to meet the need of plants, so it presents no problem for the gardener in connection with the providing of plant food. However, this is not true in soils that are excessively high in alkalinity whereby the calcium has tied up the available iron and makes it unavailable for the plant to use, even though there may be sufficient quantities of it present. Iron causes some of the characteristics of soil's color, such as red, yellow and so forth, and is a constituent of chlorophyll, the green coloring matter of plants, without which the manufacturer of food in the leaves is impossible. When the soil iron is so tied up, one runs into the condition known as chlorosis. Sometimes young shoots develop more rapidly than the iron salts can reach them.

Iron compounds are used in gardening to some extent as fungicides and weed killers. The most common of these is Iron Sulfate, though it is not as efficient as the chelate compound. Iron filings, old nails and so forth having a slight acid effect on the soil are sometimes added to it when it is desired to promote the growth of acid loving plants, or to intensify the blue color of Hydrangea blossoms. However their action is slow and somewhat uncertain. So the use of iron chelates, iron sulfate or aluminum sulfate are much more advantageous.

Earthworms

Some folks seems to think that earthworms are a direct indication of rich soil. They are segmented worms that live in the moist soil containing decaying organic matter, crawling out at night to feed, or when burrows are filled with water as during heavy rain. The worm eats the soil through which it burrows and its digestive juices break down and dissolve bacteria, leaf mold and other organic material in the soil. The indigestible remainder is discharged in the form of castings which may be abundant on the surface of the soil. It has been estimated that earthworms in an acre of land bring more than 35 pounds of soil to the surface in the year. This type of soil working and conditioning is of great value in the garden and earthworms should be left alone wherever possible. However, in some instances, too many present a problem on lawns, golf greens, etc., and mar the beauty of the turf, and thus call for their control or extermination.

One of the best compounds used to control earthworms is 5% Dieldrin granules sprinkled over the soil at the rate of three to five pounds per 1,000 square feet, and then watered in order to dissolve it so the liquid Dieldrin will come in contact with the earthworms. The same area could be sprayed with Toxaphene at the rate of one pint of 60% emulsible concentrate per 25 gallons of water. Thoroughly saturate the area in which the earthworms reside and this in itself will control the earthworm. But, unless they are in sufficient quantities to do detrimental damage to the turf, it is advisable to leave the earthworms alone as they are highly beneficial.

Soil Testing

The only true, accurate way to determine the pH of the soil, its content of organic matter, its content of nitrogen, phosphorous and potash, and soluble salts is to have a soil test run. By having your soil tested you are taking the first step toward a sound garden program. Soil tests will tell you how to fertilize a soil, what the chances are for response from added compounds such as trace elements and lime.

This information makes far more efficient fertilization possible, and it assures greater gardening profits to you. No one, regardless of what his training might be in the field of agriculture, can actually look at a soil and tell you all of these technical points without having a soil test run. So, as the old adage goes—"Nowhere can you get so much for two dollars as you can with a soil test." It is also advisable to take soil tests from the various areas in which different types of gardening are to be carried out. For instance: An individual soil test should be made for your lawn, one for your flower beds, one for your home garden, rose beds, etc. The best detailed instructions for taking a soil test can be obtained from your local county agent's office or your local fertilizer dealer. However, listed below are the sequence to take a soil sample.

1. Take a different sample for each different gardening project around the home. One for the lawn, one for the garden, one for the shrubbery, one for the rose beds, etc.
2. Make sure that you take composite samples from each of these areas. A composite sample means two, three or four samples from each individual plot, mixing these together to obtain an average or random sample.
3. You can use a spade, trowel, soil tube or other suitable instrument to take the sample.
4. Take a thin, vertical slice of soil to a depth of about six to eight inches within the area. Put this into a clean bucket and take other samples from this same area to mix together to form a composite sample.
5. After these composites have been mixed together thoroughly, remove about a pint of soil and place it in a suitable container such as an ice cream container, a soil testing bag, etc., in order to send it to the Soil Testing Laboratory.
6. Fill out a soil sample information sheet. You can obtain this from your local county agent or ASC office, or if you don't wish to go to the trouble and time to obtain this sheet, sit down and write a letter telling where the sample came from, what has been grown in the past, what fertilizers have been applied in the past, and what you plan to do with this plot of ground in the future, so that the soil chemist will have some idea as to what you are planning to grow so as to make a fertilizer recommendation to fit it.

10

7. Number your samples. Number one, for instance comes from the lawn, number two comes from the garden, number three from the rose bed. Keep a record of these numbers as your soil testing sheet will come back with information relating to sample number one, sample number two and sample number three.

8. Send your samples to the following address:

Soil Testing Laboratory—Texas A&M College, College Station, Texas.

Soil Testing Laboratory—Wharton Junior College. Wharton, Texas.

Along with each sample send $2.00, either in cash or check to cover the cost of analyzing the soil.

A soil test should be looked upon as a guide and not as a complete diagnosis of all problems that might be wrong in your soil. For instance—a soil test will:

a. Serve as a guide to intelligent fertilizer use when supported by a case history, such as the one that you relate to the chemist with the information you send to him.

b. Reveal abnormal soil conditions or excesses.

c. Give an accurate soil reaction on which to base liming recommendations or the addition of sulfur and other compounds to counteract excessive lime.

A soil test will not tell:

a. What a crop to grow on the soil or what plant to grow.

b. Whether a plant died of root disease or other disease.

c. The presence of nematodes, wireworms or other root destroying insects and pests.

But test, don't guess. A soil test is one of the best tools to use toward better gardening.

Chapter 2

Plants and Shrubs for the Home Gardner

Aloe Vera

Aloe Vera, the mystic plant of the modern space age actually was known and used before the time of Christ. Many people called the plant, a cactus, because it resembled a small century plant, but it's really a type of lily, a distant cousin of the Easter Lily and of the asparagus, and the common table onion.

Ancient history records that Greek and Egyptian women in the court of Alexander the Great used Aloe Vera as a natural cosmetic to clear their skin of blemishes and grow new and healthy tissue.

Reliable sources indicate that the Aloe originated in South Africa and later into Egypt. Everywhere the healing properties of the plant were recognized, they were cherished, exalted into mystical proportion.

History tells us that Aristotle persuaded Alexander the Great to conquer the Island Sorcota for the express purpose of gaining a supply of aloine, the medicinal property found in Aloe Vera. It has been used as a medicine since Antiquity. The aloes were first grown extensively in the new world by Spanish Padres who were positive of its healing powers, and even today if you'll browse around some of the old missions in South Texas and along the Rio Grande, you'll find the mystic plant, the Aloe Vera, still growing wild in areas where the Spanish Padres of years gone by started the plant to be used for medicinal purposes during the time of the Conquistadors.

Although many fantastic claims have been made about the curative powers of the Aloe Vera, additional research in the medicinal field must be pursued before accurate and positive statements can be made. However, the Aloe Vera Plant has been called the "First Aid" plant. The gel has been applied to burns, scalds, cuts, abrasions, bruises and insect bites. It is soothing and pain-arresting. Physicians have used it successfully in the treatment of X-ray burns. The gel has been investigated by a number of Universities and the United States Department of Medicine and to date there have been many medical research reports put out on the medicinal powers of Aloe Vera. In fact only recently, an Independent Laboratory in Dallas has certified Aloe Vera as being safe for human consumption.

In the Aloe Family there are 250 different species, but there is only one true Aloe called Aloe Vera Barbedencia—this is a plant that when it is full grown waist high and its individual leaves will weigh as much as 2 to 2½ lbs. and they are filled with gel. Not only does the plant offer the home owner many medicinal curative powers as mentioned above but it also make a very beautiful decorative plant and one that is certainly a center of conversation.

In growing the Aloe Vera one must remember that it is a subtropical plant and will freeze. That is the only major point that one has to worry about in producing this plant at home or in the garden. It can be grown in a flower pot—it can be grown in a flower bed—it can be grown inside and outside, however it does need a sandy loam soil, one that drains well and it does need filtered shade. Even though the gel of the plant has been proven to be highly effective in arresting sun burns, its quite ironical that the plant itself will become sunburned if set out in the open sun. The Aloe Vera needs very little fertilizer and watering only slightly. Most people kill it by watering it too frequently. When you do water it, always water it by underneath or below the leaves never into the rosettes and do not over-fertilize. Make sure that you bring it in during the cold weather to keep it from freezing and set it back outside again in the summer under the shade of tree and leave alone and it will do quite well. Very few insects or diseases prey upon it, however there is a leaf blight and stalk rot that can invade it and there is no control for this except destruction of the plant once it appears. However, most of this is taken care of by Inspectors for the Texas Department of Agriculture as the majority of the plants are transported in from Mexico are grown in the valley under strict supervision so that this disease does not spread to home owners stock.

A lot of gardeners refer to this plant as a home medicine chest and would not dare be without one.

Amaryllis

This is a type of a South African bulbous plant which bears large lily white, pink, white, rose, red or purple flowers on a single, solid stem in mid-Summer. It can be grown inside, but for indoor flowering it requires a soil of fibrous loam, leaf mold and sand with liquid manure during the blooming season. Most of our Amaryllis bulbs today are hybrids; they are now being commercially produced in enormous quantities in the southern states, and of course most of the amateur gardeners are finding that Amaryllis hybrids do a beautiful job in the garden. They are excellent landscape subjects for use as individual specimens, in mass plantings, in flowers beds or for border planting around home grounds and in park plantings.

The Amaryllis is one of the simplest of plants to grow for indoor beauty. The reason for a number of failures by amateur gardeners lies in the care given the bulbs, not so much in the potting as in the watering in the beginning and subsequent care after blooming. Blooming the first season is proof that the bulb was mature blooming size and had formed bloom buds previously in its growth.

To water a bulb too much after the growing starts, may cause it to rot because there will be no assimilation of the moisture. A newly potted, dormant Amaryllis should be kept fairly dry after an initial watering to settle the soil around the bottom of the bulb until signs of life show. For best production of Amaryllis, one should grow bulbs for the inside or out with the mixture of three parts mixed loam, one part of well rotted leaf mold, with some sand and bonemeal, and another part of thoroughly rotted cow manure. Set the bulb 1/3 in the soil, water it carefully. As the bloom bud clears the neck of the bulb, use a liquid formulation of fertilizer, such as a tablespoonful of 13-13-13 dissolved in a half-gallon of water. Applying once a week or every 10 days, depending upon the growing conditions, until the color begins to show up on the blossom buds through the sheath. Full sunlight is best for sturdiness, and normally a temperature of between 55° and 60° grows them well. It is best to tie the bloom stem loosely to a stake to prevent it being broken. The blooms can be used for cut flowers. The cut plant is given less water and kept some cooler for a while. As weather becomes hotter the feeding of liquid manure is started again, or if you can't do that, you can work some cottonseed meal in and around the base of the bulb, which would help to feed it without chemical burn. Amaryllis can be grown successfully almost any place in the South and are worth the simple care that they require. They offer beauty either as a cut flower or a potted plant and an opportunity for initiative in the art of breeding your own seedlings. The color range, size, shape and blooms all offer mixed variation for experimentation, and the young gardener gets a great deal of fun out of trying to grow different types of Amaryllis.

Insofar as insects are concerned, dusting with Malathion or spraying with a Malathion liquid emulsible concentrate at the rate of 2 teaspoonsfuls to a gallon of water oftentimes will control most of the insects that infest Amaryllis.

Varieties of Amaryllis

There are a number of different varieties of Amaryllis that are adapted for the Southwest, and can be grown very profitably by almost any amateur gardener if normal care and general cultural practices are carried out. The varieties that are well known are Amaryllis equeastre. This variety is a solid pink that grows abundantly in the Southern part of the nation, especially along the Texas Gulf Coast, and adapts itself well to home and greenhouse conditions. The next one is Amaryllis formosissima, commonly known as Jacob Bean Lily, a native of Mexico. It forms black skin bulbs and bears bright crimson flowers above strap shaped foliage. The next one is Amaryllis johnsoni. This particular Amaryllis bulb is characterized by large red flowers with white veins.

14

Diseases of Amaryllis

The primary disease of an Amaryllis is leaf scorch, a fungus that apparently overwinters on the bulbs, which should be treated with a disinfectant prior to the time that they are planted. Bulbs showing the black resting bodies of the botrypis fungi should be discarded. The most typical sign of the disease is the fuzzy, greyish mold produced on the leaves and flowers, but small black resting bodies may be found on the bulb scales and on plant debris in the soil.

Sanitary measures such as removing all blossoms as soon as they fade, cutting off the leaves on the surface of the ground as soon as they ripen, generally is the best means of control.

Spraying the plants with a weak Bordeaux mixture several times in the spring, starting when the first shoots appear, is quite beneficial. As has previously been stated, it is almost mandatory that the bulbs be treated prior to planting.

First, thoroughly inspect the bulbs that have been bought from the nurserymen and discard any badly diseased bulbs. Soak the rest of them in a one to 1/1000 solution of corrosive sublimate for one hour, or in 0.25 per cent liquid Semesan for six hours.

When basal rot threatens, the hot water used to treat Narcissus, Iris etc. for the control of nematodes and bulb flies, should contain a fungicide such as one ounce of Semesan to four gallons of water, or one ounce of Corrosive Sublimate to eight gallons of water.

Arborvitae

Arborvitae is the common name for the Genus Thjua, a group of hardy evergreen trees of compact pyramidal or columnar form. They grow best in cool locations, either in wet soil, sandy loam or sand, with water near the surface or where water can be applied quite frequently. They suffer from both heat and cold in dry situations. The foliage of the Arborvitae is normally thin, scale-like and waxy to the touch, and fragrant. The lower branches are retained even in severe exposures, but growth is more luxuriant in sheltered positions.

In the Southwest Arborvitae is found growing in almost any section of the yard. However, they perform better where plenty of moisture can be applied to them, and they are best utilized in our gardens in the Southwest when used as part of the garden plan to set off corners of the home or in the corner of the lot to serve as a boundary line.

Arborvitae can also be used as hedge material, requiring little clipping because of the low growth and compactness of the shrub. Of course, there are dwarfed forms particularly desirable for borders, providing a substitute for other plants in the garden plan. In foundation plantings it is a common error to plant closely for immediate effect and fail to separate the plants every two or three years. Another

15

failure is to arrange the tall growing varieties and the dwarfs in correct relationship to the house. The result is that they will become unsightly and overcrowded with each other, and as a result do not respond.

Arborvitaes can be propagated by a number of methods: by seeds, cuttings and by grafting. The smaller sizes, especially the dwarf type Arborvitae, are readily transplanted because of a fibrous root system.

Cultural Practices

In general, in the Southwest little needs to be done to enhance the growth of Arborvitae other than to see that they receive ample moisture at all times and sufficient plant food to keep them in a green growing condition. In extreme hot weather it is advisable to soak the soil around Arborvitae at least twice a week because they do utilize a great deal of moisture. It is also advisable to mulch around the underside of the drip line of the Arborvitae in order to retain the moisture on hot humid days during the summertime. The plant food requirements of these particular shrubs are not as high as some of our other faster growing plants, but do need to be taken into consideration. Naturally a liberal application of a fertilizer similar to 12-24-12 or 13-13-13 will generally take care of what plant food is needed. Normally, for an average size Arborvitae, one pound to two pounds of either one of these two materials—applied in a trench around the drip line of the Arborvitae and soaked into the soil will be sufficient to keep the plant in a lush growing condition.

Enemies of Arborvitae

About the greatest pest is Red Spider, followed by the Bag Worm. You'll find a complete section for control of these insects in the chapter on Insects and their Control.

A minor enemy, needle scale is hard to see. It is a bug and not a disease. See how to recognize it in the Insect chapter.

Aster

Aster is a name meaning "Star," which refers to two distinct plants, both of which are members of the Composite or the Daisy family. Hardy Asters are usually characterized by leafy stems and opposite, often spear shaped leaves, ranging from one inch to three or four inches in length. The small flowers are daisy-like with orange or yellow centers and fine, often thickly growing petals. The stems are frequently much branched near the top, producing large clusters of flowers, which individually range from less than one inch to two inches across. The colors range from deep purple through lavender, blue, pink and rose to white. Most varieties bloom in the late summer and fall when many other plants are finished blooming. For this reason, and because of their variation in height (from six inches to six feet) which makes them adaptable to so many purposes, they are rightly considered plants of outstanding value and a number of our Southwestern gardeners enjoy growing them. These Asters have been developed and used far more extensively abroad than here in the United States, however, I might add, in spite of the fact that some of the principal parents used in creating the modern forms are natives of the United States.

CULTURAL PRACTICES: Most Asters under cultivation like full sun, many of them enjoy moist situations, although they do not like to have their roots standing in water as they become water logged quite easily. But, they will usually accept the average garden condition, with an open exposure. A good, average garden soil is more satisfactory than one which has been made very rich by a great deal of fertilization. Asters are used for several purposes in the garden. In the flower border the taller varieties may be used as background flowers, the smaller ones in front of them. As the taller varieties naturalize well, they may be used satisfactorily along the edge of fields to divide the mowed lawn from the cultivated areas. They are also delightfully effective, as well as happy, along the edge of a natural pond, bog or brook, as long as their roots are above the waterline.

The dwarf type Aster makes an ideal rock garden plant, some blooming in the fall when there is scarcity of flowering plants in this type of garden, and others blooming in early summer. Wherever planted, the effect of Asters is charming rather than striking. They blend with the landscape, yet are very much in evidence. When planted in the border the taller varieties will often need staking because of the heavily branched spikes and the heavy flower head which has a tendency to weight them down.

Asters are usually raised from seed and almost invariably bloom the next year after a spring sowing. If one should buy Aster plants from his local nursery to set out in the garden, these mature specimens should be spaced at least two feet apart. This is a common mistake a lot of folks make—they crowd them and put them too close together.

Most hardy Asters thrive best when they are divided each year, in spring, and in this way the supply can be increased very rapidly. Also, they can be increased by cuttings made later in the spring when the growth has reached the height of about three inches.

Enemies of Asters

The most serious of the insects is the Tarnish Plant Bug, a flying insect that punctures the new growth just below the flower buds causing them to droop or become deformed. Then there's the Blister Beetle which attacks almost everything. You can find how to control these in the Insect Control chapter.

A virus disease called Yellows is responsible for severe Aster losses. The plants turn yellow and if the buds open at all they are malformed and greenish. Also watch out for the ever prevalent stem rot. See how to combat these in the Disease Control Chapter.

Azaleas

Azaleas belong to the family Ericaceae and are closely related to the huckleberry, cranberry and sparkleberry. Their nearest relatives are the rhododendrons.

Azaleas are very widely distributed. Prior to the beginning of World War I they were produced by the millions by growers in Europe, notably in Germany, Belgium, Holland and England. In the U.S.A. Azaleas are grown from the eastern shores to the sunny lands of the Gulf Coast. The largest collection of Azaleas is in the National Arboretum, Washington, D. C.

Varieties of Azaleas

The deciduous azaleas are highly valued for the beauty of their brilliant flowers, ranging from creams and whites through yellows, oranges, pinks and flame reds. There are many native American species that are rarely seen in Texas gardens, but are widely grown both here and abroad. The most famous of these are the Ghent hybrids and various hybrids of Azalea mollis.

The semi-deciduous azaleas are equally outstanding. They have flowers of medium size, full color, are hardy and develop into large shrubs. Their flowers have a tendency to fade in full sunlight and they also should be planted in partial shade. The Kaempferi hybrids are the most outstanding of this group.

The indica azaleas grown in Texas and throughout the lower-South are perhaps the best known of the evergreen azaleas in this area. These varieties have been derived from many species and varieties of evergreen azaleas. Most of the Azalea indica forms developed in the South have single flowers in a wide range of colors, and grow into tall shrubs which may reach 30 feet. These also are closely related to the double-flowered Azalea indicas which are used widely as potted plants by florists.

The Kurume azaleas also are evergreens and are the loveliest of all azaleas. They produce compact well-shaped plants which are covered with vast quantities of delicately covered small flowers in shades of white, light pink, rose, lavender, salmon and scarlet. Their blooming period is longer than the indica type.

Soils & Climate for Azaleas

Azaleas cannot be grown successfully in dry soil. They thrive and do best in a damp atmosphere. The climate of the southeastern and southern U.S.A. is well suited to them, but when there are dry seasons, artificial watering is beneficial.

Azaleas thrive better in an acid soil, high in organic matter and a soil light in texture. The soil must be well aerated and retentive of moisture, but at the same time well drained. Very few soils meet all these requirements, therefore it is generally necessary to make special soil preparations for the successful culture of Azaleas.

A good soil mixture for Azaleas consists of equal parts of cured manure or peat moss and sandy loam soil, with ½ cup of sulphur added to each bushel of the mixture. The sulphur should be thoroughly incorporated in with the mixture. *Never* use manure that is not well rotted as there is danger of burning the plant roots. Since each individual bed will vary in the soil reaction, and because of the many factors involved, it is impossible to say exactly how much sulphur or iron sulphate, or aluminum sulfate should be used to bring about a given soil change. Therefore, experience of the gardener and accurate observation are necessary to accomplish the desired results.

The high pH or alkalinity of our soils present many problems to gardeners in their efforts to grow Camellias and Azaleas. In areas of Texas the soils usually contain lime in amounts injurious to the plants, and the free soil-water is also likely to contain lime. Where these conditions exist the culture of Azaleas and Camellias is not likely to be successful without special attention to soil preparations and the use of lime-free water.

LIME INJURY: The Azaleas show this injury first in the foliage. The new leaves are undersized and present a peculiar, unmistakable appearance. In the earlier stages the veins are still green, but the spaces between are yellowish and the leaves mottled. Later, as the condition progresses, they become brown and dead on the edges. Still later they drop off, the twigs die back, leaves produced lower down are smaller and these in turn die prematurely. Eventually the plant dies. The disease is not difficult to diagnose, and it is not likely to be confused with anything else—except yellowing due to starvation. Treatment consists in changing the soil from an alkaline to an acid reaction. This is best done through the use of aluminum or iron sulfate. Apply either of the compounds at the rate of ¼ to ½ pound to a square yard, or about one pound per 100 square feet. A second application of the same amount after an interval of sixty days may be advisable. If the injury is severe, it may be best to take the plants out and reset them in peat or mulch, to which aluminum sulfate has been added at the rate of a six-inch pot full to a wheelbarrow of soil. Handled in this way they usually make a good recovery, unless too severely damaged.

Planting and Cultivating Azaleas

Azaleas grow best in semi-shaded location. Although large trees offer sufficient shade, they also compete with the plants for food and moisture. Avoid planting close to building foundations as alkaline soil conditions may exist from the lime and other materials used in construction. Adequate drainage must be provided if the plants are to grow normally. A good plan to follow in setting the plants, is to dig the holes twice as wide and twice as deep as the ball of earth surrounding the roots. Discard the soil removed, place some coarse drainage (rocks and gravel) into the hole about 2 inches deep and use the specially prepared soil (½ manure-½ sandy loam and ¼ to ½ cup of sulphur) beneath and around the plant ball. The top of the ball of roots should be about one inch below the ground surface. Pack the prepared soil firmly, but avoid breaking the ball. Make a basin around the plant large enough to accommodate several gallons of water and water immediately.

Azalea roots need more than the usual amount of air. It will not do to set the plants too deep. If planted too deep they may die outright, and if they recover—they do so by developing a new set of roots nearer the surface of the ground.

Azaleas are shallow-rooted. The roots are fine and fibrous and occupy only a few inches of surface soil. For that reason they cannot be cultivated with a hoe and rake without injury to the root system. Weeds should be pulled up. Instead of cultivation, the ground should be mulched to conserve moisture. Mulching of three or four inches is not too much. As this decays and becomes reduced in thickness, more material should be added to maintain the original depth of mulch.

A good formula to use in preparing a mulching material to add to the soil around Azaleas and Camellias is as follows:

1 bushel of peat humus, leaf mold or steer manure
5 pounds of cottonseed meal
1 pound Ammonium Sulfate, or if a balanced fertilizer is desired—13-13-13 or 10-20-10, etc.
1 cup sulphur or sulfur soil

These ingredients should be thoroughly mixed and mulched around the plants in the spring. One gallon of this mixture per foot of height or spread of the plant is the proper rate of application. If additional fertilization is required to promote growth and vigor, dissolve 1 pound of 13-13-14 into 10 gallons of water and apply at the rate of one gallon for each foot of height or spread of the plant.

Watering

After planting, Azaleas should be watered freely and frequently. They require large amounts of soil moisture. Infrequent, heavy waterings are more effective than frequent light ones. Several gallons of water per plant, per week are basically sufficient during the summer months, depending upon the rainfall. Syringing the tops and foilage of the plant is particularly beneficial. The plants respond to free watering and sprinkling of their tops. It must be borne in mind that syringing the plants will not take the place of, but be in addition to, thorough wetting of the soil. Watering should be done in the late afternoon or early morning, rather than during the hotter part of the day.

Pruning

In habit of growth Azaleas differ. Some have compact tops or heads and are densely branched; while others are open and spreading because their branches are fewer in number, longer and furnished with a lesser number of twigs or short branches. If allowed to grow at will in the garden, Azaleas *require little pruning*. Sometimes branches are crowded and killed by shading. This should be removed by cutting out close to the point of origin.

The number of flowers that an Azalea puts on can be increased greatly. All well placed branchlets of the season's growth on a well grown and healthy Azalea, should develop flower buds on their tips late in the season as growth ceases. By nipping back the tips of vigorous shoots earlier in the year and causing lateral buds to push out into shoots or branches, the number of branches or branchlets tips can be increased, resulting finally in added development of flower buds. Nipping to increase the number of flower buds must not be undertaken and prolonged too late in the season. Late pruning may leave too short a time for lateral shoots to push out and form flower buds on their tips before growth stops in early autumn. Plants grown in the Southwest may be pruned this way with safety up to the first of September. The time at which pinching back may be started each spring will vary with growth conditions. All branches are not ready for nipping back or shortening at one time. It is necessary to go over them several times.

After flower buds have set, and particularly toward the approach of the blooming season, new shoots frequently shove out. If plants are being produced for a maximum of bloom, these should be broken off as soon as they have shoved out an inch or so. With careful attention the heads may be made as round as a ball, as smooth on the outside as the surface of an umbrella and with all of the flowers showing on the outside when they come into bloom.

Insects and Diseases

For specific control recommendations, see the chapters on
Insects and Diseases.

Azaleas may be injured by several insects, but red spiders and Azalea lace bugs are the principal pests. Red spiders are small mites which rasp the surfaces of the leaves and feed on the juices. Injured leaves take on a reddish brown appearance, and at times may seem to be dusted lightly with salt and pepper.

Azaleas lace bugs are small insects about $\frac{1}{8}$ inch long and have lace-like wings, marked with brown or black. They are sucking insects and feed mostly on the under surfaces of the leaves, causing them to show a mottled grey color. This is due to the destruction of the green coloring matter of the leaf.

21

Flower spots attack only the petals of the plant. It appears as whitish spots on opened flowers. All flowers on the plant may suddenly wilt.

Chlorosis, or yellowing of the foliage of an Azalea may be caused by a shortage of available iron or insufficient acidity of the soil. Apply sulphur or iron sulfate to increase the soil acidity, or spray the plants with a solution of iron chelates to correct iron deficiency. $\frac{1}{4}$ teaspoonful of iron chelates in one gallon of water is proper dosage. Remember when the proper soil acidity is maintained (pH 4.5-5.5) iron deficiency seldom occurs. *So, get a soil test made* ! !

AZALEA PETAL BLIGHT: This disease is most damaging to some of the Indica varieties and types of azaleas than to the native azaleas. The first symptoms of this disease, on the flowers, are tiny spots about the size of a pinhead, and one must examine the petals very closely, in order to determine the advent of this disease. These tiny spots are pale or whitish on colored petals, or rust colored on white petals. These round spots enlarge into irregular blotches, the affected tissue becomes soft and eventually the whole flower collapses, thus losing the beauty of the azalea plant.

The disease cycle usually starts with the first bloom in the spring. Low hanging flowers, the first ones to open, become infected by spores produced on old dead flowers laying on or in the soil beneath the plants. Infestation can be cut down by keeping the soil under the plants as clean as possible and preventing return to the soil of the fungus causing the disease.

LEAF BLOTCH AND TWIG BLIGHT: Plants affected by winter injuries, sun scald or malnutrition or severe insect injury, are susceptible primarily to leaf blotch and twig blight. This particular disease is characterized by brown or bronze leaves, excessive leaf drop, and the appearance of small black fruiting bodies on the leaf lesions.

To control these diseases one should grow the plants in a favorable environment to avoid winter injury or sun scald, and follow a regular fertilization program and prevent insect injury. By a regular fertilization program, one should fertilize on a regular periodic basis, rather than try to feed the plant all it needs at one time, and then to shut it off. The advent of a heavy application of a chemical fertilizer to such a plant leaves the plant wide open in so far as resistance is concerned to these two primary diseases.

Most gardeners have found that periodic applications of a balanced fertilizer (like 12-24-12) at the rate of one to two tablespoons per plant, about 30 to 40 days apart throughout the growing season will be the best fertilization program that one can follow.

LEAF AND BUD GALLS: These diseases are caused on Azaleas by mold-like, air-borne fungi, and are wide spread and quite common during periods of high humidity—such as experienced along the Texas Gulf Coast.

This disease causes the leaves to become thickened or curled, fleshy, pale green to white, or pink in color, and frequently with a white powdery surface. Flower parts may also be affected.

In the average home garden, where few plants are involved, these diseases are controlled most easily by hand picking and destroying the galls by burning. There is actually no chemical control that will control the leaf or bud galls after they have formed.

Bougainvillaea

Bougainvillaea, although not particular as to the soil it grows in (either sand or clay) can be frustrating when it comes to blooming. The truth is that a Bougainvillaea, to do its best, must be given a southern exposure in full sun. If it is growing on the north side of your home, or in the shade, it will develop huge shoots of leaves, but never a bloom. Some of the best adapted varieties to put in are: Sanders, purple blooms; Afterglow, salmon blooms; Texas Dawn, florescent color; Crimson Lake, red blooms; Barbara Karst, red blooms. Barbara Karst is especially hardy. Bougainvillaea makes an excellent tree or shrub, as well as a woody vine. It takes training to make it into a tree shape. It will freeze, however Bougainvillaeas on the south side of Houston area homes have prospered for years without freeze damage.

In general, insects do not bother Bougainvillaeas, nor do they suffer from nutritional deficiencies. Occasionally a plant may develop chlorosis—which can be corrected with iron chelates or iron sulfate. Manganese deficiency shows up in the plant leaf and this can be corrected by the application of manganese sulfate.

As a tip that might work to shock a Bougainvillaea Vine into producing blooms, try applying a pint to a quart of plain vinegar (white or apple), apply to the soil around the feeder roots and work into the soil. This may or may not work. Give it a try.

Camellias

Camellias are artistic shrubs which produce one of nature's most perfectly formed flowers. The plants are exceptionally long-lived and, with ordinary precautions, a minimum of care in the preparation of soil, insect and disease control and adequate water and nutrients, these plants will give the home gardener years of satisfaction.

Camellia fanciers estimate there are 15 to 40 types or species, but the exact number is not known accurately.

As grown by most gardeners, Camellias are of one or more of three principal groups or species—*Camellia japonica, Camellia sasanqua* and *Camellia reticulata.*

23

Camellia japonica

The most popular species in Southern gardens today is *Camellia japonica*. Several hundred varieties of this species are available. The forms of the flowers range from singles through semi-doubles to doubles, and the colors vary from white to many shades of red and pink, including a wide assortment of variegated colors. Most blossoms of this species have no scent, but those of a few varieties have a fragrane after the blooms have been open several days.

Camellia japonica varieties have evergreen leaves which range in shape from long and narrow to almost round.

Camellia sasanqua

The second largest number of varieties grown in American gardens today are of the *Camellia sasanqua* species. Most have single flowers which range in color from red to white, but several varieties have double flowers or variegated blossoms.

Camellia sasanqua varieties generally are hardier to cold than those of *Camellia japonica* and can be grown more successfully in colder climates without winter protection.

This species constantly increases in popularity because many varieties bloom earlier than the average *Camellia japonica* varieties and at a time when few other plants are in bloom. Most sasanqua varieties are fragrant and nearly all grow rapidly.

Camellia reticulata

The latest species to become adapted by gardeners is *Camellia reticulata*, although it has been popular in English gardens since about 1800. Its growth is almost entirely terminal and the plants do not branch well when the terminal growth is removed. The leaves are thick, flat, long and narrow and are a dull green.

The flowers are semi-double, 6 to 8 inches in diameter, and have large ruffed petals. This species is much more difficult to propagate by cuttings than the other two species mentioned, but it is not difficult to propagate by grafting.

Your local nursery can provide full information about colors, blooming form and blooming season for varieties in each group judged best for this area.

Insects and Diseases

While the number of insect pests which attack Camellias is comparatively small, some are serious and care should be given to their control.

Scale

The most common group of insects likely found on Camellias are various species of scale. They infest the twigs, branches or undersides of the leaves, depending on the species present.

Scale infestation may be identified by a peculiar light spotting of the leaves on the upper surface, by an abundance of ants on the plants or by observation of the scale insects on the plants when they become encrusted on the leaves or branches. Fungus also is often found growing on the honeydew secreted by some scales, which gives the plants a dirty, black, sooty appearance.

The maximum hatch of most scale insects under Texas conditions usually occurs in the spring soon after the danger of the last frost is over.

Aphids

At least two species of aphids infest the young growth of Camellias. When these attacks are not detected and treated early, a curling and distortion of the young leaves occur. These insects are controlled readily with any all-purpose spray used for roses or other garden plants.

Thrips and Mites

Both red spider mites and thrips, under certain climatic conditions, may become a nuisance on Camellias, especially during the summer.

The presence of red spiders or thrips is indicated by a peculiar light spotting or graying on the upper surface of the infested leaves.

Leaf-eating Insects

Occasionally leaf-feeding insects may attack Camellias. Most of these are night-feeders and are rarely found on the plants during the day.

Physiological Disorders

The best control for physiological disorders is its prevention by shallow planting, avoiding annual heaping applications of heavy mulches, applying sufficient water to keep the soil moist, but never saturated, and by providing excellent drainage for the plant roots.

Die Back

Die back or twig blight, sometimes called phomopsis, is a common disease of Camellia and has been prevalent in the Gulf Coast area of Texas. It causes a dying back of twigs or branches and occasionally larger limbs. At least three species of fungus have been associated with this disease. The primary cause of this injury has not been determined.

The control suggested is to remove the infected twigs and branches, being certain to cut back well beyond the injured area. Even though a fungus is responsible, it is well to keep the pruning tools disinfected. Spraying the plants with a 5-5-5 strength of Bordeaux mixture in the early spring about the time knew growth starts also is recommended in areas when this disease is known to exist.

Blossom Rot

A disease known as Camellia blossom rot is increasingly prevalent in the Southwest. It occurs in the late winter during wet weather and is evidenced by wet, brown discolorations on the petals of the flowers. It may occur on partially opened buds as well as on flowers in full bloom.

Sanitation or the picking up of all affected blooms and flowers that fall to the ground is recommended.

Spraying the ground around the plants with a mixture of 1 pound of Ferbam to 100 gallons of water and thoroughly wetting the soil is effective for about 14 days. Make frequent spray applications during the flowering period if rains occur.

Bud Drop

Excessive shedding of buds by some Camellias often is caused by unfavorable growing conditions rather than by disease. Diminishing the supply of food and moisture, even for a short time, especially in the dry fall when the buds are large, may retard growth, keep buds from developing fully and cause them to drop later in the season. Camellias planted too deep, in heavy soil or where poor draining exists also are susceptible to bud drop.

Sudden cold spells, especially those followed by warm sunny days, are another cause of bud shedding. This is especially true when early warm spells have caused the buds to swell prematurely.

Many varieties of Camellias often set more buds than even the most robust plants are able to develop to maturity. When disbudding is not practiced, this retards the growth of all buds and results in bud shedding and undeveloped blooms. When large amounts of readily available fertilizers are applied, but shedding and plant injury also may result.

Chrysanthemums

The Chrysanthemum is widely grown throughout the Southwest, in most instances with good success. Most all of our present day Chrysanthemums originated from hybridization of varieties obtained from China, India and Japan. The Chinese and Japanese Chrysanthemums are the tallest, often obtaining more than four feet in height and producing handsome, erect, many branched plants.

In recent years a number of new, extremely hardy, charming and useful garden varieties have appeared and won widespread popularity. Their lovely pastel and brilliant colors in wide variety make them ideal for cutting, as well as for outdoor display. These newest varieties are commonly called Korean Hybrids. Profuse bloomers and growing about two feet tall, the Korean Hybrid reach their peak generally in the month of September.

26

Varieties or Kinds of Chrysanthemums

Thriving in ordinary good well drained garden soil, the plants prefer a sunny location and require thorough watering. There are at least a half dozen classes listed according to cultural methods, and they include:

GARDEN ANNUALS: These Chrysanthemums are the late summer blooming type and are of the robust habit and easy to grow from seed, which are generally sown in the open ground as soon as it can be worked. They have masses of colored type blooms, and they may be grown thickly in order to give a border appearance. However, they do their best and provide lovelier blooms when thinned to a stand of 12 to 24 inches apart and given an open sunny location.

PERENNIAL BORDER KIND: Chrysanthemums in this group prefer sunny locations where they bloom profusely in a wide range of color, even after other flowering plants have been killed by the first frost. These plants are put in well drained soil. They may be kept from year to year in almost any climate, if given a covering of loose litter during the winter. In most instances they will come through the winter in pretty fair shape. Propagation of this particular variety is by seeds which give flowering plants the second year.

FEVERFEW: These are forms of the perennial, exceedingly hardy and easily cultivated Chrysanthemums. They are grown from seed and they flower the second season, producing an abundance of small white rayed heads with yellow centers. Plants generally in this class are dwarfed and compact and the foliage is crisp and yellow tinged.

PYRETHRUM: These plants are distinguished by their long simple flower stems arising from crowns of attractive foliage and are frequently grown by florists for cut flowers. They bloom from spring until midsummer, and bear daisy-like flowerheads, the colors ranging from white to lilac, rose to red. If the flowers are cut regularly in the spring and summer, the period of bloom may be extended until autumn. Propagation of this particular specie is by seeds which give blossoming plants the second year.

MARGUERITES: These belong to the specie often called Paris Daisy. They are generally propagated by cuttings, which if taken in the spring give flowering plants the following winter and spring, depending upon what type of cultural practices are carried out, whether grown under hothouse conditions or not.

Soils for Chrysanthemums

There isn't any one type of soil that Chrysanthemums particularly favor, but there are some rules of management and cultural practices that are quite important. Most important among these is the matter of humus, or as a lot of folks call it, organic matter. A hard, poorly

27

aerated soil just won't grow good Chrysanthemums. A good soil should have a loose open texture. When water is applied it should soak into the soil rather rapidly and not run off. It should be possible to push one's fist down into a section of soil if it is the right consistency and has the right amount of humus in it. A good soil that will grow Chrysanthemums to an excellent degree won't crack as it dries. Most any good field or garden soil can be made into this kind of a porus, open growing medium by adding organic matter. Peat moss, decomposed leaves, manure and others will do an excellent job in changing the texture of the soil to grow good Chrysanthemums.

CULTURE: Chrysanthemum beds need to be prepared about 10 inches deep unless natural drainage is poor. An extra 5 to 6 inches is then dug and normally a layer of coarse gravel is laid in the bottom to assure adequate drainage. Good drainage is essential for safe wintering of the plants. Plants that are alternatively frozen and thawed or frostbitten and thawed rarely survive an average winter. It would be advisable as we hit the excessively cold weather of winter, normally around January and February, that a light mulch be placed over the roots or burlap bags be layed over them to protect the root system from freezing and eventual damage. Do not cover the plants excessively as they are easily suffocated and they might die from this. If the season is dry, regular and deep waterings are necessary to prevent the stems from becoming woody.

LOCATION: Location is a very important factor in the growth and flowering of the Chrysanthemum. It is best to plant the flower in a spot that is protected from strong winter winds. They should also be protected from a cooking sun which may destroy plant tissue. In most instances a Southwestern exposure is the best—with a house, wall, fence or shrubbery behind for a windbreak. Actually, in this particular instance, protection against extreme summer temperatures is of greater importance than protection against wind, as the plants do not have to sustain the severe thrust of northerly winds as in the north.

PROPAGATION: Hardy Chrysanthemums may be propagated by division, cuttings or by seed. The most popular ones used by gardeners in this area are by dividing and by cuttings. Cuttings are normally taken in the month of March and April and are rooted in sand, and divisions are done as early in the spring as possible, normally in this area around March or April again. The younger Chrysanthemums are, the better blooming job they do. After the division process has been carried out, or cuttings established, you should plant the newly started plants in the bed about 12 to 18 inches apart, and after the spring resetting when the plants have six leaves—pinch the tops out to induce side branching. As each new branch develops six leaves, pinch these also and continue this practice up to about the first part of July and then let the growth go on, otherwise flower formation may be greatly delayed and sometimes no flowers at all. Those plants received by patients in the hospital or at home from friends generally should be set outside, out of the pot, in the spring when the ground has warmed up and of course the ground should have been worked.

Pot Plant Production of Chrysanthemums

Pot plants can be raised from cuttings taken at any time, although the best time seems to be in early April. They should be rooted in the cutting pan, propagating box or hotbed, and then placed in small pots in a soil mixture of equal parts of sand, fresh loam, leaf mold and well rotted manure. After being potted the plants should be well watered and placed in a mildly warm hotbed, or in a warm section of the garage where they should be given air daily—after the second day—and watered carefully.

After they have made a dozen good leaves, the top buds should be pinched off to induce branching. As the pots begin to fill with roots, lift the plants to large pots and place in a cold frame or where they can get plenty of sunshine. As the branches grow, continue to pinch them back, removing the terminal bud. After the plants have reached the desired growth, they should be placed outside in a location sheltered from severe winds.

Generally by the first of July or August the plants will be ready for a shift into a 5 or 6 inch pot, which should at all times be protected against cut worm infestation. The best thing to use is a 50% DDT dust applied around the plant at the groundline. Meanwhile, continue watering the plants carefully, and as the shoots form flower buds you should stake the plants, tying their branches up. Before the first frost, which generally occurs in this area in November, or maybe thirty days before that time, the plants should be taken inside and placed in a light airy place and keep them cool. They will shortly begin to blossom (within 30 to 40 days) and continue to bear flowers until well in the winter, around Christmas time.

During the flowering period, an occasional watering with a weak solution of liquid fertilizer will help. It is a general practice that after they have finished flowering the first year in these pots, most folks like to set them out in their beds in the spring. With the type of weather factors we have in the Southwest they will do alright if given the proper amount of fertility and correct cultural practices in the flower bed.

Diseases of Chrysanthemums

(For Control Practices, See Chapter 9)

LEAF SPOT seems to be the most serious of all diseases of Chrysanthemums. The small dark brown to black spots gradually increase in size until large leaf areas are involved. This disfigures the foilage and causes defoliation. The lower leaves are attacked first, often shriveling

29

and drying, although these symptoms may also be caused by unfavorable physiological conditions present in the soil.

POWDERY MILDEW also affects Chrysanthemums, and the best control measure for Powdery Mildew is to dust the leaf surface of the affected plants with sulfur.

FUSARIUM STEM ROT in Chrysanthemums introduces slow fading and withering of the leaves from the bottom up.

Insect Pests of Chrysanthemums
(For Control, See Chapter 8)

The major insect pests that affect Chrysanthemum production are the Red Spider; Pill Bugs; Leaf Hoppers; Tarnish Plant Bugs and Aphids. It is advisable to carry out a preventive approach to insect control. Once an infestation has built up, much of the damage is already done. Furthermore, it takes more effort to put down a serious build up than it does to prevent it ever happening. Then too, the fellow who waits for trouble to appear often must spend a lot more time just looking for it; therefore, a preventive control is the cheapest and best.

Day Lilies

Day lilies are native Asian plants. They have been cultivated for centuries in China, where the flowers of some kinds are used for food. In the beginning there were very few varieties. But today the number of varieties have been increased until actually there are hundreds of them named, propagated and distributed. Not only have new colors been secured, but the height and size of the plants, and the forms of the flowers have been changed to such an extent that it is hard to believe they belong with those varieties of former years. Day lilies bloom from April to October, May and June being the best months.

Propagation

Day lilies can be propagated and increased in numbers from seed, by dividing clumps into smaller parts and by planting shoots that sometimes develop on the main flower stems (scapes) of certain varieties. Seeds are produced frequently by some kinds, by others infrequently and not at all by some. Seeds from hybrid plants, are not likely to reproduce true to parent type. To make seed production more certain, pollen should be placed by hand on the stigmas of the flowers shortly after they open. Plants true to parent type are secured by dividing clumps. A clump is dug and taken apart. If the variety is abundant and the clumps large, this may be done by simply cutting them into sections with a sharp knife. Separation can be done by breaking the clump apart with the hands. A cluster of several plants may be left together, or the clump can be separated into single plants, each with its own leaves and a few roots. The leaves should be cut back half way, and the small plant is ready for planting.

Planting Day Lilies

Day lilies should be grown in full sunshine or light shade. They do not do well in dense shaded areas. Planting day lilies is not difficult. In the beds, it is best to dig the clumps, divide them and transplant immediately. In our area, this can be done at any time, but on the whole, the best season is immediately after flowering, or when growth ceases in the summer. Set the clumps not more than an inch deeper than they grew, pack them in place and water thoroughly. Smaller grown plants should be set at 18-inch intervals, larger one at 24 inches. A planting can be left undistrubed for four or five years before it becomes advisable to divide and separate them.

Care and Culture of Day Lilies

Day lilies will respond to good soil preparation before planting, and fertilizer, water and freedom from weed competition afterward. *Something for nothing is not a good garden rule.* The soil where they are to be planted should be dug and pulverized to a depth of a foot, and organic matter should be worked into the soil. Steer manure or compost are excellent additions to mix with the soil. Addition of commercial fertilizer after planting will help greatly in the growth and blooming of the plants.

It is advisable to fertilize day lilies at least twice a year, March and June, and also it is advisable to fertilize again in the fall (October). Use 13-13-13 or 12-24-12 at the rate of two to five pounds to 100 square feet of bed surface, spread evenly over the bed and watered in immediately.

Leaves that die from time to time usually are covered by green ones above them, but if they show too much, they can be pulled out easily. Water during dry weather. They should be given water to keep the plants supplied as there is every indication that alternating dry and wet periods are not good for day lilies. They will take and use water in liberal amounts.

There are few, if any, insects or diseases that harm the day lily. This, truly, is the most pest-resistant, the easiest to grow, plant in your garden.

Iris

Garden Irises are hardy, long lived perennials that need minimum care. They are an established backbone of home gardeners because they bloom when few other plants do, after spring flowering bulbs, Peonies and Phlox. Easy to grow, Iris varieties adapted to every region of the United States including the Southwest, are available. They produce graceful flowers and a wide range of shapes, sizes and color. The Iris—Bearded, Beardless and Crested—grow from thick underground stems called rhizomes that store food produced by the leaves. Rhizomes grow slightly below the surface of the ground or at the ground level, many small roots penetrate the soil deeply. Every year underground offshoots develop from the original rhizomes. Offshoots may be divided and transplanted to grow new Iries. There are many thousand different varieties of Irises available and you should select varieties that will provide the colors that you want in your garden. Many new varieties are produced each year, but be sure and pick those from a reliable concern.

Planting Irises

Irises may be planted in triangles, clumps, borders or in beds with other garden flowers. The best time to plant Irises is in the early fall. They should be established before Winter. Most garden supply stores sell rhizomes only during the planting season, but if you order Irises by mail you receive rhizomes before planting time recommended for the locality.

One thing to remember about this plant is the fact that it needs full sunshine, so select a sight with a southern exposure and good air circulation. Bearded and Crested Irises need a lime soil with good drainage, and most of our soils here are adapted for growing of Irises, but drainage is a problem. Beardless types need moist soil that is slightly acid.

Preparing the Soil for Planting

A person should prepare the bed one to two weeks before planting time arrives in order to allow the soil time to settle. Dig and loosen the soil at least 18 inches deep and thoroughly break up all clumps or clods. Use commercial fertilizer to enrich poor soil in the Iris bed, and use organic material such as peat moss, litter, etc. to improve the soil structure and productivity. For rather poor soil—use about ½ pound of commerical fertilizer for every 5 to 10 foot area, and thoroughly mix the fertilizer into the soil so that the lumps of it do not touch roots. In a well prepared bed dig a shallow hole large enough to receive the rhizome or clump of rhizomes that you are planting. Form a cone of earth in the center of the hole for the planting base. The height of the planting cone or planting depth is determined by the type of garden soil.

In a heavy soil build a cone even with the ground surface, the top of the planted rhizome should be slightly above ground. Place the rhizome on the cone, parallel with the ground surface, carefully spread the roots around the cone and do not wad the roots together. Fill the hole with soil and press it firmly in place around the rhizome. Water immediately. Thoroughly soak the soil around the roots.

In order to obtain a good display of Iris color, use at least three rhizomes of the same variety in a triangle or a pattern that alternates plants in rows. Plant rhizomes about 18 inches apart, point each fan of the leaves away from other plants in the group. If you want to produce masses of flowers quickly, plant undivided rhizome clumps or set three individual rhizomes eight to ten inches apart. You should water the plants often enough before blooming time to keep the soil moist but not wet, and be sure to remove all weeds and grass around the plants.

32

Before the plants bloom, loosen the surface soil with a hoe or hand cultivator, be careful not to injure the root system. Cut the flowers as soon as they fade unless you want to obtain seeds. Plants that are growing well with good green foliage usually do not need fertilizer. However, if they show some yellowing conditions and they are slightly stunted, the application of a commercial fertilizer might be called for. In the early fall, prior to winter, cut the leaves 6 to 8 inches from the ground. All Irises need mulching the first season after planting. Apply a light mulch of straw, peat moss, mulch of any type, above the ground during the wintertime in order to protect it from freezing etc.

Insects on Iris
(See Chapter 8 for Control Practices)

The Iris Borer causes more damage to Iris than all other insects. The pink caterpillar-like larvae have rows of black spots along their sides; they are about 1½ inches long when full grown. The Iris Borer adults are large brown moths with black markings.

The first symptoms of borers are pierced veins and chewed leaf edges that appear on leaves in the early spring. The Iris later develop loose rotted bases and holes in the rhizomes. Borer larvae hatch in the early spring from winter eggs. These caterpillars pierce the leaves and tunnel into the stems, them bore into the rhizome where they remain to' feed and grow. At maturity the larvae leave the rhizome and pupate in the soil.

APHIDS OR PLANT LICE—Aphids or small plant lice are small green, pink or mealy white insects that attack many plants. Aphids may appear on Iris plants in early spring. They pierce leaves and suck the juices, when they feed they may transmit the virus which causes Iris Mosiac.

IRIS THRIPS—The larvae and adult of the Iris Thrips pierce the surfaces of young leaves and leaf sheaths. They suck the juices that ooze from the wounds and dry wounds become straw colored spots, flower buds blackened, plant tops weakened. Iris Thrips are especially injurious to Japanese Iris. The larvae of the Iris Thrips are milky white, the black bodies of adults are usually wingless, they are about 1/25 of an inch long when matured.

Poinsettia

This plant with its characteristics of large red flowerlike bracts is one of the most favored Christmas flowers. Likely some of your friends may present you with such a flower at Christmas time. The Poinsettia, although a tropical specie of a plant, is most popular as a pot plant and is considered a shrub, growing in some instances from 10 feet to sometimes twice that height in the proper conditions.

Propagation of this plant is accomplished generally by cuttings. The tops which are removed before the plants are repotted are suitable for cuttings. Divide them into four to six inch lengths and place in warm water for about 15 minutes. This stops the sap from flowing too freely, then dip the lower end into powdered charcoal and insert the lower third of the stem into sand for rooting. A temperature of 65° F should be maintained during the rooting process. Keep them in a sunny location. When roots have formed on the tip ends of the stems, set the young plants into small pots, water and keep shaded for a week or two. As the top growth increases, repot into larger containers. From that stage on they are handled as any other standard Poinsettia plant.

SPRING AND SUMMER CARE: Generally, in this area, about the month of April or the first part of May the Poinsettia plant should be repotted. Take the plant out of the pot and repot in fresh rich soil. The soil should consist of garden loam, sand, leaf mold, or a general potting soil that can be purchased on the market. It should at least have some organic matter in it, particularly sheep manure or dried cow manure. Cut the stems to within 2 or 3 eyes from the base, water and sink the new pot with the plant repotted in it outside in a sunny spot, level with the soil surface.

Soon after placing outdoors you will notice that new shoots and new growth will grow from the eye. All during the summer the plants will grow into large well branched specimens. The plants should be placed where they will receive full light and sunshine throughout the day, but not excessively hot sunshine as we experience in the Southwest. In our area it would be more or less like a semi-protected area with ample sunshine, but not direct. These plants require lots of moisture; so keep them well watered.

CARE DURING BLOOMING: One should keep the Poinsettia from being set in a draft, keeping it within a temperature of 70 degrees during the daytime and not lower than 63 degrees at night. Generally a sunny window, preferably protected by a storm sash to prevent cold drafts, is a good place to keep the Poinsettia as they require a lot of sun. Water every day from above with slightly warm water, never let the soil dry out, yet don't keep it excessively wet either. The utmost care must be taken in watering this plant as excess moisture is sure to shorten the period of the plant's attractive display. Even if kept under perfect condition the plants will drop their leaves later in the wintertime, until only the red bracts remain at the top. This is a natural behavor and amateur gardeners should not become alarmed and think that their plant is dying. Actually the Poinsettia requires a resting period after it has bloomed, and this is the stage it goes through. When the lowest leaves begin to drop, withhold the water gradually and finally keep altogether dry. When only the naked stems remain, store the pot in a warm dry place until early next spring without applying any water to it.

Geranium

Geraniums are a favorite flower grown in the Southwest by some folks with success, others with great difficulty. Geraniums are generally

34

perennials or biennials, but there are a few annual varieties available. The common garden Geranium is not a true Geranium at all but is a member of a different family.

CULTURE: Geraniums are not difficult to raise. They need only a moderate amount of water, fairly cool, well drained, moderately rich soil, but must be placed where there is plenty of sunshine. Normally in the Southwest a half day's exposure of the Geraniums to the sun should be enough to make the plant bloom freely without excessive sun burning. Top dressing of decayed manure or rich compost, or any type organic matter is advisable in order to stimulate the Geraniums. This plant has the characteristics of being rather drouth resistant, therefore it is no great concern to florists and gardeners in the Southwest.

POTTING: The standard recommended mixture for potting Geraniums is generally considered two parts of loam soil, one part leaf mold or compost, like steer manure, and one part sand. Some folks like to add 1 teaspoonful of bonemeal to the pot in which the plant is to be put. If the soil outdoors where you plan to put the Geraniums is excessively heavy, the soil should be lightened by mixing a mixture of sand or leaf mold in order to make the soil more pliable and easily worked—thus the roots of the Geranium easier to penetrate into the depth of the soil.

PROPAGATION: The average home gardener is going to be most successful by propagating from cuttings, normally taken in September or at the beginning of the early spring. The sequence to follow for successful propagation of this plant is to take a three or four inch cutting of the leaf bud (not the flower bud). Use a very sharp knife and make a cut straight across—just below the bud. Never use pruning shears for this purpose as there is a danger of crushing the delicate tissue, thus ruining the cutting before it is ever transplanted. Do not allow your cuttings to get dry, but set them in moist, sharp sand immediately. Then, you should protect them with a muslin, or some type of cloth, shade. Do not allow them to dry out while they are taking root. As soon as roots are formed, which should be in about three to six weeks, you should pot the newly started plant using a potting soil that is not too highly fertilized as far as chemical ingredients are concerned. From the pot they can be transplanted outside or grown as an inside plant.

BLIGHTS AND DISEASES OF GERANIUMS: If the leaves of a potted specimen begin to turn yellow you can take your choice of three possible causes. Not enough sun, to much water, or an iron deficiency called chlorosis. Once in a while the indoor Geraniums may develop a leaf spot, particularly if you have been wetting the foliage when you water. If the presence of such a disease is detected, isolate the sick plants for the sake of the healthy ones and place them where they will get plenty of light and fresh air, and where the humidity is low. Remove the affected leaves and flowers and burn them. It is advisable not to wet the foliage of this plant as you water it, if it is an inside plant.

35

For mealy bugs which seem to favor this plant, the application of a Diazinon spray oftentimes will control mealy bugs and other sucking type insects that might get on this plant.

Usually the greatest problem involved in the production and growth of Geraniums are Aphids and Leaf Blight. If one will follow the secret of keeping water off the leaves, the problem of Leaf Blight will be very, very nil. If they should become infested with a fungus—use Captan or a fixed copper compound like Bordeaux Mixture to overcome the ravages of the fungus growth. In so far as insect pests are concerned, normally the application of Diazinon will control the biggest majority of them.

Gardenias and Cape Jasmine

Gardenias or Cape Jasmine are shrubs that enhance the beauty of any home. However, there are problems that go with growing this shrub.

There are about 70 species of the Genus Gardenia. Some are shrubs, but there are also vines and trees. Gardenia jasminodes, called Cape Jasmine, (Blooms in the spring) is the most popular one grown in this area. Your nursery offers many types—dwarfs, low growing, climbing or shrub forms.

To grow a beautiful Gardenia or Cape Jasmine, here are a few suggestions to follow in order to produce a healthy shrub and loads of flowers.

1. Prepare a good bed into which the shrub is to be transplanted. These shrubs love an acid soil, so mix some sand or sandy loam in with regular soil found in the bed, if it isn't already of that class.
2. Make sure that the soil drains well. These shrubs can drown out relatively easy.
3. Set the plant in the bed, giving it ample room for it to spread both from the above ground portion, as well as the root system.
4. After the shrub has been set, scatter at least a cupful of iron sulfate (copperas) in a band just under the outer tips of the branches.
5. Apply a starter solution made by dissolving 2 pounds (a pound coffee can) of 12-24-12 fertilizer into 10 gallons of water. Thoroughly soak the soil around the shrub with this solution.
6. Go a final step. Apply 2 or 3 coffee cans of agricultural sulfur around this area and mix into the soil. This should be applied prior to putting on the starter solution.
   The sulfur and iron sulfate is applied to prevent a condition called chlorosis. This is a condition brought about as a result of a deficiency of Iron. In shrubs such as these, when the leaves turn yellow, this is a sign of iron deficiency and either iron sulfate or sulfur should be applied.

When the weather gets hot, a mulch of either pecan leaves, rotted saw-dust or well cured manure should be applied around the shrub to protect the root systems from the intense heat. Protection given by the mulch is a very important item.

As soon as the blooming period is over, branches should be pruned to keep them in bounds, and poor wood is removed.

Gardenias in general like humidity in the air, acid soil, shading from hot summer sun. They may be planted most any time during the winter months. There are several new varieties on the market today, but if possible, buy one of the new varieties that have been grafted onto Gardenia Thunbergia rootstock, which is said to be Nematode and Alkali resistant.

The black sooty fungus growing on Gardenias is caused by the White Fly. The fly leaves a sugary media on the leaves in which the fungus grows. See Chapters 8 and 9 for control.

Insects

Insects that bother this shrub are: Aphids, Soft Brown Scab, White Fly and a weevil-like insect that attacks the flowers. Chapter 8 tells how to control them.

Roses

Of all the garden plants grown today, roses are probably the most popular of all, the reason being that they are adapted to many purposes, and are grown in almost every section of the country.

There are many different varieties available on the market for planting on lawns and borders, for arbors, trellises, bedding, hedges, ground covers and those strictly to produce cut flowers. Roses are generally classified into groups according to similarity in habit of growth, form of flower, hardiness and other characteristics. Actually there is no sharp line of difference between all of the various types because plant breeders have crossed and recrossed varieties from different sections until many of our modern day roses now possess characters of two or more groups. Mainly for the amateur gardener, there are two main classes of roses, bush roses and climbing roses. These two classes are based entirely on habit of growth. The bush rose grows from one to six feet in height and requires no support, climbing roses produce long canes each year and must be provided with some type of support for them to do their maximum good.

Under the classification of bush roses there are many different types, depending upon flowering habits, winter hardiness and other traits that have been bred into them. The types most commonly found under bush roses are the hybrid teas, the floribundas, polyanthas, hybrid perpetuals, shrubs, old fashions, tree or standard and miniature roses.

Climbing roses, like rose bushes, are also grouped into several classes, and there is much overlapping among classes. However, generally speaking, most of the climbing roses are classified as ramblers, large flowered climbers, everblooming climbers, climbing hybrid teas, climbing polyanthas, climbing floribundas and trailing roses.

Culture of Roses

Roses are not difficult to grow. However, they do have to be protected against disease and insects, and soil conditions must be taken into consideration. If one will follow the listed rules below—generally you can look for success.

1. Buy good roses.
2. Select the location where you have sun at least half of the day, and protect them from roots of other plants—such as trees.
3. Plant the rose bush properly.
4. Prune them in the early spring.
5. Start weekly cultivation and dusting early in the spring. Fertilize according to recognized procedures and give them adequate protection if severe winter should cause damage.

Roses obtain their best growth in full sunshine, but good results may be obtained if they are exposed to sunshine at least a half a day. If it is impossible to avoid shade, it is far better to have it on the plants in the late afternoon than it is in the morning. The reason for this being that if the plants are in morning shade the plants will remain wet with dew for a few hours longer than if in direct sunlight, and the presence of moisture on the leaves causes favorable conditions for a number of leaf diseases, as well as fungus growth.

Good drainage is most important for the successful growing of roses, poorly drained soils, or a location where water accumulates after a rain will not produce good roses. Any good garden soil will normally do the job in producing a bountiful crop of blooms. However, where we have a heavy type clay soil, it is advisable to add to this heavy soil, organic matter or some lighter type sand. Organic matter including such things as peat moss, leaf mold, or steer manure, all worked into the layer of soil—12 to 18 inches deep—to assure a type of soil that is best for rose production. Actually the top four to six inches is not so important, but the next 12 inches of soil in the bed should contain the plant food, and of course generous quantities of well decayed organic matter in this zone—because this is where your roots generally feed.

If excessively heavy clays exist in the area in which you are planting the rose bed, it may be advisable to remove a portion of the soil—12 to 18 inches deep—and mix it thoroughly with well rotted manure in the proportion of about 6 bushel of soil to one bushel of manure. It is also usually advisable to mix thoroughly with this seven bushels of soil and manure about a half pound of phosphate—either 0-450 or super phosphate.

The rose bed should be well removed from the hungry, marauding roots of shade trees, as these go far in search of food, and sometimes after gaining entrance a single root will spread out to fill the whole bed and rob the roses of the food that they need. Roses should be planted where there is air movement, but they must be protected from high winds. Any well drained garden soil, mixed with this organic matter as explained previously, can produce good roses. The soil should be slightly acid to neutral. Highly acid or highly alkaline soil is unsuitable for growing roses successfully. In the Southwest, one of our biggest problems is the fact that we have a high alkaline soil, and where this persists our roses are confronted with a toxic lime condition and generally show up wtih chlorosis. It probably would be advisable, as the bed is being prepared, to work in about two to three pounds of agricultural sulfur per 100 square feet of bed space.

Planting and Spacing of Roses

In general, fall planting or early spring is the ideal time to plant roses. As a rule of thumb, generally the months of November through March are accepted as the time for transplanting or putting out roses in this area. The spacing of rose plants depends on several factors, including the variety of the rose, the climate in which it is grown, the methods of pruning to be used and the type of bush to be desired. One must remember that plants that have ample room produce more and better flowers than those that are crowded.

Roses in cans—and this is a growing practice—can be planted anytime.

As a general rule of thumb—hybrid teas, polyanthas and floribundas should be planted at two to three feet apart, preferably three. The hybrid perpetuals should be spaced three to five feet apart. Climbers anywhere from eight to ten feet apart. In any case, enough space should be allowed so the plants can develop fully and receive as much sunlight and aeration as possible. Such spacing provides room for good culture and for spraying or dusting operations to control diseases and insects.

Rose plants should be set out as soon as they are received. If this is not possible, the plants should be unpacked, unwrapped and examined to see if the roots have dried out. If the packing material about the roots is dry, it should be moistened and replaced, providing planting is not delayed more than a few days. If it is necessary to delay planting due to inclement weather longer than a few days, the plants should be unpacked and heeled in. That is, placed in a trench and the roots covered with moist soil. If the roots are dry when received, they should be soaked in water for several hours before heeling them in. If the stems of the plants are also dry, the condition of the plants may sometimes be improved by burying them for a few days in moist soil. When all preparations for planting have been made, the roots of each plant should be carefully examined. All dead growth should be cut off; the top should also be pruned if needed. However, generally, most nurseries cut back the roses to about 12 inches before they ship them. If stems are cut back to less than ten inches—flowering oftentimes is usually delayed.

The proper procedure for planting a rose is make sure that the hole that you dig to transplant the rose in, is large enough that the roots can be spread out in a natural manner, spreading out from the stem like the fingers of a hand. Build a mound of soil in the center of the hole and arrange the roots over it, press down around the plants to force out any air pockets remaining in the soil mound. Cover the roots with topsoil and tamp firmly. Never plant when the soil is extremely wet, or as a rule of thumb—so wet that it cannot be pressed into balls the plant, then water it thoroughly. When new plants are set out in that will not crumble. When the soil has been firmly tamped around the fall—cut back all the canes to 12 inches from the ground. When the buds begin to swell in the spring, cut all the strong canes or stems down to six inches from the ground and remove all the weak or spindly growth. When plants are set out in the spring, cut the canes to six inches above the ground at the time of planting.

Fertilizing

Roses are oftentimes overfed—much more than underfed. The average gardener wishing to obtain the finest flowers oftentimes believes he can rush up the process of producing blooms by the application of fertilizer. Roses prefer a slightly acid soil. In general, roses grow best when the pH of the soil is from 5.5 to 6.6, generally considered slightly acid. It is generally best to apply a complete fertilizer around the rose bushes. It is advisable to apply this during the growing season—several times. The first application should be made when the new spring growth is well established and all danger of severe freezing is past. The best rose material to use is about 1 teaspoonful of balanced fertilizer around a fully grown rose bush during the early spring season. Spread the fertilizer evenly and scratch it into the soil, preferably just before a rain or prior to watering the rose bed. This treatment should be repeated every 60 days. Generally one should not apply fertilizer after September or October as this will interfere with the normal process of the rose bush going into a semi-dormant state during the winter months. Do not use more than the recommended amount of these balanced fertilizers, because if this is done—oftentimes it will cause a chemical burn.

Of necessity, it may be advisable to treat for chlorosis in our roses throughout the growing season, and the best way to determine that is to watch the foliage of your plants. As they begin to turn a yellowish-white, this is a sure sign of an iron deficiency. Use one ounce of iron chelate to two gallons of water sprayed directly onto the foilage of the plant.

Phosphorous is a compound that is essential in the formation of blooms, and a deficiency of phosphorous will show up not only in the leaves, but also a shortage of blooms. A lot of good gardeners have found that the application of bone meal oftentimes will supply the correct amount of phosphorous to overcome this shortage. A balanced fertilizer will supply the needed amount of phosphorous that the plant must have. But stressing once again: DO NOT OVER FERTILIZE YOUR ROSES.

Rose Diseases

(For Control Practice, See Chapter 9)

Roses, like most other plants, are subject to attack by disease producing organisms such as fungus, bacteria and nematode. Furthermore, certain rose diseases are due to viruses or to physiological disorders. The disease of greatest economic disorders to gardeners are Black Spot; Powdery Mildew; Dieback; Ground Gall; and Root Knot. These will be discussed individually.

BLACK SPOT IN ROSES: Black Spot is principally a disease of the leaves, it may also occur in the leaf petioles, flower peduncles, and even on the canes. It is one of the most important of all rose diseases, occurring wherever roses are grown. The disease causes a weakened condition of the plants, through loss of the leaves, consequently normal food supply which is developed in the leaves to be transferred to other parts of the plant is maturely decreased. Black Spot oftentimes is the result of poor growth, not only during the current season, but also following the season that has been attacked by the fungus. It can be recognized on the leaves of the rose bush by the black colored lesions, nearly circular shaped, and is differentiated from other leaf spots by the generally fringed margins, and also by the darker and more uniform color. The size of the spot varies from less than 1/16 of an inch or more in diameter.

POWDERY MILDEW: This is another widespread and important disease of roses in this area. The white or grayish-colored mold on the young leaves, flower buds and tender canes is easily recognized. All classes of roses are affected. The effect of Powder Mildew is to curl and distort the leaves and decrease the rate of growth of the plant. Flower buds are dwarfed and misshapened, often the tips of the cane are severely affected. It is seldom that mildew causes the death of a plant, but it retards the normal growth processes, and the end result is a weakened condition—which affects flower production and the ability to produce blooms.

RUST: This particular malady is characterized by the orange or yellowish-orange spots on the leaves of the plant. Although not widespread, and apparently unknown in the commercial fields of East Texas, this disease has been observed at other places throughout the country. Generally this disease is not prevalent to any great extent in this immediate area and does not warrant sufficient coverage of it.

STEM DIE-BACK: Die-back is a prevalent cane disease and it causes the canes to die from the tip downward, frequently beginning in the flower stem. The diseased wood and bark turn brown or black in color and appear somewhat shriveled from drying. Investigations indicate that varieties of roses which are most subject to Black Spot are also most seriously affected by Die-back.

CONTROL: Practices which increase the vigor of the bushes will reduce the amount of Die-back present. Just budding or pinching off the flower blossoms have been found effective in helping build up healthy rose bushes, and thereby reducing their susceptibility to this disease. Fungicides such as dusting sulfur, Captan and Phaltan, which control Black Spot, will likewise improve the condition of the plants and thereby prevent Die-back to a certain extent.

ROSE INSECTS: There are a number of rose insects such as aphids, plant lice, leaf miner, and others that attack rose bushes. There are also a number of general, all-purpose, combination insecticide-fungicide dusts and sprays on the market that will do an excellent job. One of the best insecticides to use on roses for the control of various insects is Diazinon. This is compatable with your fungicides—such as Captan and Phaltan—to the extent that they can generally be combined in the same spray material and applied at one time. A program of prevention is the best practice in controlling insect and disease injury to roses. Spray or dust on a regular schedule, and apply it as soon as possible after each rain, or at least once a week. This prevents infection and protects the new foliage from becoming infected. *DO NOT WAIT UNTIL INSECTS AND DISEASES ARE PRESENT BEFORE CONTROLS ARE USED.*

Wisteria

Wisteria ranks among the best of the ornamental vines for temperate regions and often obtains a good old age and large size. They are actually decidious twining shrubs that are native in North America and Asia, belonging to the Pea family.

While Wisteria will grow in almost any soil, they thrive best in a deep, rich loam that does not get too dry. They are at their picturesque best when allowed to grow at will up an old tree, old wall or building. It is best to pay some attention to training the growth. They will also do quite well on a cyclone fence. They are sometimes grown in standard form and also forced readily in pots. As their roots are long, but not fibrous, the plants are best transplanted when small or from pots rather than the field.

Wisterias often disappoint by not flowering for many years. These non producers are seedlings, and it is highly uncertain as to when they will reach the flowering stage. Restriction of the root run and shortening back the long shoots in mid-summer may aid in the formation of flower buds, but the best thing is to plant only grafted or layered plants from flowering specimens. The spring crop of flowers is born on spurs, and in severe climates the buds are often winter killed. A small crop of flowers is often produced in late summer on young growth of the current season. They are hard to transplant after making any appreciable growth. After they get fully grown it is very seldom that a Wisteria vine can be transplanted as a grown shrub without it dying back. Always plant a

Wisteria vine in the full sun because the seedlings take years to begin blooming. It is best to buy grafted, potted plants from local nurseries.

The soil should be prepared three feet deep, with a third of it rotted manure. Manure should also be used to mulch the plant each year. Young plants when first transplanted, should be tied to a support until they begin to vine.

Very few insects infest the Wisteria vine, however large sucking bugs called Lantern Flies are often found on Wisteria. They lay their eggs in slits in the bark and cover them with masses of white-wax secretion. If the injury becomes serious one should spray the plants with a Malathion spray. The large spotted "Skipper," which is a butterfly, feed on the Wisteria. Both can be controlled very easily by using Malathion spray.

Wisterias, as well as any other shrub, will respond to fertilizer treatment. Oftentimes the leaves will begin to yellow, which is a definite sign of chlorosis, or a lack of an iron element, and therefore sufficient iron compounds in the form of iron chelates or iron sulfate should be applied around the feeder roots of the Wisteria vine. In so far as fertilizer is concerned, the same fertilizer that you use to fertilize your lawn will do an excellent job if a cupful is applied around a fully grown Wisteria vine. This should be done preferably in the fall so as to build an excellent root system for the plant to come out and do their maximum amount of blooming next Spring.

Growing Houseplants

Any plant which will grow under the adverse conditions of aridity, temperature, and light encountered in an ordinary house, generally is classified as a house plant and needs specific attention and care. Of all factors involved in the production of plants in a home, whether it be ivy, ferns etc., moisture and sunlight are the two most important ones. Except Cacti—all houseplants need more atmospheric moisture than is available to them in an artificially heated home. Water is constantly evaporating from all the foliage of such plants. Though the rate of evaporation differs according to the leaf structure of various varieties, usually plants with smooth leathery foliage will loose less water through their leaves than those with hairy or spongy textured leaves. Because of water expired by each plant, a group of plants in a small area may be surrounded by a more moist atmosphere than one single plant by itself. Therefore a group of plants in a planter box or set on a window or shelf will oftentimes improve the atmospheric conditions for all of the plants.

A bulb spray syringe may be used to spray water over house plants daily if the surroundings will not be damaged by the moisture, or they may be moved to a sink or tub periodically (on a weekly basis) for a spray bath of all the foliage. Most house plants benefit from a weekly soaking in a tub with water up to the pot rim. After it has absorbed enough water to make the surface moist, the plant should be thoroughly drained before being returned to its window or setting place. The amount of water given between soakings will differ according to the plant, the size of the pot and the accidental clogging or plugging of the drainage hole in the bottom of these pots that takes place after it is filled. Most plants should not be allowed to stand in saucers filled with water that is drained after their daily watering. However, if their need for moisture is greater than can be supplied in any other way, the plant saucer may be filled with pebbles which are kept moist and the plant will stand on the pebbles above the water line. Oftentimes excessive watering and water logging of plant roots is of greater detriment to the plant than a lack of water. Here again it will depend upon each individual variety and the care that is taken of it, coupled with the atmospheric conditions in the home itself, and one can only learn this by trial and error methods.

TEMPERATURE: The ideal conditions for most house plants is about the same as those for human being. Temperatures of 65 to 70 degrees in the daytime and 50 to 55 degrees at night are optimum. Higher or lower temperatures than these are detrimental to the plants. Temperatures in a plant window may fluctuate much more than this, especially if curtains or dividers behind the plant prevent circulation of air from the room. During the day the sun will quickly heat a small enclosed space to shoot the mercury up 10 to 25 degrees. Unless the glass is doubled between the plants and the winter cold, the temperatures in a deep window may drop to freezing near the glass on a very cold night. When plants grow in too hot an atmosphere, even though they are given plenty of moisture and food, the growth is too soft, it is easily injured and is easy prey for insects, and the plant does not do well.

LIGHT: Light is important to almost all plant life. It is essential in the manufacturing process that goes on in the plant itself. Just as some plants thrive outside in the shade or half shade, house plants may not want more than a small amount of sun filtered through a thin curtain or screen, while other varieties demand a great deal of sun. Ideally, house plants should be supplied light on all sides. This can be obtained by constant turning of the plants periodically throughout the week so that all sides receive the same amount of light. One should see to it that ample sunlight is provided for all of the plants. Artificial light oftentimes is not enough, African Violets, of course, will respond in so far as blooming conditions are concerned with artificial light. Other plants though must have the rays of the natural sun in order to prosper and grow as they should.

SOIL: Potting soil is of utmost importance in the maximum production of house plants, and here again different varieties of plants desire different types of potting soil. Some plants can be grown in water, while others must be planted in rich organic soil. As a general rule of thumb—suggestions for the mixing of a potting soil that will be ideal for most plants that are to be grown in the home, we suggest the following:

General Potting Soil Mixture

Two parts good garden loam, one part compost, leaf mold or other organic material, one part of clean coarse sand. To the above mixture add some cotton seed meal (preferably about ¼ cupful per mixture), supply the necessary chemical nutrients through the medium of a liquid fertilizer. As a suggestion, dissolve a tablespoonful of fertilizer into ½ gallon of water, or—if you desire a larger amount of this mixture—take two pounds of this material and dissolve into ten gallons of water, and once every three weeks water your plants with this mixture.

Chapter 3

Annuals in the Garden

Annuals in the Garden

Those plants which grow from seed, obtain their growth, and produce seed in one year, or less, then die—thus having completed their life cycle—are called annuals. Many annuals appear to be perennials, seeming to live on from one year to the next, but in reality they reproduce themselves by scattering seed that live through the winter and then rise up to give new plants. Thus thy perpetuate themselves. Also, there is a misconception on a number of gardeners part to think that plants of a biennial or perennial classes which bloom the first year from seed are considered annuals, but this is not true.

The annual flowers and plants that we grow in our gardens come to us from all over the world. Properly chose they can provide bloom and fragrance in the garden from early spring till late fall. Annuals come in many forms, heights and colors, and then lend themselves to many uses.

Annuals may be divided into three main classes. (1) *hardy annuals* which can withstand the light spring frost and can thus be started from seed sown in the open as soon as the soil can be worked.

(2) half hardy annuals, which require a long season to attain maturity and therefore must be given consideration to get an early start, normally starting them off in a greenhouse or hot bed.

(3) tender annuals which require still an earlier start in the greenhouse or hotbed, and cannot be transplanted into the open until the ground is warm and all danger of frost or freeze is past.

Hardy Annuals

From our previous description as to a hardy annual, these seed can be sown outdoors in the early spring without fear of getting the young plants killed from an early frost or freeze. Those plants which can be done this way include the folowing:

Alyssum	Evening Stock	Phlox
Baby's Breath	Larkspur	Poppy
Batchelor Buttons	Lupine	Sunflower
California Poppy	Mallow	Sweet Pea
Candytuft	Marigold	Verbena
Chinese Delphinium	Pansy	Viscaria
Evening Primrose	Petunia	Zinnia

Seed of these hardy annuals, which are sown in the open, should be planted in well prepared loamy soil in which compost, well rotted manure, or other type organic matter have been dug into the soil the fall before. The surface of the soil in which they are planted should be light and fine enough so that tender seedlings may break or penetrate through the outer crust easily.

If the soil is stiff or heavy, one can utilize a mixture of sand or humus to help lighten the texture, thus enabling the small seedlings to break through the outer crust.

Some of the annuals that I have named resent being transplanted and therefore should be spaced and planted according to how one prefers them to grow when seeding is performed. Among those are the Lupine, Mallow, the California Poppy, the Poppy and the Sweet Pea. Therefore this should be taken into consideration when planting is done.

Half Hardy Annuals

These plants can be started normally in flats, hotbeds, greenhouses or other utensils whereby they can be given partial protection. Oftentimes folks will move them in and move them out to get them tempered or hardy to sustain themselves under environmental conditions in which they are to grow. Half hardy annuals that are grown in the Southwest flowers gardens are:

Asters	Phlox	Snapdragon	Sweet Sultan
Petunia	Sage	Swan River Daisy	Wallflower

If one desires to start these plants in a flat in order to move them in and out so that they can be tempered to meet the rigors of the environmental conditions in which they will grow later on, this can be done by using a tomato crate or some other type of flat in which the soil and other organic matter can be mixed. You need a flat with the depth of at least four inches. Partly fill the box with coarse sand, finishing off with the top inch of the soil consisting of fine silted loam mixed with humus or other compost material, and then pack it to make a firm seed bed. Sow the seed in rows in these flats. The rows should be about one inch apart. Very fine seed may be covered with burlap, which should be kept watered in order to keep the humidity high, aiding in germination. After the plants have reached the desired height and have been tempered or strengthened by introduction of a periodic nature to the environmental conditions in which they grow, they can be transplanted into the flower beds for growth.

Tender Annuals

These plants should be started the same way as the half hardy annuals, but normally much earlier and this requires either a greenhouse or the protection of a garage where the temperature and the humidity can be maintained. Those flowers which generally fit this classification are:

Annual Poinsettia	Balsam Apple	Canary Bird Vine	Castor Bean
Balsam Chrysanthemum— (the annual)	Dwarfed Morning Glory	Scarlet Sage Scarlet Runner Bean	Torenia

These plants should be planted as previously mentioned for the half hardy annuals, and the plants should be shifted in and out of doors quite frequently in order to make them more stocky and hardy—so to withstand the rigors of outside environment when they are transplanted. As soon as several true leaves have appeared on the plants in the planter box or the greenhouse, the seedlings should be pricked off into small individual pots or into another box or flat. An old kitchen fork is an excellent tool to use in this work, or one could use a small garden spade.

These transplanted seedlings form a better root system much quicker and grow more compact and steady rather than tall and slender, which is a hazard of plants growing too close togther. Once the outside temperature has warmed up to be conducive for their growth, transplant them into their beds in which they are to grow.

Nurseries offer bedding annuals quite inexpensively, saving you all this trouble.

Climbing Annuals

Annual vines are ideal as a cover for fencing, decorative purposes, covering up unsightly objects or to form a screen for privacy. They grow quickly and provide beauty while performing these other necessary tasks. One of the most beautiful is the Moon flower vine, whose fragrance resembles that of a Magnolia. Another one that grows profusely is the Aerial Tuber—which makes huge leaves and grows profusely throughout the spring and summer months. One of the fastest growing climbers is the Cup and Saucer vine—whose purple and white blossoms, resembling the Canterbury Bells, bloom profusely for the amateur gardener. Nor can we ignore the old fashioned Morning Glory too, which is known throughout this area, as well as vines of the gourd family. Hanging tea kettles, baskets and window boxes are also a feature of a number of homes, Annuals here are used as a decorative purpose. The Clock Vine, the Dusty Miller, Marigolds, Petunia, Phlox, Pansys and Verbena are all popular flowers to be used in this decorative purpose.

Two basic principles must be remembered in growing annuals. The first is the necessity of obtaining the best seed from a well known reputable established firm, one that you can trust and one that has been in business for a long time. Normally the seedmen servicing the garden trade have pride in the strains that they bring out, which designates their own individual personality in the strain. Normally if you buy from reputable seed breeders you can safely count on the right color and the desired quality of the plants which grow from their selected seed. Or buy already grown bedding plants for easy transplanting.

The second thing to remember is that if you wish to prolong the blooming period of an annual, the flowers must be picked before they fade or immediately thereafter in order that the seed do not have a chance to form. A true annual plant has a slight root system as it stores no food for future seasons, and it lives to bloom quickly, set seed and finish its existence. Therefore constant picking of the flowers conserves this energy and prolongs its growth and beautification by the production of flowers. That, along with normal cultural care, insect control, proper watering and fertilization—annuals are a part of everyone's gardening program.

Chapter 4

Home Vegetable Garden

Home Vegetable Garden

A small home vegetable garden can become feasible in almost anyone's backyard, and the production of fresh vegtables can certainly lighten the food bill as well as furnish for those who love to till the soil an opportunity to work and reap the benefit of his work by furnishing their families and the deep freeze with plenty of fresh green vegetables during the 12 months of the year.

The first step in planting a garden is to select the best possible location. Of course, oftentimes this is restricted to a point where folks only have a small plot in their backyard. But, in selecting a garden plot to produce good vegetables the following points should be considered.

1. *Convenience*—The garden site should be located near the house so that it is easy to work and harvest the vegetable crops.

2. *A good soil*—This is a factor that the home gardener cannot control completely, but in most cases it is a matter of choosing the most suitable soil available on the home grounds and then improving that soil so it will produce the type of vegetables that you want.

3. *Water Supply*—Of course where you have access to city water this is no problem at all.

4. *The lay of the land*—Oftentimes the home gardener in town has no choice over this other than to provide proper drainage to take care of excess rainfall that may come.

5. *Adequate light*—Most vegetable crops require much sunshine for the best growth. Location that is shaded by trees, shrubs, walls or buildings most of the day should be avoided. Leafy crops such as lettuce, mustard, collards, spinach, chards and kale tolerate more shade than most of the fruit bearing crops—such as tomatoes, egg plants, squash, cantaloupe and peppers.

6. *Competition*—Competing vegetation in the form of large shade trees and ornamental shrubs can seriously reduce the yield of a home garden. If the root systems of these plants are growing in the garden area, they will take up large quantities of fertilizer and moisture needed by the vegetable crop for satisfactory growth.

Making Garden Plans

For even an experienced gardener, a plan on paper is quite helpful for choosing the desired kinds of vegetables before planting time. If certain varieties are not available locally, they can be ordered from various seed producers. There is no perfect plan, of course, that fits all gardens, but it is best to group vegetables according to the proper time for planting. In general, vegetables are divided into three groups— early—mid-season and late. The early group such as English Peas, carrots, spinach, beets, cabbage and onions should be planted in another part and late vegetables in still another part. If at all possible, the low growing type of vegetable should be planted so that they are not shaded by the tall ones. The garden fence may oftentimes be used to an advantage in providing a trellis for pole type beans and other vegetables of this type.

Soil Preparation and Improvement

PREPARING THE SOIL: The location, type of soil, drainage, physical condition and the season of the year, the amount of rainfall and other factors alter the procedure in preparing garden sites. An old garden site of deep, open sandy soil needs only light, shallow cultivation. However, if a new site is selected on poorly drained spots or tight shallow soil, or rocky and heavy sodded land, it should be cleaned off, drained and broken thoroughly as soon as the weather will permit. It is best to prepare such a plot in the winter before spring vegetables are to be planted. After the sites have been plowed and prepared, the soil should be thoroughly broken to a depth of eight to ten inches. In breaking plots one can use a rotary type tiller, or if a large enough plot is available, one can use a breaking plow with a tractor. Or if a small plot of say 200 square feet, one can use a spading fork.

As spring gardening time approaches the roughly plowed garden should be pulverized several times well in advance of planting. Rows should be prepared to suit the location and the type of vegetable to be planted. For most vegetables, 18 to 36 inch rows are adequate. The running type vegetables such as cucumbers and watermelons, of course, require more space. In general, flat culture requires less work and is better than growing the crops on raised beds or ridges. However, if the soil should be poorly drained, it may be that ridges or beds should be prepared so that the plant can grow above the normal soil line, giving it adequate drainage. Soils should not be worked when too wet; this results in poor condition of the land and in general a poor soil.

USING COMMERCIAL FERTILIZERS: Commercial fertilizers are good for vegetable production in light sandy or sandy loam soils. Generally a combination of barnyard and commercial fertilizer is better than either alone. The more organic matter worked into the garden plot, the better the plot will become. On small plots, such as for those who garden in town, commercial fertilizers may be broadcast and thoroughly raked into the top three or four inches of soil. When fertilizer is used in drills beneath the row, it should be placed about two inches to one side and slightly below where the seeds are to be planted. The amount of fertilizer to use in the row will depend a great deal on the analysis of the fertilizer.

For those who use a 13-13-13 or 12-24-12, about two pounds per 100 feet of row should be mixed in thoroughly with the soil a week or ten days prior to planting. This should be ample to carry the vegetables through the biggest part of the growing season. The application of a nitrogenous compound as the plant is growing, as a side dressing, often-times will pay great dividends and faster production. Such nitrogen fertilizer should be in the form of either urea or ammonium sulphate.

In side dressing plants, place the fertilizer well away from the base of the plants, out in the feeder root area, work it well in the soil and water thoroughly. For plants that will be transplanted into the garden, such as peppers and tomatoes, it is advisable to use a starter solution—made by dissolving two pounds of 13-13-13 into ten gallons of water.

Place about one pint of this starter solution around each plant. Normally it will take five or ten gallons of this mixture for 100 feet of row space, depending upon the spacing of the vegetables. In soils that are excessively alkaline, it would be advisable to work in some soil sulfur. It is advisable to work the sulfur into the soil at the time of preparing the garden. The amount to use—about five pounds per 100 square feet of garden space will be ample. This will help acidify the soil and make it more desirable for those vegetable plants that love an acid soil.

Local Market and Home Grown Varieties Adapted for The Southwest

Quite frequently gardeners will become confused as to the best adapted varieties for this immediate area. As a result they will order a variety from north or west, and they are completely dissatisfied with the results they get, due to the fact that they are not adapted and will not perform according to their specifications in our climatical conditions or soils. Therefore, the varieties which have been recommended for local market or home gardens have been compiled by the Texas Agricultural Experiment Station and Texas Agricultural Extension Service for the Gulf Coast area. It would be advisable when you go to buy your vegetable seed to follow this recommendation to make sure that you plant those varieties that are adapted for this area.

Varieties and Planting Guide for The Southwest

Name of Vegetable	Variety to Plant	Seeds or Plants Per 100 Ft. of Row	Rows Apart (In.)	Plants Apart (In.)	Depth of Planting	No Days Ready for Use	Hardiness
Asparagus	Martha Washington	60–80	24–36	15–20	8–10	2–3 years	Very
Beans, snap, bush	Top Crop, Tendergreen, Pearl Green, Seminole (Fall)	1 pint	24–36	2–4	1–2	48–55	Tender
Beans, snap, pole	Bluelake, Kentucky Wonders	½ pint	24–36	4–6	1–2	55–65	Tender
Beans, lima, bush	Fordhook 242	½ pint	24–36	3–4	1–2	55–65	Tender
Beans, lima, pole	Florida Speckled	½ pint	24–36	4–6	1–2	75	Tender
Beets	Detroit Dark Red	1 oz.	24–36	2–3	1	60–65	Hardy
Broccoli	Early Green, Sprouting Texas 107	66	30–36	18	2–4	60–80	Hardy
Cabbage	Marion Market, Early Round Dutch, Golden Acre (Early)	75–100	30–36	12–18	2–3	70–75	Hardy
Carrots	Red Core, Chantenay, Danver's Half-Long	1 oz.	24–36	2–3	½–¾	70–75	Hardy
Chard, Swiss	Lucullus	1 oz.	24–36	6–8	½–¾	50	Hardy
Collard	Louisiana Sweet	¼ oz.	30–36	12–18	½–¾	75	Hardy
Corn, sweet	Aristogold Bantam, Evergreen, Calumet 57, Ioana	¼ pint	30–36	18–24	1½–2	80–90	Tender
Cucumbers, slicing	Stono (Disease resistant) A & C	1 oz.	48	48–72	1	65–70	Tender
Cucumbers, pickling	Ohio MR 17, Earliest of All	1 oz.	48	48–72	1	55–60	Tender
Eggplant	Black Beauty, Florida High Bush	⅛ oz.	30–36	18–24	½	80–85	Tender
Kale	Scotch Curled, Siberian	¼ oz.	24–36	6–8	½–¾	55	Hardy
Lettuce, head	Great Lakes	½ oz.	24–36	4–6	1–¾	80	Hardy
Lettuce, leaf	Grand Rapids, Salad Bowl	½ oz.	24–36	4–6	½–¾	40–45	Hardy
Muskmelon (Cantaloupe)	Smith's Perfect Rio Gold	1 oz.	60–96	24–36	1–2	85–95	Tender
Mustard	Tendergreen (Early) Florida, Broad-leaf Giant, Southern Curled	2 oz.	24–36	1	½–¾	30–40	Hardy
Okra	Louisiana Green Velvet, Clemson Spineless	1 oz.	30–36	24–36	1	55–60	Tender
Onions	Excel, Crystal White, Granex	400	24–36	3–4	1½–2½	80–95	Hardy
Parsley	Moss Curled	⅛ oz.	24–36	2–3	½–¾	70	Hardy
Peas, Southern	Extra Early Blackeye, Purple Hull, 49 Cream 40 Cream 12	1 lb.	24–36	6–8	2–3	60–65	Hardy
Peas, English	Laxton's Progress, Little Marvel	2 lb.	24–36	3–4	3–4	60–65	Hardy
Pepper	Yolo Wonder, Early Calwonder	50–75	36	12–24	2–3	70–80	Tender
Potato, Irish	Bliss Triumph, Red Pontiac, La Soda, Sebago	5–8 lb.	30–36	12–15	3–5	75–100	Half-Hardy
Potato, Sweet	Allgold, Texas Porto Rico, Red Velvet	50–75	36–42	12–18	3–5	120–150	Half-Hardy
Radish	Scarlet Globe, White Icicle	1 oz.	24–36	½–1	½–¾	20–30	Hardy
Spinach	Bloomsdale Savoy	1 oz.	24–36	3–5	½–¾	40	Hardy
Squash, summer	Early Prolific, Straightneck, White Bush Scallop	½ oz.	36–48	36	1–2	50	Tender
Squash, winter	Acorn	½ oz.	60–72	36	1–2	85–90	Tender
Tomatoes	Texto 2, Pritchard, Firesteel Porter (Summer) Summer Prolific (Summer)	35–50	48	30–36	2–4	60–85	Very-Tender
Turnips	Purple Top Shogoin (Greens)	½ oz.	24–36	3–5	½–¾	35–55	Hardy
Watermelon	Charleston Gray, Pride O'Texas, Tendersweet, Sugar Baby	½ oz.	84–96	36–48	1–2	85–95	Tender

Transplanting

In almost any flower or vegetable garden there are occasions for a certain amount of transplanting, even if it is only to readjust the spacing between plants which have come up irregularly from seeds sown directly in the garden.

The basic rule for moving plants are very simple. Disturb the roots as little as possible and use plenty of water. To these ends it is desirable, if the soil is not already moist, to water your flower bed or vegetable garden the day before you intend to do any transplanting. This gives the soil a chance to become uniformly moist, not just muddy on the surface, and makes it easier to firm the soil around the roots of the transplants, which is highly essential.

Before you remove the plants from the flats, make sure that they are well watered to encourage the soil to adhere to the roots and hold together when you lift it with your trowel or your hand. If the plants are to be moved from flats where they have been grown from seed, they will probably be growing about two inches apart in the flat. This is the ideal spacing, of course, because you can cut an adequate square of earth around each plant, lifting the plant roots and soil in one complete unit, thus not disturbing the root system. The lucky plants moved this way hardly know what has happened and go on developing without hesitation.

Even better transplanting conditions result from the use of compressed peat pots, which are fine for starting plants and which are set directly in the soil, plant, pot and all in one unit. The roots grow right through the wall of the pot and continue on into the garden soil. If the ball of earth around the roots crumbles by accident during the transplanting operation, there is no need to despair for even bare rooted plants will adjust to a new situation and make growth again. In fact, a number of our tomato and pepper plants are of this nature, as you may get them bare-footed, wrapped in a moist newspaper.

In setting any plant in its permanent location it is important to make the hole deep enough so that the roots need not be curled or folded back in setting them in position. Extremely long roots ought to be pruned rather than crumpled. Plants should end at the same level in the garden as they were growing in the flat or pot in which they were started.

Once in place it is very important for you, the gardener, to firm the soil around the roots, eliminating air pockets and wedding the garden soil to that moved along with the transplant. This you can do with the pressure of your fingers and by watering. Of the two, watering is the most important, for all the crevices are filled, the soil particles silted into position, and the plant situated in the new location by this action.

In addition to this, the watering can be supplemented or replaced by the use of a starter solution around such plants. A discussion on starter solution will follow. It is better to do your watering by pouring around the base of the plant. Sprinkling the leaves may cause them to stick to the soil, and it is hard for them to break loose once again.

Starter Solution

Starter solutions have been used in the past by vegetable farmers to surround recently transplanted plants such as tomatoes, peppers and sweet potato slips. The basic advantages in using a starter solution are: (1) It decreases the shock in moving the young plants. (2) It stimulates root growth and hastens the plant toward growing to maturity. (3) It increases yields by increasing earlier maturity. (4) It provides earlier maturity for the vegetables.

The simplest way to formulate a starter solution is to take a fertilizer that is completely water soluble and high in the P₂O₅—phosphoric content. This is the element of importance because it has a great deal to do with stimulating root growth, and this in turn has a direct bearing upon the absorption and utilization of the other major and minor elements in the soil. Therefore, as a suggestion for formulating a starter solution to be placed around recently transplanted plants, I suggest that you take two pounds of 12-24-12 fertilizer and dissolve into ten gallons of water. This is equivalent also to 20 pounds to 100 gallons of water. In the diluted form there will be no danger of chemical burns if this materials is used right. Water soluble fertilizer will immediately go into solution; stir it up, and as you transplant the pepper plants, tomato plants, potato slips and so forth, pour about a cupful of this material around each one of the plants. If the plants are smaller than the ones that are mentioned above, then use proportionately smaller amounts.

A number of gardeners have found that this is the ideal way to apply fertilizer to their shrubs, also roses and flowers to enhance fertility into the soil and keep them growing at a maximum rate by using this material about every three weeks in place of a regular watering. One should not apply this material to the foliage of the plant as it may be in concentrated enough form to cause some chemical burns. Best to apply it around the feeder roots of the plant and then, if need be, apply additional water after the starter solution has been poured around the feeder roots of the plant. It will do an excellent job; it is very simple to formulate as any gardener can see. Some folks keep a 55 gallon barrel around the place and keep on hand a starter solution at all times.

A Gardeners' Guide for Converting Tons or Pounds Per Acre Into Pints, Cups, Tablespoons, or Teaspoons Per Row or Plant

Books and bulletins on agriculture and gardening usually give a recommendation for the use of fertilizer in tons or pounds per acre, or in pounds per 1,000 or 100 square feet. The gardener oftentimes finds difficulty in converting these weights into the measures needed for small plots or for single row or single plants. Frequently he has no scales for measuring pounds; therefore it must be in a form converted to cups, pints, quarts. The following table makes a conversion for him, using the common household measurements of pints, cups, tablespoons and teaspoons. This table has been worked up by the U.S. Department of Agriculture. Therefore, after determining the type of fertilizer that is to be used and its normal recommendation in Table 1., read across to the various tables such as the volume measure per 100 square feet and then turn to Table 2. and determine the amount to apply per row space. Weights of various fertilizing materials per acre, per 1000 square feet, and per 100 square feet and the approximate equivalent-volume measures for 100 square feet, grouped according to weight in comparison with that of water.

Weights of various fertilizing materials per acre, per 1,000 sq. ft., and per 100 sq. ft. and the approximate equivalent-volume measures for 100 sq. ft. grouped according to weight in comparison with that of water.

MATERIALS	WEIGHTS SPECIFIED PER— Acre	1,000 Sq. Ft.	100 Sq. Ft.	Volume Measure for 100 Sq. Ft.
	Pounds	Pounds	Pounds	Pints
	1,300	30	3	3
	870	20	2	2
	435	10	1	1
Weight about the same as that of water............... ←				Cups
Examples: Cal-Nitro (or A-N-L), manure salts.	220	5	½	1
	110	2½	¼	½
				Pints
	5,660	130	13	10
	3,485	80	8	6
	870	20	2	1½
Weight about 1 1/10 that of water.................... ←			Ounces	
Examples: Ground lime-stone, ground dolomitic lime-	565	13	21	1
stone granular sodium nitrate, potassium sulfate.				Cup
	280	6½	11	1
	Pounds	Pounds	Pounds	Pints
	1,740	40	4	5
Weight about 9/10 that of water.................... ←	650	15	1½	2
Examples: Epsom salts, bonemeal.			Ounces	Cups
	175	4	6½	1
				Tbs.
	44	1	1½	4
			Pounds	Pints
	1,740	40	4	6
	1,525	35	3½	5
Weight about 7/10 that of water.................... ←	650	15	1½	2
Examples: Activated sewage sludge, urea, ammonium			Ounces	
sulfate, granular ammonium nitrate, aluminum sul-	300	7	11	1
fate, granular borax.				Cup
	150	3½	5½	1
				Tbs.
	44	1	1½	4
		Ounces		
	11	5	½	1

Materials	Weights specified per- Acre	1,000 sq. ft.	100 sq. ft.	Volume Measure for 100 sq. ft.
	Pounds	Pounds	Pounds	Pints
	1,300	30	3–	5
Weight about 6/10 that of water	545	12½	1¼	2
Examples: Cottonseed meal, sulfur, fish scrap.			Ounces	
	260	6	10	1
				Cup
	130	3	5	1
			Pounds	Pints
	1,100	25	2½	5
Weight about 5/10 that of water	435	10	1	2
Example: Hydrated lime.			Ounces	
	220	5	8	1
				Cup
	110	2½	4	1

Approximate equivalent-volume measures of materials to use in the row and per plant at various rates per 100 square feet.

Rates per 100 Square Feet	Rates per 10 feet, Rows Spaced—			Rates per plant, Spaced—		
	3 ft.	2 ft.	1 ft.	5 x 5	2¼ x 2¼ ft.	2 x 1½ ft.
Pints	Pints	Pints	Pints	Pints	Cups	Cups
10.........	3	2	1	2½	1	½
	Cups	Cups	Cups	Cups		
6..........	3½	2½	1¼	3	(h) ½	(h) ¼
5..........	3	2	1	2½	½	¼
					Tbs.	Tbs.
4..........	2½	1½	¾	2	6½	(h) 3
3..........	1¾	1¼	(h) ½	1½	5	2½
2½........	1½	1	½	1¼	4	2
			Tbs.			
2..........	1¼	¾	6½	1	3¼	1½
1½........	(h) ¾	(h) ½	5	¾	2½	(h) 1
1..........	½	Tbs. 6	3¼	½	1½	Tbs. 2½
Cups						
1½........	½	5	2½	6	1	1½
1..........	5	3¼	1½	4	2½	¾
½..........	2½	1½	¾	2	1¼	½
Tbs.						
4..........	1¼	2½	1¼	1	½	¼
Bushels						
1..........	1	(h) ½	1/3	¼	1/6	1/12
	Bushels	Pecks	Quarts	Bushels	Quarts	Quarts
2..........	(h) ½	1½	6	½	3	1½
	Peck			Peck		
1..........	(h) 1	(s) 1	3	1	1½	¾

h—slightly heaped.   s—A trifle less than full.

Vegetable Insects

No garden is free of insects. Regardless of the vegetable growing or the time of year. The gardener must maintain a constant watch for insects. Insects and their control have become a perplexing problem. What insecticide to use? How to use it? How long to wait after application before consuming the vegetables? The Tables below will assist you in answering these questions.

Common Vegetable Insects
(See Chapter 8 for Detailed Control)

INSECT	Insecticide	No. Days from Last Application To Harvest	REMARKS
		BEANS (Snap or Lima)	
Aphid	5% Malathion	1	Sprays are more effective than dusts. Apply insecticides at 5-7 day intervals until control is obtained

57

INSECT	Insecticide	No. Days from Last Application To Harvest	REMARKS
Flea Beetle	5% DDT	7	Flea beetles may cause severe damage to seedling plants. Toxaphene dust may be used within 7 days of harvest if beans are washed.
Leaf hopper	5% Malathion	1	May attack seedling or older plants. Repeat treatment as needed.
Thrips	5% Malathion	1	May cause damage to seedling plants. Toxaphene and parathion dust may be used 15 days before harvest if beans are washed.
Corn earworm	5% DDT	7	Attacks blossoms.
Cabbage looper	20% Toxaphene	*	Toxaphene and parathion dust may be used 15 days before harvest if beans are washed. Begin treatment when first ragging of leaves appear.

BEETS

INSECT	Insecticide	No. Days	REMARKS
Beet webworm, beet leafhopper leaf beetle	5% DDT		Do not apply DDT after seedling stage if tops are to be used for food of feed. Apply insecticides at weekly internals for beet leafhopper control.

CABBAGE, BROCCOLI AND CAULIFLOWER

INSECT	Insecticide	No. Days	REMARKS
Aphid	5% Malathion	7	Sprays are more effective than dusts. Early detection and control measures are important. Diazinon may be used on broccoli and cauliflower 5 days before harvest. Phosdrin may be used on broccoli and cabbage 1 day before harvest.
Flea Beetle	5% DDT	*	Methoxychlor may be used on cabbage 3 days before harvest and 7 days before harvest on cauliflower. Toxaphene may be applied on cabbage 7 days before harvest if outer leaves are to be stripped. If outer leaves are not to be stripped do not apply after heads begin to form.
Cutworm	20% Toxaphene	*	Sprays are more effective than dusts. Cutworms are early season pests. Refer above under remarks for use of Toxaphene. DDT may be used on cabbage 14 days before harvest if outer leaves are removed.
Harlequin cabbage bug	20% Toxaphene	*	Toxaphene may be applied on cabbage 7 days before harvest if outer leaves are stripped.
Cabbage worm	20% Toxaphene + 2% Parathion	*	Toxaphene plus parathion may be used on cabbage 21 days before harvest if outer leaves are stripped. Phosdrin may be used on cabbage and broccoli 1 day before harvest. Toxaphene plus malathion may be used on cabbage 7 days before harvest if outer leaves are removed.

CANTALOUPES, WATERMELONS, CUCUMBERS AND SQUASH (Do not use DDT, toxaphene, sulfur, BHC or chlordane on cucurbits)

INSECT	Insecticide	No. Days	REMARKS
Squash bug	5% Malathion	3	Do not apply dusts to cucurbits when plants are wet. Remove excess residue of lindane from squash and cucumbers. Parathion may be used on melons 7 days before harvest.
Darkling beetle	1½% Dieldrin	*	Do not apply dieldrin to melons after blossoming. Dieldrin may be used on summer squash 7 days of harvest and 14 days before harvest on cucumbers.
Thrips	5% Malathion	1	Parathion may be used on melons 7 days before harvest.
Cutworm	20% Toxaphene		Early season pest. Apply insecticides to soil only.
Aphid	5% Malathion	1	Sprays are more effective than dusts. Thorough coverage is important. Trithion has not been approved for cucumbers and squash.
Melonworm	2% Parathion	7	Parathion may be used on melons up to 7 days of harvest.
Leafminer	2% Parathion	7	Parathion may be used on melons up to 7 days of harvest. Sprays are more effective than dusts.
Spider mite	5% Malathion	1	Parathion may be used on melons up to 7 days of harvest. Trithion has not been approved for use on cucumbers and squash. Sprays are more effective than dusts. Thorough coverage is important.
Cucumber beetle	5% Methoxychlor	7	Do not apply dieldrin to melons after blossoming. Dieldrin may be used on summer squash 7 days before harvest and 14 days before harvest on cucumbers. Endrin has not been approved for use on melons.
Leafhopper	5% Malathion	1	Parathion may be used on melons up to 7 days of harvest.

CARROTS

INSECT	Insecticide	No. Days	REMARKS
Flea beetle	20% Toxaphene	0	Do not use treated tops for food or feed.
Cutworm	20% Toxaphene	0	Do not use treated tops for food or feed.
Beet webworm	20% Toxaphene	0	Do not use treated tops for food or feed.
Leafhopper	20% Toxaphene	0	Do not use treated tops for food or feed.

* Do not spray or dust after edible portions begin to form.

58

INSECT	Insecticide	No. Days from Last Application To Harvest	REMARKS

EGGPLANT

INSECT	Insecticide	No. Days	REMARKS
Flea beetle	20% Toxaphene	5	Apply when insects first appear.
Spider mite	2% Parathion	15	Sprays are more effective than dust. Thorough coverage is necessary.

LETTUCE

INSECT	Insecticide	No. Days	REMARKS
Aphids	5% Malathion	10	Sprays are more effective than dust. Thorough coverage is important.
Cucumber beetle	5% DDT	See Remarks	Do not apply toxaphene after seedling stage for leaf lettuce. Seven days for head lettuce if outer leaves are stripped at harvest.
Cutworm	20% Toxaphene	See Remarks	Do not apply after seedling stage.
Cabbage looper	20% Toxaphene	2	Do not apply toxaphene after seedling stage for leaf lettuce. Remove outer leaves of head lettuce when toxaphene-parathion is used.
Corn earworm	10% DDT	See Remarks *	Do not apply DDT after seedling stage for leaf lettuce. Seven days for head lettuce if outer leaves are stripped. Do not apply TDE to leaf lettuce after seedling stage.
False chinch bug	5% Malathion	10	Malathion can be used on head lettuce 7 days of harvest and 14 days of harvest for leaf lettuce.
Leafhopper	5% Malathion	See Remarks 10	Do not apply DDT after seedling stage for leaf lettuce. Seven days for head lettuce if outer leaves are to be stripped at harvest. Apply at weekly intervals starting when plants are young and continue until within 10 days of harvest for aster yellows control.

MUSTARD AND TURNIPS

INSECT	Insecticide	No. Days	REMARKS
Aphid Harlequin cabbage bug	5% Malathion	7	Sprays are more effective than dusts for aphid control. Thorough coverage is important.
Flea beetle	5% DDT	*	DDT can be applied within 21 days of harvest on mustard greens intended for processing.
Cabbage looper	5% Malathion	7	Sprays are more effective than dusts. Thorough coverage is important.
False chinch bug	5% Malathion	7	Apply when needed.

OKRA

INSECT	Insecticide	No. Days	REMARKS
Aphid Spider mite	2% Parathion	21	
Corn earworm	5% DDT	7	Apply when needed.

ONIONS

INSECT	Insecticide	No. Days	REMARKS
Thrips	5% Malathion	3	Do not apply toxaphene or dieldrin to green or spring onions. Dieldrin can be used on bulb onions 14 days of harvest. No restriction for use of toxaphene on blub onions.

PEAS (Blackeyes or Cowpeas)

INSECT	Insecticide	No. Days	REMARKS
Aphid	5% Malathion	3	Sprays are more effective than dusts. Thorough coverage is important.
Curculio	20% Toxaphene	10	The adult weevil must be killed before egg laying begins. Treat when first pods are $\frac{1}{3}$ inch long and repeat after 7 days. Single applications are not effective. Toxaphene dust may be used within 10 days of harvest if peas are washed.
Cabbage looper	2% Parathion	See Remarks	Toxaphene plus paration dust can be used 10 days before harvest if peas are washed.
Corn earworm	20% Toxaphene	See Remarks	Do not apply to varieties with edible pods after blooms appear. Do not use treated vines for forage.
Leaf miner	2% Parathion	21	Control not necessary on seedling plants.
Stink bug	20% Toxaphene	3 See Remarks	Toxaphene dust may be applied 10 days before harvest if peas are washed.

PEPPERS

INSECT	Insecticide	No. Days	REMARKS
Cutworm	20% Toxaphene	5	Begin treatment when plants are small.
Flea beetle	20% Toxaphene	5	Begin treatment when damage first appears.
Darkling beetle	1½% Dieldrin	7	Only seedlings are damaged.
Leafhopper	20% Toxaphene	5	Apply at weekly intervals.
Leaf miner	2% Parathion	15	Apply at 4-day intervals until control is obtained.
Weevil fruitworm	20% Toxaphene	5	Apply first treatment when fruit begins to set. At least 3 treatments at weekly intervals should be used.

* Do not spray or dust after edible portions begin to form.

INSECT	Insecticide	No. Days from Last Application To Harvest	REMARKS

POTATOES (Irish)

INSECT	Insecticide	No. Days	REMARKS
Aphid	5% Malathion	0	Apply as needed and cover plants thoroughly.
Colorado potato beetle Flea beetle Leafhopper Blister beetle	10% DDT	0	Increase dosage for blister beetle control.
Potato psyllid	5% DDT		Begin treatment when insects first appear. Three or four treatments at 2-week intervals may be needed.

RADISHES

Aphid	5% Malathion	5	Sprays are more effective than dusts. Thorough coverage is important.
Flea beetle	5% DDT	0	Thorough coverage is important.

SPINACH

Flea beetle	5% DDT	21	Do not apply DDT after seedling stage (21 days on greens intended for processing).
Leafhopper	5% Malathion	7	
Cabbage looper	5% Malathion	5	Sprays should be applied at the rate of at least 15 gallons per acre.

SWEET CORN

Budworm	50% DDT Dusts not effective		No restrictions on use of corn kernels for human food. Do not ensile treated corn. Do not feed stover from sweet corn receiving late applications. Do not feed treated forage to dairy animals.
Corn earworm	5% DDT		See chapter on insect control.
Flea beetle	5% DDT		Do not feed treated forage to dairy animals or animals being finished for slaughter.

TOMATOES

Cutworm	5% DDT 20% Toxaphene	5 5	Remove excess residues of toxaphene at harvest.
Flea beetle, Potato beetle Stink bug	10% DDT 20% Toxaphene	5 5	Apply when insects first appear.
Darkling beetle	1½% Dieldrin	7	Apply when insects first appear.
Blister beetle	10% DDT 20% Toxaphene	5 5	Remove excess residues of toxaphene at harvest. Apply when insects first appear.
Hornworm	10% DDT 20% Toxaphene	5 5	Remove excess residues of toxaphene at harvest. Apply when worms are small.
Leaf miner	5% Malathion	3	Apply when insets first appear.
Fruit worm	10% DDT	5	May require three applications at 7-day intervals beginning at fruit setting. Examine for worms and eggs and continue treatment if necessary.
Suckfly	5% DDT + 40% Sulfur	5	Apply when insects first appear.
Spider mite	5% Malathion	3	Sprays are more effective than dusts. Thorough coverage is important.
Leafhopper	10% DDT	5	In areas where beet leafhoppers appear begin control with DDT when plants are small and continue at 7-day intervals until approximately 2 weeks of harvest.

MISCELLANEOUS INSECTS

Armyworm Fall armyworm	20% Toxaphene		Refer under specific crop for information on the number of days from last application to harvest.
Grasshopper	20% Toxaphene		Apply when grasshoppers are small.
Harvester ant and fire ant	10% Heptachlor		Treat individual hills. Follow directions on manufacturer's label.
Salt marsh caterpillar	20% Toxaphene		Refer under specific crop for information on the number of days from last application to harvest.
White grub, wireworm, southern corn rootworm, seed corn maggot	10% Chlordane		Apply chlordane at the rate of 2 to 3 pounds of technical material per acre follow manufacturers directions.

Chapter 5

Home Orchards and Fruit Bearing Vines

Home Orchard Management

More and more people in the Southwest are becoming interested in growing some variety of fruits for the home, whether it be one tree or whether it be a small orchard. Everyone likes to raise some fruit around the home and harvest the fruits of his labor.

According to the A&M College System one-half to one acre planted to a variety of fruit chosen to ripen in succession will supply a family of five with fresh fruits in season and a surplus to can, dry, preserve or pickle for the winter. They say that it costs only a few dollars to prove that you can produce fruit on a small scale. One must, of course, have some land—either his own or some that he can lease, and with this at the start and the willingness to spend a few odd hours during the year attending to the trees and plants, almost any Texas backyard gardener can produce fruit in abundance, a quantity that will provide each family member two servings daily, 300 pounds yearly, needed for nutrition.

LOCATION: Some spots are better than others for growing fruit. If possible, the orchard or few trees should be located within easy reach of the house and laid out so as to add attractiveness to the home grounds. In areas of heavy rainfall, an orchard should be located where good drainage is provided. In areas of limited rainfall, the orchard should be planted where it will catch water. Livestock quickly ruins trees, which suggests that some places should be avoided as orchard sites. Most places should be fenced to prevent damage from livestock.

Select healthy soil as best possible. Avoid old orchard sites because serious diseases may often be found in the stumps of old trees. That is why it is not advisable to replant where one tree has died, to replant another one.

During the growing season, prior to setting the orchard, pull up and examine the roots of plants growing where the trees are to be planted. If nematodes are present in the soil, they will be found on the tip ends of the root systems of the plants that are growing there. When nematodes are found in the soil, do not plant fruit trees there as most of the trees will be killed by this pest. Also, avoid planting the orchard where cotton has died. This is a sure sign of cotton root rot, a disease which attacks most fruit trees.

Fruit trees, whether they be figs or peaches, will grow in many types of soil. But, if it can be found, a deep sandy loam is the choice.

Heavy soils bake, they crack and become very dry, while loose soils of reasonable fertility hold moisture more uniformly throughout the season to promote root, top and fruit development. Heavy soils may be improved, of course, by plowing under a green manure crop, the addition of manure under the trees and to the soil. Any form or method of putting organic matter into the soil is advisable. After the site has been selected for a small orchard, intensified cultural practices should be carried out in order to break the soil, to break up the hard pan, to clean the soil of all debris and disc or spade it so that it will be ready for the transplanting of the fruit trees. This can be done with a garden tractor, or if nothing else is better—a spading fork. But break the soil to where it can aerate—the hard pan, if possible, should be broken, too. Remember, always, the soils where the trees are to be planted must be thoroughly prepared, even though the planting be delayed in order to do so. This is true whether it be one tree or a thousand trees. Deep plowing is advisable and should be done in the fall or early winter, at which time a cover crop such as vetch, clover, rye or oats may be sown in order to build up organic matter of the soil.

BUYING SELECT VARIETIES: The first consideration in buying a tree is to get a vigorous one. One that is adapted to your area.

It is advisable that you follow these variety recommendations in order to stay out of trouble.

The second most important factor is to get a tree grafted onto the right kind of root stock. The cheapest and most profitable trees in the long run are those of medium to large size, free from disease when planted. Spindly or weak trees are expensive at any price. No better general suggestion for buying fruit stock can be given than to get it from a recognized reliable nurseryman.

Choosing the Right Variety
for Gulf Coast and South Texas

Fruit	Variety	Comments
Apples	Not Adapted	
Blackberries	Brazos	A new berry; large berry
	Dallas	Ripens May and June
	Early Wonder	Commercial variety
Cherries	Not Adapted	Wrong climate
Cherry Plum	Not Adapted	Wrong climate
Dewberries	Young	Ripens May and June
	Boysen	Ripens May and June
	Regal-Ness	Ripens May

Figs	Celestial	Ripens June
	Magnolia	Ripens July
	Texas Everbearing	Commercial; Ripens July

Grapes	Scuppernong	Ripens July
	Thomas	Does extremely well in test
	Carman	Ripens August
	American	Ripens August
	Fredonia	Similar to Concord

Peaches	Maygold	Ripens late May; yellow clingstone; requires 650 hours of 45° temperature or below
	Hiland	Early June; yellow clingstone; requires 750 hours cold weather
	Red Cap	Early June; yellow clingstone; requires 750 hours cold weather
	Coronet	Mid-June; yellow semi-freestone; 800 hours of 45° weather required
	DixieGem	Mid-June; good quality; cold weather for 800 hours of 45°
	Keystone	Late June; yellow freestone; high quality; 750 hours cold weather required
	Redskin	Yellow freestone; good quality; cold requirements of 750 hours
	Frank	Yellow clingstone; excellent for pickling; requires 650 hours of cold weather
	Sam Houston	New variety only released; good quality; cold required, 500 hours; most reliable of all varieties
	Early Amber	Patented peach from Florida; adapted for South Texas; requires only 450 hours of cold weather

White Peaches	Extremely low Chillers but not as high in Quality as yellow Flesh Varieties.	
	Luttichau	Ripens June
	Melba	Ripens June
	Dallas	Ripens July
	Montopolis	Ripens June

Pears	Orient	Good for yard planting; good quality; ripens August
	Garber	Long lived tree; large fruit
	Keiffer	Bears at young age; fair quality; very productive; ripens August
	Douglass	Ripens August; good canning and preserving fruit
	Amity	Good eating pear; ripens August

Pecans	Stuart	One of the best dual purpose, both shade and nuts; requires 50 nuts to weigh a pound and runs almost 50% kernel
	Desirable	Resistant to scab; large nuts (less than 50 nuts a pound); runs 54% kernel; not as strong as Stuart
	Success	Large nut (52% kernel); good quality; has some resistance to scab, but shows some disease in a wet year
	Mahan	One of the best shade trees; bears at an early age; nuts are poorly filled in many seasons; runs high percent of kernel in many seasons because of thin shell (55-57%)
	Moore	More of a pollenizer tree; ripens in August and September
Persimmons	Tanenashi	Ripens October; large cone shaped fruit; sets fruit without pollination, so therefore is seedless
	Eureka	Ripens October; roundish, oblong fruit; excellent quality
	Hyakume	Ripens August
	Zengi	Ripens August and September
Plums	Bruce	Ripens mid-May; large red fruit, very acid; excellent for preserving; self sterile; must have another variety for pollination
	Methley	Ripens mid-June; purple fruit; good fresh eating plum; best pollinator for Bruce
	Excelsior	Ripens June; large red fruit; very dependable
	Santa Rosa	Good quality; ripens mid-May
Lemons	Meyer	Ripens August and September
	Pondorosa	Ripens August and September
Oranges	Navel	Ripens October
	Joppa	Ripens December
	Valencia	Ripens January
Grapefruit	Ruby Red	Ripens November
	Marsh Seedless	Ripens November
	Marsh Pink	Ripens November
Strawberries	Ranger	Has large berries of high quality; heavy yielder and does well in South Texas
	Missionary	Same as above
	Florida 90	Same as above
	Dixieland	Same as above

Varieties for Central and North Texas

Fruit	Varieties	Comments
Apples	Holland, Starks Earliest Golden Delicious San Jacinto	Ripens August
Blackberries	Lawton Brazos Early Wonder	Commercial variety Heavy producer; large berry Commercial variety
Cherries	Early Richmond Montmoreney	Adapted to Panhandle only
Cherry Plum	Sapa	Ripens June
Dewberries	Austin Mays Young Boysen	Ripens May and June Ripens May and June Ripens June
Figs	Green Ischia Celestial Texas Everbearing	Ripens June Ripens July Commercial variety; ripens July
Grapes	Carnan Delaware Portland Favorite Fredonia	Ripens August Ripens July Ripens July Ripens August Ripens August
Peaches	Dixie Red DixiGem Halehaven Burbank Elberta Cardinal Texaberta Red Cap Ranger Frank	Commercial variety Commercial variety; yellow freestone; ripens June Commercial variety; yellow freestone; ripens July Commercial variety; yellow freestone; ripens June and July Good quality; yellow clingstone; ripens June Commercial variety; yellow freestone; ripens July Yellow clingstone; ripens June Commercial variety; yellow freestone; ripens June Commercial variety; yellow clingstone; ripens August

	Suwannee	New variety requiring only 750 hours of 45° weather in winter months
White Peaches	Extremely low chillers; more dependable, but not as high in quality as yellow flesh varieties	
	Montopolis	Ripens June
	Babcock	Ripens June
	Early Red	Ripens June
Pears	LeConte	Good quality; ripens July
	Orient	Hardy pear; ripens September
	Kieffer	Bears at young age; fair quality; ripens August
	Bartlett	Commercial variety; ripens July
Pecans	Stuart	Same as for South Texas; ripens October and November
	Desirable	Resistant to scab; large nuts (less than 50 nuts to a pound); runs 54% kernel; not as strong as Stuart; ripens October
	Success	Large nuts (52% kernel); good quality; has some resistance to scab, but shows some disease in a wet year; ripens October
	Western	
	Schley	Ripens October
	Burkett	Ripens October
Persimmons	TaneNashi	Ripens August; large cone shaped fruit; sets fruit without pollination, so is seedless
	Yemon	Fruit; ripens September
	Eureka	Ripens October; roundish oblong fruit; excellent quality
	Tamopan	Fruit ripens August and September
Plums	Bruce	Ripens mid-May; large red fruit; very acid; excellent for preserving; self sterile; must have another variety for pollination
	Methley	Ripens mid-June purple fruit; good fresh eating plum; best pollinator for Bruce
	American	Fruit ripens June
	Santa Rosa	Good quality; ripens June
Lemons	Meyer	Not adapted, too cold
	Pondorosa	Not adapted, too cold
Oranges	Naval	Not adapted, too cold
	Joppa	Not adapted, too cold
	Valencia	Not adapted, too cold
Grapefruit	Ruby Red Marsh	Not adapted, too cold

66

	Seedless	Not adapted, too cold
	Marsh Ping	Not adapted, too cold
Strawberries	Ranger	Has large berries of high quality; heavy yielder and does well in North Texas
	Klondyke	Same as above
	Missionary	Same as above
	Gem	Same as above

It is always difficult to recommend peach varieties for South Texas. The ones we have listed in the yellow flesh group have the lowest cold requirement of any peach varieties that we have. These varieties have performed well on the southern edge of the peach growing belt. Most of them have been tested at College Station and have made a good record. We would like to point out that some years even the extremely low chillers will not fruit in the Gulf Coast section of the state.

Our feeling is that if people are going to plant yellow flesh peaches come what may, it would be better for you to have these varieties. They at least have a reasonable chance to produce, rather than to have the medium and high chillers that are often sold such as Elberta, Hale Haven, Cardinal and Dixired.

Treatment of Trees on Arrival: In this area it is preferable that most fruit trees be planted during February. Trees should be unpacked immediately upon receipt from the nursery, or mail order house, from which you buy it. Every precaution should be exercised to prevent the roots from drying out. If the trees cannot be planted at once, they should be heeled in by digging a trench sufficiently wide and deep to receive the roots. In covering the roots with soil, care should be taken to work the soil into the spaces where the roots are massed together, otherwise there is a possibility of them drying out even though the tops of the roots are apparently well covered. If the soil is dry, a few pails of water poured into the trench may prevent the roots from drying out.

Occasionally the trees may be frozen in transit. Upon arrival such trees should be buried completely, tops and roots, in moist soil so that they may thaw slowly. Normally if trees are bought in the Texas area this is not likely to happen. Avoid wet spots where the soil is poorly drained, as a site for heeling in trees because where water stands on the root systems it could cause them to start decaying.

But—container grown or balled and burlapped fruit trees are available anytime, can be planted anytime.

Laying Out and Planting an Orchard: In laying out even a small orchard, spacing between the trees should be decided carefully. Where terraces are needed they should be prepared sometime before the trees are planted to allow the soil to settle. A terrace for each tree row is a sure way to avoid loss of moisture and plant food. Trees planted on top of terraces do especially well.

If the trees are not to be planted on terraces, the row should follow the contour of the terraces.

In areas where the topography of the land is level, the trees may well be planted by the square method. Where the trees are planted in squares, cross cultivation may be employed, thereby making the task of cultivating the orchard much easier. Suitable planting distances and the number of trees or plants that may be planted per acre, by the square or triangle methods, according to planting distances are shown in the accompanying table:

Apples	30-40 feet apart
Pears	30-40 feet apart
Pecans	40-60 feet apart
Peaches	25-30 feet apart
Plums	20-25 feet apart
Figs	20-25 feet apart
Grapes	12-16 feet apart
Black Berries	Plant three ft. apart in rows six ft. apart
Dewberries	Plant four ft. apart in rows six ft. apart
Strawberries	Plant ten in. apart in rows 2½ ft. apart

Trees should be cut back at the time they are planted to maintain more nearly a balance between the roots and tops. Cutting back should be done to the height of which the branches are expected to develop. A small tree, 12 to 14 inches in height, need not be pruned when planted. Medium to large trees should be pruned at planting time as follows:

Apples	Cut back to 30 inches
Citrus	Bare root trees—cut back 26-30 in.
Figs	Cut back ½ to ⅓ of the top
Grapes	Cut off except one branch, leave one-three buds
Peaches	Cut back to 18 to 20 inches
Pears	Cut back to 30 inches
Pecans	Cut back ⅓ top of the tree
Plums	Cut back 18 to 20 inches

Oftentimes when young trees are put out, either in the backyard or in a small orchard, rat and rabbit damage occur. This normally occurs from rodents gnawing on the trunk, thus cutting the cambium layer, preventing the newly planted trees from ever budding out. The damage is not only disfiguring to the appearance of the tree, but it is also detrimental to their growth and development and sometimes causes total loss of a newly set orchard.

Young fruit trees that have just been set out in the orchard may be wrapped with several thicknesses of newspaper or wrapping paper around the slender trunk. This protective covering of paper prevents the rabbits from gnawing on the tender bark and damaging the tree.

On larger fruit trees the trunk and lower branches may be treated with a repellent solution to prevent rabbit damage. This formula has been used successfully by orchard owners. It would be advisable that it, or a commercial compound be used:

Two pounds sulfur	¼ pint linseed oil
Two pounds of yellow ochre	One ounce asafetida
¼ pint turpentine	Four eggs
½ pint wheat flour	

Mix all these ingredients together with skim milk and apply with a paint brush.

If one desires obtaining a commercial repellent, I would suggest that you use Goodrite Z.I.P., mix according to directions on the container and apply it to the basal section of the newly planted tree just as soon as the trees have been put out.

Setting Out the Tree

The precautions carried out in transplanting a newly secured tree can oftentimes mean the difference whether the tree will grow or die. Before peach trees, or any type of fruit tree is planted, any broken or diseased roots should be pruned off. Any further reduction of the root system is not necessary. In fact, it is not advisable because if too much root system is cut away, it may shock the tree to where it will never put out substantial root systems to start growing.

If the roots of a tree have dried out in storage or in transit, (which is seldom because nurserymen shipping the tree normally will package it in moss and keep it moist) they should be soaked in water for several hours.

Care should also be taken to keep the roots of the tree from drying out during the planting operation. If the trees should be obtained during a spell of bad weather when it is impossible for the operator to put them out in the orchard, then the advisable thing to do is to heal them in.

This can be accomplished by digging a trench large enough to accommodate the root systems of all of your trees, and then covering the root system back over with a layer of soil to keep them moist and vital until the weather corrects itself to where they can be transplanted.

In setting out a tree, hold it in place in the hole at a level about two inches lower than it grew in the nursery. Fill the soil into the empty space around the roots. The removal of air pockets around the root system of a newly planted tree is one of the most important steps, whether it be a peach tree, pecan tree, or a shrub that goes into the yard. These air pockets can cause rapid decay of the root system and ultimately cause death.

Since the top soil generally contains organic matter and mineral nutrients more so than the sub-soil does, you should fill in around the system of the tree using this material rather than the sticky type gumbo clay or black gumbo that is normally present as a sub-soil in most of our orchards.

This operation should be done while the main stem of the tree is being held upright. As the soil is applied, in and around the root system, one should tamp the soil down around the roots to bring soil particles in contact with the roots. Above the firmed topsoil a person should shovel in additional top soil if it is conveniently available, otherwise, he could use the sub-soil, the clay, that has come out of the hole.

FERTILIZING THE TREES: In planting the tree, it is wise to add a shovel of well rotted barnyard manure to each three shovels of soil and fill in around the roots. If commercial fertilizer is used on first year trees, it is better to wait until the trees have begun growing before the fertilizer is applied. In using commercial fertilizer to stimulate growth in one year old trees—about one-half to three-quarters of a pound of 13-13-13 fertilizer may be worked into the soil within a radius of 18 inches from the trunk.

For second and third year trees—one and one-half to two pounds of 13-13-13 should be applied within the shade line of the trees at the time the buds begin to swell. In late summer a side dressing of one-half to one pound per tree of a quickly available nitrogen fertilizer (such as ammonium sulfate) should be applied around the 1st to the 15th of May to stimulate additional growth.

In areas of sandy soil and ample rainfall, commercial fertilizer may be used to stimulate tree growth and fruit development. This may be applied at the beginning of the growing season, at the rate of one to two pounds per inch of diameter of the trunk of the tree. It should be applied toward the end of the branches instead of close to the trunk of the tree. For a winter cover crop that is to be turned under, the commercial fertilizer may be applied just ahead of the plow and both turned at the same time.

CULTIVATION OF THE ORCHARD: Cultivation is essential not only during the spring and early summer, but throughout the entire period the foliage is on the trees. This can best be performed perhaps with a tandum disc or if you have a small orchard—a small garden tractor will be used to cultivate between the trees. Probably the most critical period of cultivation comes during July, August and early September when the evaporation of moisture is most rapid. If thorough cultivation is not carried on at this season the soil will bake and crust over, and weeds will take moisture that should go to the trees. It is not advisable to plow deep in an orchard with a turning plow during the growing season, therefore a disc, spring toothed or spike toothed harrow are desirable implements for preparing and cultivating orchard soil. Do not plow dirt to the tree row; this practice covers the roots too deep and may cause the tree to exude gum on the body. Therefore, the main thing to do during this summer cultivation is to keep the weeds down and keep the soil broken up so that it will not become compact, therefore preserving the moisture which would normally be taken by the weeds.

Pruning and Training

When a tree is obtained from a nursery, a one year old peach tree is usually three to seven feet tall and has few lateral branches large enough to be used as scaffold or frame work branches. After the tree is set out, its lateral shoots should be cut back to short stubs, having one or two buds each. This brings the top into balance with the root system and forces the tree to develop strong shoots, some of which will be selected as scaffold branches.

Trees that are set out in the spring should be cut back immediately after they are set out. In areas that are subject to severe winter cold, the cutting back of fall planted trees should be postponed to late winter or early spring as it might have an adverse effect upon the recently planted tree.

The height to which a tree is headed back depends largely upon its size and how well it is branched, and partly on the growers preference. Occasionally a one year old nursery tree has well developed laterals that can be headed back to six or eight inches and spaced to form the head of the tree. If a low and spreading tree formation is desired the central stems of one year old trees may be cut to a height of 18 to 24 inches. For normal convenience in cultivating around the trees, and doing other necessary orchard work, such as spraying and so forth, a higher framework of branches is preferable.

Where trees are headed back to a height of 18 to 20 inches, the scaffold branches usually arise close together on the trunk. If a tree has a stem, say about 36 inches long when it is planted, scaffold branches can be spaced farther apart on the trunk. This is a good reason for preferring nursery trees four feet and above in height with diameters of approximately 9/16 inch. Set trees are cut back to a height of 36 to 40 inches; their lateral shoots are cut back so far that each has only a few buds.

Pruning after the second growing season in the orchard is usually very light. Tips of outside branches are cut back to keep the scaffold branches growing in an upward and outward direction, and any surplus branches that have arisen on the trunk naturally should be removed.

71

If not all the scaffold branches were selected at the first season of growth in the orchard, others should be selected after the second season.

During the third and fourth year of growth, only correctional pruning should be done. One should remove any branches that interfere with proper development of the main scaffold branches. Some of the small shoots on the outside of the tree should be left for the first fruits are produced on such shoots.

Treatment during the first three or four years is directed chiefly toward developing the framework of the young orchard tree; this is especially true pertaining to peach orchards. Trees of some varieties may require little correction or pruning; others which naturally grow upright instead of spreading out may need more cutting near the ends of the branches to cause them to spread and keep them growing outward.

By the end of the fifth growing season, normally the peach tree that has been pruned in the right way from the very start has a good growth of fruiting wood throughout the entire tree, and as a result can bear and hold a large peach crop.

Time of Pruning a Peach Orchard

Pruning can be done with safety anytime between leaf fall and the start of growth in the early spring. Preferably, however, it is done in the late fall or early winter. Normally the months of December and January are the times when most folks prune their peach orchard. In small orchards, 10 to 15 trees or less, the pruning needed can be done conveniently just before the growth starts. However, in large orchards, it must usually begin earlier since it takes some time to prune and shape up the tree.

Pruning peach trees after full bloom, and especially after their leaves and shoots make considerable growth, prevents the trees from growing to their normal size, or from producing full yields of fruit. However, there are sometimes delayed pruning reasons until the growth has started. Where wood injury has resulted from winter cold, pruning should be delayed until growth starts. Normally this is not the case in South Texas because they do not have severe weather.

In the event this does happen, a better job of pruning can be done after growth has started because the dead limbs then can be pruned out without any serious consequences. Heavy pruning of live branches of trees that have suffered wood injury by cold usually has less beneficial effect than the use of readily available nitrogen fertilizer in encouraging regeneration and growth of new tissue. Delayed pruning has its advantage also in years when there has been winter kill of the blossoms, which once again normally does not occur in the Texas Gulf Coast. If pruning is delayed until near blossoming time, and it is found that few buds or none have been winter killed, the pruning can be heavier, reducing the number of blossoms and consequently the amount of fruit thinning to be done later on. Pruning and fruit thinning go hand in hand in order to maintain quality and the size of the fruit.

Care of the Young Peach Orchard the First Year

During the first year, after peach trees are planted, the orchard soil should be tended carefully to encourage adequate root and top growth. The soil around the trunk should be hoed two or three times during the growing season to keep down the weeds, prevent soil baking and of course to provide for water penetration. In the larger orchards the soil should be cultivated along each side of each row of trees to a distance of at least five feet.

It is not necessary to cultivate all the space in the tree middles, and annual or biennial cover crop may be grown in the cultivated strips and turned under for the purpose of building up the soil. On sites that are low in soil organic matter and subject to water run off and soil loss, cover crops are very desirable in the young orchard because they check soil erosion, and because cover crop residues make the soil more porous. Cover crops should not seriously hinder growth of the young trees by competition if they are confined to areas beyond the spread of the tree branches.

In orchards on level ground it is often desirable to grow an inter-crop during the first two or three years. A person can actually grow cotton in between rows of peach trees and the fertility that you apply to the crop in between the trees will go to supply the crop that you are trying to grow. No tree fruit is more affected by the lack of avail-able soil moisture and available nitrogen than is a peach tree.

Peach trees root rather extensively, and after about five years the roots of trees planted 25 feet apart may actually meet in the middle. Cover crops compete with the trees for soil and moisture nutrients. The greatest amount of plant cover growth from a cover crop can be obtained during early and mid-summer. This, it should be remem-bered, is also the time when the peach tree is using most of its fertility and most of the moisture available. Cultivation results in breakdown of soil organic matter and thus in the release of nutrients within it. The release of available nitrogen by cultivation oftentimes results in as much stimulation of the trees as does an application of fertilizer. In the event of an excessively dry year, it pays to irrigate, either by flood or by sprinkler irrigation system, the peach orchard so that ample water is available to the fruit.

Fertilizers

After the young orchard has been set out no fertilizer should be applied at the time the trees are set. Wait until the tree actually takes hold and starts growing, and then gradually fertilize.

Nitrogen remains the chief fertilizer element needed by peach or-chards on most soils. Potassium, of course, is perhaps the element next

73

most likely to get response. The elements necessary and the rates of which they should be applied vary widely according to soil type and other factors. Nitrogen can satisfactorily be added to the soil by applying anhydrous ammonia, ammonium sulfate or urea. Rather small amounts of ammonium nitrate are sufficient because of the high nitrogen content and this is also true with the 45% urea compound that is on the market today. Adding large amounts of nitrogen may, of course, reduce fruit color and delay ripening, particularly if it is done late in the season. Your fertilizer should be applied in a circle around the drip line of the tree, and the best time to apply it is just before or just after the buds begin to swell on the fruit tree.

The amount to apply will depend upon the size of the orchard itself, from the standpoint of the size of the tree. A small, recently transplanted tree that has taken hold and started growing shouldn't receive over, at the offset, more than a quarter to half pound of fertilizer per tree. And, again, this should be a balanced fertilizer. It would also be advisable to have a soil test made of the soil in which the orchard is growing to ascertain what is the correct level of fertility to be applied.

But, under most circumstances a quarter to a half cup of high analysis fertilizer will be sufficient to keep the tree growing in a green lush condition without chemical fertilizer burn.

As the tree grows, spread the fertilizer out near the tip of the drip line of the root system so that it can be readily obtained by the feeder roots and supplied to the main stem. After the orchard has reached about 5 years in age, actually the fertilizer could be applied into the middle between the trees and it will be taken up successfully by the root system of the orchard as by this time the root system normally will match and meet in the center. Fertilizer treatments by maintaining the vigor of peach trees make them less susceptible to winter injury.

Thinning the Fruit

This is the part that more and more peach owners are beginning to do, realizing that a tree can only produce a specific number of high quality, large size peaches. The orchard managers are thinning the crop in order to maintain the size and quality of the mature fruit. In general, the smaller the normal size of the fruit at maturity, the wider the spacing to which the fruits should be thinned on the twigs and branches.

The correct thinning distance depends largely on the leaf area per fruit and the general vigor of the tree. It takes about 40 healthy leaves of average size to produce a peach of good size and quality. Thinning should usually only leave one peach to every six to eight inches of twig. Although this may seem to be drastic and rather expensive treatment, it must be remembered that small peaches are oftentimes hard to sell and oftentimes are not near as attractive to the general public as a large peach.

74

Also, thinning lessens the labor of harvesting the crop and the danger that limbs will break under the weight of the fruit.

How many peaches should one remove from a tree in thinning? This depends chiefly upon the size of the tree and its bearing capacity. If a tree cannot bear more than one to two bushels, only enough of the peaches that can develop to desirable size, such as the diameter of $2\frac{1}{4}$ to $2\frac{1}{2}$ inches should be left on the tree to make up this quantity.

When a tree has a uniform set of fruit, it is possible to thin to a fixed basing such as six to eight inches along the twig. In most cases it is best to thin not according to a fixed spacing, but according to leaf area, tree vigor and bearing capacity. After a spring freeze sometimes the only blossoms left alive are those at the bases of terminal shoots. In such a case the fruits are not thinned even where they touch each other because the leaf area is sufficient for all the fruit that is on the tree.

Due to the cost of labor, one might hasten to ask, what would the thinning of an orchard be? If it is done by physical means, thinning of a relatively large orchard could become relatively expensive, but in recent years chemical methods have been perfected for thinning the blossoms.

Elgetol is one of the best sprays that have given most satisfactory results. Although results have not always been the same. The recommended amount of Elgetol to be used is 1 pint per 100 gallons of water and the spraying should be done when the trees are at full bloom. Of course, blossoms should not be thinned by any method where it is likely that some of them will be killed by frost. But, Elgetol seems to cut down on the labor cost of thinning the blossoms on the tree, and as a result larger and more uniform peaches are obtained.

Why Fruit Trees Fail to Bear

A fruit tree normally begins to bear fruit after it becomes old enough to blossom freely, provided other conditions are favorable. Tree health, environment, bearing habits, the cultural practices used can all directly influence its ability to produce fruit. Adequate pollination is also essential to fruit production.

If any of these conditions are not favorable, yields may be reduced, or the tree may not bear at all. A grower can, however, exercise some control over most of them.

AGE OF BEARING: Most nursery-produced fruit trees have tops that are one or two years old. The length of time required for them to bear fruit after planting varies with the kind of fruit.

Following are the ages (from planting time) at which fruit trees can be expected to bear:

Citrus	Three to Five Years
Fig	Two to Three Years
Peach	Three to Four Years
Pear	Four to Six Years
Plum	Four to Six Years

TREE HEALTH: Trees must be healthy to bear good fruit in quantity. Those that grow vigorously usually begin to bear sooner than those that do not.

If fruit trees are not sprayed at all or not sprayed properly, disease and insect pests may greatly reduce the size and quality of the yield, although the trees are seldom completely barren.

Scab fungus is typical of diseases that attack and may largely destroy the leaves and young fruits of apple and pear trees. The fungus that causes brown rot, attacks and destroys many of the blossoms of peach and plum trees.

ENVIRONMENT: Extremely cold weather during the winter dormancy may kill the fruit buds. Winter cold rarely threatens the pears and plums. Among the common fruits, peaches are the most sensitive to cold.

As the fruit buds grow and open, they are more susceptible to frost injury. Before the blossoms open but after the buds are exposed, they usually can stand temperatures of 24° to 25° above zero. But the open blossoms of practically all fruit trees will be killed if the temperature drops to about 27° above zero. Injured blossoms may appear normal after a severe frost, but if the center part (pistil) of the blossoms are killed the tree will not bear fruit.

Most hardy fruit trees require exposure to some cold winter weather as a stimulus to break dormancy and to start spring growth. Without sufficient winter cold, spring growth is delayed, and when growth starts it is irregular and slow. These conditions are not favorable for good fruit bearing.

Hardy fruit trees growing in climates considerably warmer than their native ones usually bear poorly because of insufficient winter cold. This condition is generally following mild winters in areas within about 200 miles of the Gulf of Mexico and in other mild areas such as southern California. Following extremely mild winters, the area may extend farther north.

POLLINATION: All fruit trees require pollination to produce fruit. Unless adequate pollination takes place, trees may blossom abundantly but not bear.

Persimmons and dates have male trees that produce pollen and female trees that produce fruit. It is necessary to have at least one tree of each gender to produce fruit.

Fruit trees of some species have "perfect" flowers—both the anthers, which contain pollen, and the pistils, which develop into fruit, are in the same blossom. If they bear fruit as a result of pollination from their own blossoms, these trees are called "self fruitful." However, many fruits with perfect flowers will not set fruit with their own pollen, but require the pollen from another variety to set the fruit. Such varieties are called "self unfruitful."

Nearly all citrus trees are "self fruitful." Other examples are figs; peaches, except J. H. Hale and a few others; and the European-type plums such as the Stanley, Italian and Green Gage.

PEAR: Many pear varieties are self unfruitful or partially so. It is a good practice to plant at least two varieties together. Seckel and Bartlett pears will not pollinate each other.

PLUM: Many varieties of Japanese and American plums are self unfruitful. Plant two or more varieties together.

CULTURAL PRACTICES: Fruit trees need full sunlight for best fruit production. Inadequate sunlight delays the beginning of fruit bearing and may reduce the amount of fruit the trees bear. Avoid placing fruit trees where they will be shaded by other trees or by buildings.

Fruit trees grow more vigorously and bear better if they have adequate soil for the development of their root systems. Do not plant them where roots of forest or shade trees extend into the same soil. Cultivate or mulch around fruit trees to reduce competition from weeds or grasses.

Prune trees lightly up to bearing age. Heavy pruning retards the beginning of fruit bearing age. Prune primarily by thinning out branches instead of heading back (reducing the height of the trees).

Peach and Plum Insect Control Calendar

JANUARY—Prune and remove weakened dead limbs from the orchard to reduce shot-hole borer infestations. Spray with 4 percent miscible dormant oil to control scale if an application was not made in December.

FEBRUARY—Check for aphids. If growing season is early, apply petal fall spray on plums when 75 percent of the petals have fallen.

MARCH—On plums, apply petal fall and shucksplit sprays. If growing season is early, apply first cover spray on plums 2 weeks after shucksplit. On peaches, spray when 75 percent of the petals have fallen. If growing season is early, shucksplit spray on peaches may be required.

APRIL—On plums, apply first cover spray two weeks after shucksplit and another spray two weeks later. Spray peaches at shucksplit, followed by two additional sprays at two-week intervals.
(To avoid harmful insecticide residues on fruit, do not spray plums or early-maturing peach varieties with 7 days of harvest with Sevin, or within 21 days with parathion.)

MAY—Second cover spray on peaches should be applied early this month if it was not put on in late April.

JUNE—Apply third cover spray on peaches early this month. This is the final application for mid-season varieties which ripen in July. Do not apply this spray on earlier ripening varieties. In mid-June apply parathion to trunk of tree for borer control.

JULY—Late-maturing peach varieties should be sprayed 30 days before harvest.

AUG.-SEPT.—Check for development of scale infestations. In mid-August apply second application of parathion for borer control.

OCTOBER—On peaches, apply PBD or ethylene dichloride for peach tree borer control late in the month. Check plum orchards to determine need for control.

NOVEMBER—Finish peach tree borer control applications and treat for lesser peach tree borer.

DECEMBER—Same as January.

THOROUGH SPRAY COVERAGE AT EACH SPRAYING IS ESSENTIAL FOR CONTROL OF PESTS

Propagation of Peach Trees by Seed

The average peach grower finds it to his advantage to purchase his trees directly from a reliable nursery rather than to propagate them himself. The main reason for this is the fact it is a great deal of trouble to produce the trees from seed, plus the fact that a peach variety connot be reproduced reliably from its seed. Plants grown from seed of a particular peach tree may differ considerably from it, even though there has been no cross pollination. For some varieties the progenies are more uniform than for others. In all reliable nurseries the principal purpose of germinating peach seed is to grow young trees or understocks on which to bud desirable varieties. The large majority of seed for the production for this root stock is now grown in California. Oftentimes people have difficulty in obtaining a plant from seed. Peach seed must have a rest period of about three months, the length of time depends on the variety, of course, but normally three months rest period before they can be expected to germinate satisfactorily and produce vigorous seedlings.

Early in the spring, the seeds are planted in rows in the nursery or in the garden plot. The most common practice is to plant the peach seed in the ground in the fall, at a depth of about two inches, in rows about four feet apart. Seeds so planted germinate the following spring. Too much moisture, as when the soil is poorly drained, injures the seed and prevents good germination. Special precautions must sometimes be taken with this method to avoid destruction of the seed by rodents such as rats.

Budding of desired peach varieties onto young seedlings is done during the first year of seedling growth. June is often the time chosen for peach budding in the South, and May and June is when most of the budding in this area is done. The shield or T patch budding method is used. A T-shaped cut is made near the base of the seedling and a shield shaped section of the bark of the tree of a desired variety, containing one bud, is inserted into it. The bud is then bound firmly into position with rubber bands, strips of string and so forth. The rubber bands seem to be most preferable. If string is used, it should be cut as soon as the bud is set to prevent girdling of the tree. When the inserted bud starts to grow, the seedling is cut off just above it. This is done soon after June budding, and early next spring after late summer budding. All growth except from the desired bud is removed, thus the top branches of the newly budded tree are of the selected variety.

Growing and Management of Citrus Orchards and Individual Plants

The production of citrus fruit, whether it be from one tree or an orchard, is one of the most fascinating types of farming and proves to be both beneficial and profitable. However, suitable land, good trees, plenty of water and sound management are essential in producing citrus fruit regardless of whether it is on one tree or in an orchard. Weed control, soil fertility, protective sprays or dusting to control pests and insects are absolute 'musts'.

There are many different facets of citrus orchards production since they vary so widely from the Upper Gulf Coast to the Lower Rio Grande Valley. The problem may pertain to two or three trees and it may pertain to four or five acres or more. But, briefly we will cover some of the major points of citrus production for your benefit.

Establishing the Young Citrus Orchard

Climate, soil, drainage, topography, the availability of water and climate conditions are a vital factor toward the successful production of citrus fruit. In the Upper Texas Gulf Coast climatic factors—such as rainfall, humidity, wind movement and low temperatures have an adverse effect upon the production of citrus growth. Atmosphere and wind movement are also greater near the coast line.

Since soil is important in a long time production of a citrus orchard, a soil survey, soil and water analysis may be desirable as one can build up the soluble salt content from the water used to irrigate trees to such an extent that it would kill them.

The roots of the more desirable understock (that means the root stocks) of citrus trees do not thrive equally well in all soil types. Sour Orange and the Tristeza tolerant Cleopatra mandarin, are the stocks generally used by commercial nurserymen. Both of them do fairly well

79

in deep sandy loam soil, however, the Cleopatra root stocks are affected adversely and unfavorably by high concentrations of lime (caliche) in the soil.

Growing citrus trees should not be attempted on heavy adobe clay soils, shallow soils or soils that are high in salt content. Where a relatively large orchard of a half acre or more is to be set out, topography or the elevation of the surrounding grounds is very important. Land having a slightly rolling topograph is likely to have good water and air drainage, but it is difficult to irrigate, and also it may be subject to erosion. Rolling land can be terraced, but weed control is a difficult problem in terraced orchards where cross cultivation is impractical.

Normally speaking, according to research work done by the Agricultural Experiment Station in the Valley, a two or three percent slope is ideal for orchards. The slope can be changed, of course, with modern earth moving equipment, but this too can be slightly impractical. High land is suitable for orchard use since elevation above surrounding areas assures good water and air drainage. However, it has this disadvantage in that it may be necessary to relift irrigation water to get it to the highest point, and therefore this too becomes uneconomically feasible.

By all means, you should avoid planting citrus trees in low areas where water collects following a heavy rain, as this will cause drown out. Soil drainage is important and should be taken into consideration when planting one tree or 100 trees. And, another point to remember is that the tree should not be located where it will be subject to drift from dirt or caliche roads. Dust has a highly undesirable effect on citrus trees and tends to encourage the spread of red scale pests which are difficult to control under these circumstances.

Varieties Adapted for This Area

The most commonly planted grapefruit varieties are the Ruby Red Blush, Pink Marsh and Marsh Seedless. A number of folks have encountered small fruit in the red grapefruit varieties, but good flesh grapefruit have brought the highest price over a period of years, and many growers have reported excellent yields. Of course, for a family orchard you are not so much interested in a retail value, but in the acceptability of the taste and size of fruit.

Early varieties of oranges are not equal to those of Valencia variety in shipping quality. Other varieties that seem to do well, and are early types, due to the prolific nature of the trees, are Pineapple, Hamlin, and Mars. Valencia orange encounters freezing difficulty. So, I would stick to the common varieties I have mentioned in this discussion—Ruby Red Blush, Pink Marsh and Marsh Seedless insofar as grapefruit varieties are concerned, and the Valencia variety of orange seems to be the one that is best recommended.

The use of good trees of accepted varieties on well adapted root stocks is the most important step in planting a citrus orchard. Most standard citrus varieties, when budded on the right kind of root stock, are suitable for the Texas Gulf Coast. Cold tender varieties of lemons and limes are most susceptible to freezing injury in this area (Houston and vicinity) than grapefruit, oranges and tangerines.

The age of a nursery tree is more important than its size. Trees that measure about 5/8 inch or more, nine months after budding, are satisfactory trees to set out. But, trees of comparable age that caliper, or measured 3/4 of an inch are more desirable. Over aged roots are undesirable even at reduced prices from your local nurserymen. The nurserymen that supplies the trees usually will contract his trees prior to the time they are to be delivered to his place of business, and therefore they should have balled root systems. This assures better livability among your trees.

Planting Time

Fall is the best time for planting citrus trees, but ball planting stock can be transplanted successfully almost any season, provided the young trees are given adequate care afterwards, such as moisture and fertility.

Securing good nursery trees is by far more important than the time you plan to plant them. Previous to the time that the actual planting of the tree takes place, the orchard should be graded and prepared properly before planting. This should be done by thorough breaking. Using a drag harrow, level off the orchard before planting time.

Spacing actually is a part of laying out a large orchard, and the general trend is to plant more trees per acre than formerly was thought feasible. Twenty-five by 15 ft. spacing with eventual thinning to 25 by 30 ft. is more popular. However, some people who are in the commercial business set their trees 25 by 20 ft. apart and leave them that way. This, of course, will allow about 70 to 75 trees per acre if you plan to go into large scale production.

Proper depth at which the trees are set is also very important. If you bury the plant too deeply, the bud unions may cause trouble eventually. Orchard trees should be set about the same depth as they stood in the nursery, and normally the ground line is very recognizable on the plant that you buy.

As with any other tree, one should plant avoiding air pockets in the soil as this can cause trouble. Tamping trash free soil firmly about the ball prevents air pockets near the roots of the trees, and a tamping bar, plus a person's feet, should be used to firm the soil around the roots of the newly set trees.

CULTIVATION & WATERING: Sulphur or similar materials applied at the time of transplanting the tree, prior to the root system taking hold in the soil, may set them back, kill them, or retard the tree. It is safer to wait until the tree is well established before applying any concentrated fertilizer. However, water should be applied immediately after setting the tree in order to settle the soil around the roots and to supply needed moisture, as the tree is going through a stress period at this time. Additional shoveling will be required to fill depressions that occur after the first watering as the soil settles. One should also mound several shovelfuls of dry soil around the crown roots to insulate against heat from the sun's rays and to retain moisture. Trees that are planted in the winter should be banked after the second watering in order to protect against freezing.

A citrus tree needs a great deal of watering, and for this reason all of the citrus orchards in the Valley, are irrigated substantially. But, where one or two trees are grown on the family lot, large basins or wider strips around the tree should be kept moist in order to entice the tree to increase in size. Even three-year-old trees have extensive root systems, and a soil probe will enable the home owner or the orchardist to determine whether his irrigation procedure is wetting the soil to a sufficient depth in the root zone. This is the only way it can be determined.

The rate at which the water should be applied depends upon the type of soil and how easy water can percolate through the soil. The rate of flow may be retarded on the heavier clay loam soils, while the sandy loam soils penetrate much more easily. It is easier to control the amount of water applied to each tree on level ground than it is on ground that is slightly rolling. Irrigation should be carried out only when the trees are showing need for moisture.

Cultivation, tillage or working the soil around the tree with a hoe is not essential. However, weeds interfere with the proper growth of the tree, and they take up valuable plant food nutrients and moisture which the tree needs. Weed control should be carried out and weeds kept out of the orchard at all times. If an orchard of sufficient size is set out, disking is a cheap and most efficient method of destroying a heavy growth of weeds and grasses. A tandum disc harrow, hooked behind a tractor, going through the orchard should not penetrate more than three inches deep as there is a possibility of damage to the root system lying near the top of the ground. In the first place, trees should not be planted on soils that are likely to become so compacted that deep tillage is needed. The basic principal is to keep the weeds from around the tree and keep the orchard in a tillage condition so that water can be absorbed relatively easy.

The Fertilization Program for Young Citrus Trees

Concentrated chemical fertilizers stimulate the growth of young citrus trees, especially ones that are planted on badly depleted soils. However, in many cases the improper use of fertilizers and chemicals around young citrus trees results in serious losses. Fertilizers are usually applied in young orchards to stimulate the growth of a cover crop that is grown in conjunction with the citrus trees, rather than to supply fertilizer directly to the young trees. However, after the tree has been transplanted and the root system has taken hold and started growing, it is advisable to apply a small amount of a complete fertilizer to the young trees in order to stimulate growth.

Concentrated fertilizers may be applied around young trees by hand, but care should be taken to scatter it evenly over the root zone area. Soluble concentrates, such as 12-24-12, sometimes are added to the water applied in tree basins as a liquid type fertilizer. Cyclone type fertilizer spreaders are excellent for applying concentrated dry fertilizers to orchards prior to watering. However, where one or two trees are planted, normally this can be carried out by hand.

Fertilization of the soil for the benefit of the tree should be followed by an application of water, because the added nutrients will not be available for use by the trees until they have been carried into the root zone.

Normally, trees suffer along the Texas Gulf Coast, from a deficiency of phosporous. Phosporous is a primary element in the production of fruit and the maturity of that fruit. Therefore it is advisable to use a balanced fertilizer of a 12-24-12 nature as the form of fertilizer to entice growth and production of fruit.

A discoloration of leaves may result from certain minor element deficiencies, or from excessive amounts of salt or boron. Chlorosis may be caused by a deficiency of iron, zinc or manganese. This is most pronounced on orange trees, especially those that have been budded onto the Cleopatra root stock, growing in high alkaline soils such as in the Texas Gulf Coast.

Chlorosis and mottled leaves is a definite sign of a zinc deficiency. This is pronounced on trees growing in compacted soils having poor aeration. The use of finely ground gypsum or sulphur is advisable to use around the root zones of these trees.

In some areas of the Gulf Coast it is essential that the trees be protected from cold and freezing temperatures. Individual treatment can be carried out on these trees in order to protect them from freeze. They can be wrapped with polyethylene or burlap bags to protect them from freezing temperatures. A lot of people like to bank their young citrus trees to protect the trunks against dangerously low temperatures.

Water sprouts on the trunks should be removed and all wounds should be painted with reliable wound protectants several days before the trees are banked. Trees that are past three years old, or more than three inches in diameter, are considered to be past the banking age for size. Other protective methods must be carried out to prevent freezing of these young trees.

Pruning is important in citrus orchard management, but is not as essential as it is with other fruits such as peaches and grapes. Trees having at least four main scaffold branches and no weak crotches are preferred. The first scaffold branch should be no higher than 18 inches from the ground, and the top arterial should be no higher than 13 inches from the ground.

In selecting the framework branches, those which form acute angles with the trunk should be avoided because limbs of this type are likely to break under heavy loads of fruit that the tree produces.

Young citrus trees, especially in windy locations, are likely to appear unbalanced and misshapen. Heading back in conjunction with staking and typing the tree will help overcome the effect of wind on young trees. However, wind-breaks are more effective in coping with this movement than any other cultural practices that might be carried out.

The side sprouting or suckering of young trees, prior to the time of banking, is the simple method of pruning. The cut should be made smoothly and close to the trunk to promote rapid healing, and a reliable wound dressing should be applied in order to disinfect and seal each wound which might furnish entrance of spores of of the foot rot fungus or other types of fungus disease that affect the citrus tree.

The corrective and protective pruning which a young citrus tree receives during its first years may determine largely its ability to set and mature maximum fruit crops later on.

Pruning Citrus Trees

Pruning is the act of removing unwanted branches from horticultural plants. In the case of young citrus trees the objective in pruning is to give the tree a desired shape and establish a strong framework of scaffold branches. In older trees, the objective is to establish a balance between vegetative vigor and fruitfulness which will enable the trees to produce maximum yields of fruit of the desirable sizes at reasonable cost. Other reasons for pruning are to facilitate certain grove operations and to maintain the health of the trees. Pruning of citrus trees, as it is related to fruit production, is not nearly so important as with apples, peaches and grapes. In orchards where crowding has become a factor, a type of pruning known as hedging is being used. The opening up of the tops of old trees is also being used to increase the production of inside fruit of the larger sizes.

Branches of citrus may be unwanted because of their location, number, kind and condition. Limbs that grow downward, trunk sprouts, clusters of suckers, rubbing limbs, dead, broken, diseased and cold damaged branches are the types that should be removed. The cost of removing all dead branches and twigs is quite likely to be prohibitive. The general policy in pruning is to do the minimum of essential amount consistent with good orchard management.

Formative pruning includes the removal or suppression of water sprouts, the removal of rubbing and interferring limbs and the subbing back of branches that tend to grow too long. Shortening the skirts of the trees, and hedging the sides of the trees will facilitate certain grove

84

operations, but over pruning the skirts will materially reduce yields in young orchards.

An important point to remember in pruning is to make all cuts close to the trunk, a lateral branch or a good healthy bud. Wounds that leave stubs only ⅛ of an inch long will not heal over properly.

All cuts should be made with clean sharp tools of the proper type. Dull tools may tear bark and cause slow healing wounds.

All wounds of appreciable size (larger than ¼ in. in diameter) should be sealed over with an antiseptic weather proof, insect repellant paint of the asphaltum-carbolineum type. The paint should be confined to the exposed white wood.

The best time for pruning is early spring—after the cold danger season. However, dead wood may be removed at any convenient time.

Pruning Fig Trees

In the normal growth of a fig tree, it is trained to be either a tree with a single trunk or to a bush with three to six strong leaders arising from the ground. The latter form is more commonly used by most gardeners because freezes so often kill the fig to the ground that a single trunk form is difficult to maintain.

The pruning of the mature tree or bush depends primarily on the form to which it was trained—whether a bush or a tree, the variety and the type of fruiting desired. If a fig is pruned to a bush form, all the shoots arising from the base of the plant, except the main leaders, should be removed each year, thus leaving the three to six leaders coming from the main root system, the rest should be cut out.

The pruning of the Celeste differs from the Magnolia, Everbearing and Kadota, in that the previous seasons growth on the Celeste should be headed back as little as possible. If the plant is getting excessively large, either remove the entire branches or cut the small limbs back to the lateral branches.

Commercially the Magnolia is cut back heavily to stubs. This results in vigorous growth being maintained late into the season. Also, the distance between the leaves is much greater than with less severe pruning. Since the main crop of figs is borne in the axle of the leaves, fewer fruits are formed early in the season, however, fruiting is distributed over a longer period and it is also easier to harvest figs from the low bushes. Such heavy pruning considerably lowers total yield per tree but oftentimes increases quality.

Everbearing and Kadota trees can be handled much the same as the Magnolia. However, since Everbearing is grown primarily for the local fresh fruit market and for home consumption, it is better to cut the upper most branches back lightly and keep the center thinned out. The best time to prune fig trees is during the months of December-January-February. If this type of pruning job is carried out, a good crop of figs should result the next year.

Pruning of Plums

The pruning that a plum tree receives at the time of planting and during the next two to three years after, has a great deal to do with its future. Pruning is done to maintain a perfectly balanced tree that is easy to spray, and from which fruit may be easily picked. Pruning is employed to stimulate new growth. Except in the case of one, two and three year old trees, pruning should generally be done during the dormant season—December, January and February. However, when a branch appears at the wrong place it is well to take it off at once, even though it be in the growing season. In young orchards that have recently been placed out, the selection and training of branches for forming the head is a matter of great importance. The heads of first year trees should be developed with three to five branches. The first of these branches should be eight to ten inches above the ground, with the others alternating four to six inches apart to the top.

At the end of the first growing season, prune those branches in the body that are not to become part of the permanent framework of the tree. The ends of the remaining branches should be pruned so that they all will be of approximately the same length. *DO NOT*— under any circumstances—remove more than the end growth of the tree than is necessary to give the tree a good symetrical appearance. Second and third year pruning does not vary widely from the first year except perhaps in the extent of pruning. The cutting back done at this time requires that particular attention be given to thinning out the lateral branches that are too close and shortening branches that have grown too long and out of proportion to the other branches on the tree. It is essential that some pruning be done each year. Young bearing trees should make at least 10 inches of growth each year, and a general rule for pruning bearing trees is to remove approximately one-third of the current season's growth each fall.

Pruning Pear Trees

Young pear trees run up very tall, and the branches are inclined to crowd each other. It is advisable to remove the limbs that cause the crowding during the first two or three pruning seasons. To encourage the spreading of the tree, cutting back should be done only where there are outside buds and shoots, and this cutting should, of course, be done during the dormant months of December, January and February.

Pruning Grapes

A large number of folks grow grapes for home use as well as for commercial purposes, and pruning of grapes is highly important. In constructing a four cane system trellis, set posts well into the ground— 12 to 16 feet apart, then tack a heavy wire to the posts and run the wire through the posts 40 inches from the ground. The second wire should be 60 inches from the ground, or 20 inches between the bottom and the top wire. It is important that the posts be well set in the ground and the wire stretched tightly to insure performance. After a grape vine is planted, cut it back to two or three buds on the most vigorous branch and remove all other branches.

During the first growing season, select the best shoot and keep the others pinched off. The following winter—shoots should be tied to the top wire of the trellis, at the same time it should be cut offl three to four inches above the height of the top wire. During the following summer, the strongest shoots should be selected from the growth and trained along the wires. Future pruning should be confined to cutting the vines back to four side branches—three to five feet in length. This will insure an excellent crop of grapes and confine the grape vine within its limitations.

Chapter 6

Shade Trees, Shrubs and Woody Vines

Trees

Nowhere else in the world are trees of so much value as in Texas. The primary reason is easily understood, as shade is always welcome and especially in the hot summertime. Trees reduce the glare of the noonday sun, and their green color always adds a great deal to the landscape.

Another factor most folks overlook is the fact that the moisture which the trees take from the soil and give off through transpiration into the air makes the surrounding atmosphere more pleasant and healthful. The rustling of their wind swayed leaves and branches are one of nature's most delightful melodies. As one philosopher once stated—"Anyone that hasn't heard the whispering of winds blowing softly through the pine needles, hasn't lived."

Since trees are so very, very important and so intimately connected with human life, we feel it is essential that adequate coverage be given to the protection and cultural practices necessary to keep trees growing and healthy and at the same time tips on how to establish new tree growth. Trees will grow better and live longer if given the care that they need and so richly deserve.

Varieties Adapted for Texas

There are many different varieties and species of trees that grow quite well in Texas, some faster than others, some more adversely affected by the soil conditions than others. Therefore, we will deal with those that are primarily of basic importance in this area.

OAKS: water oaks, live oaks, pin oaks, are all adapted to this area. Sycamores; Chinese tallows; Chinese umbrella and Arizona ash; as well as Pine trees, are also adapted.

One of the fastest growing varieties adapted for the Texas Gulf Coast, and one that can withstand the high calcium soils, is the Chinese tallow. This particular variety of tree is grown throughout this area. It seems to thrive quite well in the high calcium soils. They also will grow in acid soils, and are not bothered to any great extent by diseases and insect pests.

88

As is true in most localities throughout this area, many of the finest and best shade trees are natives. They are suited to climate, having become accustomed to it through many years of adaptation. Soil, climate, moisture and drainage conditions are also to their liking, and native trees may be selected to fit into nearly all situations. Some of our trees, which are of foreign origin are so different and unusual in character and appearance that they look out of place in this area. At the same time, one is asking for a tremendous amount of laborious work and culture in order to get them to exist and do well.

There are a number of trees that flower, and those most commonly planted in the South Coast are the Loquat, the Magnolia and the Chinese laurel. These are just a few of the many adapted varieties. We do not have a problem of choosing the variety as there are any number of different varieties that are adapted for this area. The biggest problems in tree production are:

1. The location and problems involved with drainage.
2. Disease and insect control.
3. Plant food deficiencies and toxic mineral deposits in the soil that causes a toxic condition in our trees.

Selection of the Type of Tree to Plant

There are a number of factors to be taken into consideration as to the variety and type of tree to plant. We must consider the suitability of the plant for the purpose for which it is to be used. First of all, it must fit our soil and soil types, and then must be adapted to the location in which we want it to grow. For this we should consider the spread, the height, the sun, the shade, texture of the foliage and etc. We must take into consideration the type of tree that will do and grow best under alkaline or acid conditions. The quickness of growth should also enter into our selection, for after all—we don't want to wait 20 or 30 years to get a good shade tree to afford maximum cover for our lawn and the areas that we want shaded. All of these factors should be taken into consideration when determining the proper variety of tree to plant.

Time of Planting

The time of planting or transplanting a tree, is determined somewhat by the selection of the material. Almost all woody deciduous plants are easily transplanted from the beginning of the dormant period in the fall until the time of sap activity in the spring. Generally, because the springtime is often crowded with a number of other outside activities, it is generally just as good to transplant your trees in the fall and winter months. If planting is done in the spring, it is best to wait until the soil warms just a little bit. The care and handling and planting of the material is of great importance. As the old adage goes— "You can plant with poor preparation and fool yourself and your friends, but you can't fool the plants."

89

The first point I would like to make is that when you purchase the nursery stock, the tree that you plan to put out, be sure and buy it from a reliable nursery. You should insist that it be properly packed to keep the roots from drying out. Container grown trees and those that are balled and burlapped can be transplanted anytime.

Second—If bare root, you should see that it is heeled into a vacant flower bed as soon as you receive it, until you can transplant it. It is also best, if the tree or shrub to be transplanted is not too large, to dip the root system into a bath of mud, which is called puddling. In Texas most of the trees are balled of course, and the puddling process is of no importance and should be disregarded. The size of the hole in which the root system of the newly transplanted shrub is to be placed, is of great importance. The hole should be excavated two feet deep and should be at least one foot wider each way than the full spread of the roots. Any increase in these dimensions will be repaid by quicker growth and plant health. The bottom of the hole into which the shrub or tree is to be transplanted should be broken up with a fork and thoroughly mixed with a water holding material—such as peat, leaf mold, or well rotted manure.

If the soil is inclined to be hard and packy, it would be good to work sand, fine gravel, or cinders, into the very bottom as this will serve to allow excessive moisture to percolate through and will protect your root system in the long run. The excavated soil should be placed upon a piece of burlap cloth or a tow-sack, with the best soil separated from the subsoil. If the plant is one that grows in alkaline soil, work into this top soil a generous quantity of bone meal and place the best soil in the bottom of the hole. Excessive use of manure (barnyard manure) should be used with care. Unless thoroughly rotted, it will burn the new growing roots. Always avoid manure in which wood shavings have been used for bedding. The wood may produce fungus growth, which causes decay on the root system.

Remember one vital word of importance; you have but one chance to cultivate under the plant, and that is when you plant it. You may cultivate around it after it starts growing, but you can never dig the plant up and cultivate the soil underneath again. After the hole has been dug and the plant has been set in, then fill in around the newly set plant with the top soil that has been excavated from the hole. Be sure there are no air pockets. Use a stick or shovel handle, as well as your hands and feet, to work the soil under and around all the roots. Use care in doing this to see that undue injury to the root system is not brought about. The roots are important as the fine fibre-like ones are feeders for the plants. If any of them are broken or diseased, they should be cut off.

Plant the tree at approximately the same depth that it grew in the nursery. You can gauge this by the ring of the dirt on the trunk line. Lay the roots out naturally, and when the hole is two-thirds filled, tramp it firmly with the feet and again flood it with water to compact the soil and destroy air pockets. Then place the balance of the soil loosely in position; do not tramp it or firm it up, but grade it so that water will drain toward the trunk of the tree. The crown of the tree should now be cut back considerably, perhaps at least one-third. However, if it has only one leader or principal stem, this should not be topped.

If the tree, that has been planted, is of considerable size, brace it to prevent wind damage until the root system takes anchor. It should be braced with guy wires run through pieces of old rubber hose where they touch the tree, so as not to injure the bark. The larger the cultivated area, generally speaking around the tree, the more quickly it will recover. It is also a good suggestion to place a mulch—straw type material—around the recently planted area to help hold the moisture until the root system and soil can seal.

Watering and Fertilization of Trees

It is highly essential that young trees and shrubs obtain a ready supply of moisture. A deficiency of moisture on recently transplanted trees can have a highly detrimental effect upon the rate of growth of the tree. One of the best suggestions for keeping water in the vicinity of the roots is to take a post hole digger and dig well spaced holes around the drip line of the tree to the maximum depth of the diggers. Keep those holes full of water at all times. One point must be remembered though—the roots of a tree grow rather rapidly and extend in all directions for quite a distance.

Few people realize the spread of the roots of a tree, 50 feet is not unusual for a root to travel to reach water and nourishment. Many feeder roots, however, are just under the edge of the branches where the drip of the water falls upon them. Nature has arranged a tree to conserve for its own use, almost all water which falls upon its surface. Part of the rainfall is siphoned down the stem of the leaf upon the branch, and then down the trunk. If the ground is properly graded this water flows deep into the soil where it is held for the use of the tap root for dry weather. The water which drips off the edge of the leaves falls directly upon the feeder roots where it can be used by the tree at once. But, there are always times during this year when supplemental water must be applied to a tree to keep it in a good health growing condition. Therefore, it would be advisable to sink supply pipes, or pieces of tile, into the soil around the drip line and keep these full of water at all times. This will percolate through the soil and come in contact with the root system where it can be picked up. You must remember, as the spread of the tree moves out, so does the root system move as well. Therefore you must move your supply pipes out with the branches, or around the drip line where most of your feeder roots are located.

Fertility has a great deal to do with the rate of growth of a tree, and since various type trees use various amounts of fertilizer at various stages in the growth period, the best rule of thumb to follow is as follows:

1. Use a water soluble fertilizer, one that is balanced both in N P & K—nitrogen, phosporous and potash—use at the rate of 1½ pounds per inch of diameter of the tree, measured 1 foot above the groundline.

   As an example: If you have a ten inch tree, measured 1 foot above the ground line, you should use 15 lbs. of this water soluble material. Either a 12-24-12 or a 13-13-13.

In order to facilitate the movement of this soluble fertilizer into the proximity of the root zone, it is advisable to make holes around the drip line of a tree using a sharp instrument, such as a crowbar or a post hole digger. Or it can be done by digging a trench around the drip line of the tree and depositing equal amounts of this fertilizer around the drip line as called for in the above mentioned formula. As an example:

   If you have a 10-inch tree—it would take 15 pounds of the above mentioned material, and this should be applied either in the holes or in the furrow around the drip line of the tree. Then fill with water for maximum diffusion and absorption by the roots.

There are a number of commercial units on the market, one called the Jet Root Feeder or Hydro-Spade and various other types that help to deposit this material into closer proximity of the root zone, thereby making it more feasible for the tree to pick up this material. Also, with the widespread root system that we mentioned previously, the tree roots are in constant competition with grass in order to get proper amounts of nutrients. Therefore, under a tree, it is advisable to top dress the grass with a balanced fertilizer periodically to supply the grass with the necessary nutrients, and the excess will be carried into the soil to be used by the tree.

One other element that is of vital importance in the production of trees is iron. As has previously been stated, the excessive amount of calcium in our soils often times causes a chlorosis condition in our trees —which is an iron deficiency. Calcium has a high affinity for iron and ties it up into an insoluble compound to where the tree cannot use it. This weakens the tree and causes the leaves to turn yellow, and as a result the entire thriftiness of the tree is affected. It is advisable periodically during the growing season to inject into the soil some iron carrying compound. Either in the form of iron chelates or iron sulfate, which is commonly called cooperas. Normally copperas should be used at the rate of ½ teacupful per inch of diameter of the tree, measured the same way as for fertility. This also should be placed into holes punched around the drip line of the tree or in trenches dug around the tree in order to facilitate the movement of the iron compound into the level in which the root system is growing.

Selected Adapter Varieties of Woody Plants Adapted for Texas*

x Evergreen   *xx Semi-Evergreen*   *xxx Deciduous*

VINES

SCIENTIFIC NAME	COMMON NAME	METHOD	HEIGHT
x Boussingaultia ramosa	Mignonette Madeira Vine	Tendrils	20′
x Ficus Pumila	Climbing Fig	Holdfasts	30′
x Trachelospermum jasminoides	Chinese Star Jasmine	Twining L to R	20′

GROUND COVERS (TO 12 INCHES IN HEIGHT)

xx Lantana callowiana Gold Rush	Gold Rush Lantana	Shrub
xxx Lantana sellowiana	Trailing Lantana	Shrub
x Trachelospermum jasminoides	Chinese Star Jasmine	Vine

DWARF SHRUBS (1 TO 3 FT. HIGH)

x Ardisia crispa — Coral Ardisia
x Zamia integrifolia — Coontie

SMALL SHRUBS (3 TO 5 FT. HIGH)

x Myrtus communis Compact — Compact True Myrtle
xx Thunbergia erecta — Bush Clockvine
x Viburnum suspensum — Sandankwa Viburnum

MEDIUM SHRUBS (6 TO 9 FT. HIGH)

x Ardisia japonica — Japanese Ardisia
xx Erythrina crista-galli — Cockspur Coralbean
x Fatshedera Lizei — Fatshedera
xx Hibiscus rosa-sinensis — Chinese Hibiscus
x Myrtus communis — True Myrtle
xx Tecomaria capensis — Cape-Honeysuckle

LARGE SHRUBS OR SMALL TREES (10 TO 25 FT. HIGH)

x Evergreen   *xx Semi-Evergreen*   *xxx Deciduous*

x Cycas revoluta — Sago Cycas
xx Duranta stenostachya — Brazil Skyflower
xxx Fremontia mexicana — Sandiego Fremontia
x Pithecellobium flexicaule — Ebony Apes-Earring
xxx Tetrapanax papyriferus — Rice Paper Plant
xxx Albizia julibrissin — Mimosa

*There are many, many plants that thrive here in Texas—far too many to list here. All these will do well. But your best source of information on varieties is your reliable nurseryman.

x Acacia decurrens dealbata	Silvergreen-wattle Acacia
xx Brachychiton populneus	Kurrajong Bottle Tree
x Cinnamomum camphora	Camphor Tree
xxx Firmiana simplex	Chinese Parasol Tree
xxx Fraxinus Uhdei	Shamel Ash

Trees (30 ft. and over)

xxx Pistacia chinensis	Chinese Pistache
x Podocarpus macrophyllus	Yew Podocarpus
x Quercus agrifolia	California Live Oak
xxx Quercus facata	Southern Red Oak
x Quercus ilex	Holly Oak
xxx Sapium sebiferum	Chinese Tallow Tree
x Pinus taeda	Loblolly Pine
x Pinus caribaea	Slash Pine
x Pinus palustris	Longleaf Pine
xxx Platanus occidentalis	Sycamore
xxx Liquidambar styraciflua	Sweetgum
x Magnolia grandiflora	Southern Magnolia
xxx Quercus phellos	Willow Oak
x Quercus virginiana	Live Oak
xxx Cornus florida	Flowering Dogwood
xxx Carya illinoensis	Pecan
xxx Salix babylonica	Weeping Willow
xxx Quercus stellata	Post Oak
xxx Quercus palustris	Pin Oak

Pruning of Trees

No one single practice, connected with the handling of plants and shrubs, is so necessary as *pruning*. May I hurriedly say that none is so poorly understood, so badly executed, or so entirely neglected. Plants may be cultivated, well arranged, watered and fed right, but seldom are they pruned right.

Garden trees and shrubs cannot be kept in good condition and appearance without being pruned from time to time. There are very few shrubs or vines that will not grow out of bounds, out beyond space given to them. When shrubs and trees begin to outgrow their space, either the group planting must be taken up and rearranged or the pruning saw and shears must be used severely enough from time to time to keep them in bounds.

Oftentimes this pruning job is too long delayed and the plant dies back of its own accord, or shrubs become unkept and straggly. Pruning should be timely; it should be a regular part of good garden maintenance, not done as a last resort or put off from month to month or year to year.

As a rule of thumb . . . the best time to prune any shrub or tree is during the dormant season. This, of course, would occur during the months of December, January and February in Texas. This is true not only with trees that are dormant, but also trees and shrubs that are evergreens.

In order to do a satisfactory job of pruning, every gardener should know the different parts of trees and shrubs and the work done by each. If one could look at a cross section of a tree or shrub, one would find the heart-wood—the sap-wood and the cambium layer (working from the inside out). *Or,* if the reverse order was carried out from the outside near the bark: this is the cambium layer, next to it would be the sap-wood and in the middle of the tree would be the heart-wood.

The heart-wood strengthens the plant, helps it to carry its weight of leaves and branches, contains moisture and in some measure, by its nearness, helps to maintain an equal supply of moisture in the sap-wood in which it is surrounded. However, heart-wood has nothing to do with the life activities of the tree. It does not change its character, it increases in size only as it is added to by the sap-wood.

Through the sap-wood, by which the heart-wood is surrounded, water carrying crude plant food is taken up to the leaves and other green parts of the top. In them, through the action of sunlight on the green coloring matter, called chlorophyll, this crude food, taken up by the root systems and carried up through the sap-wood, is combined with carbon taken by the leaves from the air. Starch, sugar and other plant foods are manufactured. This prepared food then is sent downward again along each twig, branch and trunk out into remotest roots, through what is called the cambium layer—laying directly between the sap-wood and the bark.

How to Prune

Every precaution should be taken to prevent unnecessary injury or damage to a tree when a branch or limb must be removed. Many cases of decay and permanent injury to trees can be traced directly to faulty pruning. One of the most common mistakes that gardeners make is leaving stubs of twigs and branches when they are cut off. When a branch, whether it be large or small, is removed, it should be cut away just as close as possible to the trunk of the tree or the branch of the main limb. When stubs are left they interfere with proper healing of the wound and may cause permanent damage to the tree. To insure close cutting of a limb or branch, pruning shears or a pruning saw should be used.

One of the greatest problems, most amateur gardeners run into when pruning a tree, is that they will start from the top of a limb and try to cut all the way through. When you cut about half way through the limb, the weight of the limb will break it, tear strips of wood and bark down the trunk and branches. This can be prevented quite easily. Out a few inches from the base of the branch, one should cut upward on the underside of the limb until the saw begins to pinch; remove the saw and cut downward at the proper place. The weight of the branch will cause it to split away between these two cuts without injury to the trunk.

When small branches are pruned, it is best to cut with a sloping cut —just above the bud. The slope should not be too long, nor should it be too short. The direction of the new shoot at the tip of the remaining portion of the branch can be influenced and directed by cutting away a bud pointing outward and away from the center of the shrub.

As has been stated previously in other chapters, the best time to prune shrubs and trees is during the dormant season.

Pruning Wounds and Their Protection

When the pruning process takes place, unless safety measures are carried out, one leaves an open wound on the side of a tree or branch that could become an infestation for fungi as well as insects that could permanently injure your tree.

With the exception of a few groups like the palms, all common trees and shrubs are protected on the outside of their woody parts by what we call bark.

The outer parts are dead; they crack and slough off from time to time as growth proceeds. The inner parts are made up of living cellular structure. So long as this bark remains in a good healthy condition and completely covers the woody structure within, there is no danger to a shrub or tree. But, if it is broken, through mechanical means or weather, immediately the way is open for bacteria and fungi to gain entrance and for decay to begin. The eventual result is damage to the tree, a shorter life of the tree and perhaps death for the tree.

Pruning wounds are as dangerous as any other kind—whether it be mechanical, weather or so forth, and is very necessary that they be made properly and that the exposed surface should be protected until the wound heals. The healing of a wound takes place with the formation of callus—a ring of woody tissue covered with bark that grows out from the edges of the wound. It covers the cut surface, eventually healing it over, but it has no living connection with the base of the severed branch. The rate at which a wound is healed over, depends upon its size, its position on the tree and on growth conditions. Large wounds may take several years, whereas smaller ones can cover over quite quickly. Until the callus covers the wound, the cut surface should be protected from decay. Within four to five minutes after the removal of a branch, the edge of the wound where the bark and wood meet should be coated with a type of shellac or wound sealer. Some tree surgeons use an asphalt paint made for that particular purpose and works quite well. If one should put shellac on, let it dry and then coat the entire area with a good paint (*not lead*) or with some other protective covering. The shellac should always be put on the bark also as a narrow band around the wound.

An excellent coating may be made from asphalt by reducing it to the proper consistency with benzine. The asphalt may be melted over a fire, removed to be a safe distance and allowed to cool slightly. Enough benzine should be stirred in to bring it to the working thinness of good paint. A liquid or melted grafting wax, or paraffin, are sometimes recommended for covering wounds, but they are not sufficiently permanent to be effective in southern climates. Often times they will melt off by direct rays of the sun. So, for this immediate area, I would recommend the asphalt wound paint that can be bought at almost any feed, seed or fertilizer dealer.

Preventing Wounds

Many wounds can be prevented completely on a small tree if regular inspection is made. The presence of dead bark, the work of borers, small wounds of any kind, should be noticed and proper care given to them. If such an area should be found, the dead bark should be removed and a coating of the wound paint placed over this area to prevent further damage.

When young trees are set out they should have care and attention from the very beginning. If they are worth planting, they are certainly worth taking care of. A number of wounds and damage to a tree are caused by improper planting, staking next to the main stem of a newly planted tree and then tying wire around the stalk to stabilize the tree. The wire is never removed, and as a result the cambium layer grows over the wire, eventually constricting the movement of plant food nutrients and causing the death of the tree.

When stabilization of a tree is needed insofar as a recent transplant, it is advisable to use a connecting cable around the tree by using strip pieces of inner tube and belting that will not cut into the cambium surface as the young tree sways with the breeze. This, of course, can then be attached to a guy wire attached to some stake in the ground to hold the tree stable. Never use a straight piece of wire to wrap around a tree, because oftentimes one forgets it and before you know it, the cambium layer has been cut by the wire and ultimate damage has been done to the tree.

Treating Tree Wounds and Damaged Areas

Within the past ten or fifteen years a new profession has come into being, and it is referred to as tree surgery. May I hurriedly add that the term is not misapplied because many of the principles underlying the practice of animal surgery, such as the process of removal of dead tissue, the corrective measures for disinfecting wounds etc., are applied in tree surgery as they are in animal agriculture. In most instances this line of work is handled by a group of specialists equipped by training and practice, to take care of trees in ways that require attention, cultivation, feeding, spraying, pruning and so forth.

One of our biggest problems with trees are cavities. This is decayed wood, dead tissue that must be removed completely—otherwise it will spread as a cancer through the tree. The tree surgeon performs this by taking a drill, chisel, gauge, a flaming torch and a scraper to all decayed and diseased parts to make sure that they are thoroughly removed. When the task of removing diseased wood is finished, the whole surface of the cavity is generally disinfected and painted thoroughly. Such material as creosote, carbolineum, crude carbolic acide, bichloride of mercury and Bordeaux paint are commonly used for this process.

If a true carbolic acid is used, you should use it at only half strength by mixing it with water in which laundry soap has been dissolved—one pound to a gallon.

If creosote is used, it should be used with great care in treating large areas of exposed wood, and its application should be limited only to the surfaces affected.

Oftentimes it is amazing to find two different tree surgeons with varying viewpoints. Some tree surgeons say that all cavities should be filled, while others say they should be disinfected and left open. Each has his own viewpoints, and of course good points. For instance: The open method permits examination of the wound from time to time, and any further decay that may appear is readily detected and cared for. Healing does not take place so readily over deep open wounds, but callus forms and rolls inward along the edges. The most common material used for filling wound cavities is concrete, however, one of its greatest drawbacks is the fact that oftentimes it will frequently crack and let air and moisture get through the crack, thus carrying on the decaying process behind a wall of protection.

In order to prepent this cracking and chipping of the concrete a patented process filling with concrete in sections, separated by three ply roofing at intervals of about 8 inches apart, has been brought into use and has been proven to be very satisfactory. These separations slope downward toward the outer surface of the filling. This will give space between the concrete, letting it give with atmospheric pressure, temperature changes and with the swaying of the tree; thereby preventing cracking of the concrete.

Concrete should be made properly with clean sharp sand and rock if you plan to do the job yourself. A good formula is to use 1 part of fresh concrete, two parts sand and three parts gravel or crushed granite. It must be well packed into the cavity and properly finished off on the outer surface. This surface should be rolled into the level of the cambium layer, all around the cavity, and it should conform to the shape of the trunk—but at the level of the cambium. It is quite a chore to do this and for that reason if you have a cavity, I would sincerely recommend (rather than taking a chance on you doing it and not doing it right) that you call a tree expert or tree surgeon to perform the job for you. But, if one intends to do it yourself—to treat cavities—remember—

1. Scrape and cut out all the damaged and decayed wood.
2. Treat the inner surface with a disinfectant—such as creosote— carbolic acid—or Bordeaux paste.
3. Mix your concrete and apply as has previously been mentioned.

Oftentimes this will save a very valuable tree and will definitely not harm its performance in any way.

Pruning Frosted Trees and Shrubs

After trees or shrubs have been damaged by the cold, the question arises as to how they should be pruned and when. This invariably arises each year after a banana tree has been killed back, as well as other shrubs. Many folks believe that the presence of frozen parts will damage the remainder of the plant. This is not true. However, dead parts, often with foliage hanging to them, are very unsightly. For that reason removal is desirable. Within a very short time after the frost or freeze occurs, the extent of damage to twigs and branches may be determined approximately by cutting into the bark here and there with a sharp knife. The bark will show discoloration where the part has been frozen or killed back. The branch then should be cut back to the point of the lowest injury into the wood that has not been damaged. Later it will be necessary to go over the injured plant again for a final pruning, after the exact extent of the damage has been completely ascertained and when new growth starts. Shrubs, such as hibiscus, may be pruned severely at the first cutting back because they soon grow out and form new heads. In most instances we recommend that hibiscus and banana trees be cut back to the ground line from which they will put out next spring.

Diseases and Insects of Trees

One of the big problems we have with our trees in Texas is borers. This is being covered in the insecticide fact sheet, much more thoroughly· than can be covered here, so we suggest you check in the insect section for a borer control to fit your need.

Another problem in the insect line is called gall—leaf gall and stem gall. Most people consider galls as a disease or malformation of the leaf. Actually, insect galls are swelling or deformities of plant tissue resulting from the irritation caused by the feeding of insects, or a toxin injected during the feeding process. Such plant deformities are normally recognized by most gardeners as blisters or projections on the leaves, swellings on the stem or twig, bud gall, flower galls, or root galls. In the insect world there are some 2000 American insect galls (805 of these are the work of gall wasps, nearly 700 are caused by gall midges, 80 by aphids and the rest by soil flies and beetles).

There is no control after the gall has been formed because this is the aftermath of the infestation of the insect itself. To control the formation of galls on leaves and stems, it must be done as a preventative control measure. Chlorinated hydrocarbons can be used or some of the phosphate insecticides applied to the foliage of the tree to prevent the insects that cause the galls from infesting the tree. One important word: you must, by all means, apply this before the insect can infest the tree, otherwise the gall will form and it is too late. Therefore, as a rule of thumb, we would suggest that you spray your trees early in the growing season, just as soon as the leaves begin to form on the tree, with either DDT, Toxaphene, Chlordane, Diazinon or Malathion.

Any one of these insecticides will adequately prevent the formation of the galls. The amount to use will depend upon the strength of the insecticide involved, but as a normal recommendation—about three tablespoons of 50% DDT or Toxaphene will give adequate control. If Diazinon is used—four tablespoons of the liquid (25% Diazinon) per gallon of water should be sufficient.

On oak trees, one of the big problems that we have in keeping our oaks healthy, is anthracnose. Anthracnose is caused by fungus, and several different species of oak trees are attacked. Damage is most severe on the white oak. Premature defoliation is common in wet seasons. Diseased leaves show small scattered brown spots, or large brown areas that tend to follow the veins to the margin. Twigs are also attacked but not seriously damaged.

The best control measure for anthracnose, in the shade oak tree, is to apply a Bordeaux mixture at three different applications. Make the first application when the buds burst, and later ones at intervals of 10 to 14 days. Sanitation in pruning is also beneficial, and all dead or cancerous twigs should be carefully pruned out and burned.

General Suggestions for Preventing Disease in Shade Trees and for Treating Mildly Diseased Trees

There is immediate concern about the increased susceptibility of depressed shade trees to parasitic fungi and other pests which do not commonly attack trees in vigorous health. For example, on Live oaks and Spanish oaks from which the bark has loosened and started to slough off, there is a cream colored layer of fungus growth beneath the bark which extends a quarter of an inch or more into the wood. The cambium, which is the vital growing zone in a tree trunk, was killed. When the killed zone girdled the trunk at any given level, it was almost inevitable that parts of the tree above that level died. The fungus in these cases was tentatively identified as a species of *hypoxylon*. Hypoxylons are rotters of dead wood, generally having very little real parasitic ability. Some of them, however, are notorious as attackers of trees suffer-

100

ing the stress of severe drought. This situation is typical of a number of kinds of troubles that may beset shade trees that are not in good health.

Since we tend to notice these troubles only after they have inflicted considerable injury on the tree, and since the best way to control them is by action beforehand to keep the tree so thrifty that it will resist the attacks of parasites, the following suggestions are offered as a program which should be beneficial in many of the situations that have been referred to in this book:

1. Remove any dead limbs, cutting back to live wood. Make the finishing cuts smooth and paint the cut surfaces with asphalt paint thinned to light brushing consistency with kerosene. This disinfects the wound, seals it against invasion by wood-rotting fungi and promotes healing.

2. Inspect the trunk and principal limbs for evidence of any abnormality, such as sloughing bark, conks of bracket fungi, burls or pockets of wood rot. If rots are present, the treatment will depend on the extent of the rot. Small rotted zones can be chiseled out, having care to cut down to clean, healthy wood and leaving the cut surfaces smooth. Pockets that will collect water should be reformed by further cutting so that complete drainage is permitted. Finish by painting the wound with asphalt-kerosene as indicated above. Large rotted zones present a more serious problem, because removal of much wood may so weaken the tree that it will break. Treatment may involve bracing the tree with timbers while the work is in progress, cleaning out the rotted wood, allowing drainage, disinfecting and sealing cut surfaces and filling the cavity with reinforced concrete for adequate structural strength. Such operations are often best done by reputable firms specializing in this work.

3. Feed and water the tree by some method appropriate to the situation. The following method is feasible in many locations.
    a. Build a circular dike of soil around the tree sufficient to hold water 4 inches deep in the basin thus enclosed. The diameter of the basin should equal that of the shade canopy of the tree. For very small trees or shrubs a diameter of 6 feet is suggested.
    b. Spread a commercial fertilizer over the soil within the dike. The formula and rate of application will depend on the inherent fertility of the soil. As a starter one-half pound of 12-24-12 per 100 square feet of soil surface is suggested.
    c. Fill the basin with water to a depth of four inches and allow to soak in. During the hot, dry part of the year the watering can well be repeated every week or 10 days but discontinued during wet seasons.
    d. Repeat the fertilizer application every 30 days during the

101

growing season, withholding fertilizer as the tree starts to go into dormancy. Always water well every time fertilizer is added.

A word is in order about lawn grasses in relation to shade trees. A thick turf of grass, such as St. Augustine and Bermuda, is probably beneficial to the mat of tree feeding roots in the top soil, because the cooling effect of the turf tends to protect tree roots from excessive heat in the summer. On the other hand such grasses are powerful competitors for plant foods in the topsoil, and grass roots and tree feeding roots are intermingled, questing for needed materials in the same soil zone. It would seem then that a good turf around the base of a tree is generally a desirable thing, but that fertilizer should be applied in amounts allowing for the needs of both tree and grass.

In some instances trees have become victims of the cotton root rot fungus. Previous instructions cannot help appreciably in these cases. A tree dying from attacks by the cotton root rot fungus can *sometimes* be saved by following the instructions under section 3 above, substituting fertilizer grade *ammonium sulfate at one-half pound per 10 square feet* for the commercial fertilizer suggested. After the first application of ammonium sulfate and water, repeat 10 days later with the same amount of chemical and water. Thereafter, no more ammonium sulfate the rest of the growing season but frequent and abundant watering.

Wood Rot of Shade Trees

Wood rots occur in all areas of Texas and attack most shade trees. Toadstool or mushroom type growths on the trunk or limbs of the diseased tree are a reminder that the disease is present. These growths form microscopic fungus seed or spores which can be carried to other trees by wind or insects. The spores germinate and enter the tree through unprotected wounds.

The great damage caused by wood rot fungi often occurs over a long period. When the tell-tale mushrooms appear, the rot may be quite extensive inside the tree. The fungus weakens and makes the infected tree more susceptible to wind damage.

Oaks, hackberry, ash, elm and other shade trees may be damaged by different kinds of wood-rotting fungi. Hollow trees generally are caused by this disease.

Prompt treatment of hail, ice or wind damage, insect injury or any mechanical damage will help prevent wood rot infection. The application of a combination Zineb and Captan spray immediately after a damaging hail storm is suggested.

Badly bruised, cut or splintered wood should be given prompt surgical treatment. Edges of wounds should be smoothed with a sharp knife to promote healing. Injuries should be treated as needed with a disinfectant tree paint.

Where extensive wood rot has already occurred, the rotted wood should be completely removed. The cavity should be filled with a special filling. Cavity filling by an amateur may prove more injurious than beneficial to the tree.

An Economical Method of Removing Spanish Moss and Ball Moss from Trees

Spanish moss is the most widely distributed representative of the tropical and sub-tropical family "Bromeliacea." It hangs in long strings from trees, wherever the moisture supply is sufficient to support it.

Although it is supposed by many people to be parasitic, it has been proven that it lives entirely on the plant food which is derived from the air and rain. To what extent it affects the tree on which it lives is not known. That it cuts off the air supply and reduces the sunlight however is very evident, but just how that may affect the tree would of necessity have to be determined by experimentation over a long period of time. It is usually not propagated or spread by seed, but by fragments of these strings—called festoons which are blown about by the wind. The source of water supply of Spanish moss is the water in the atmosphere. Dissolved in this water are the necessary salts which are derived from the dust in the air. The entire plant is covered with fine scales and these fine structures are ready to absorb moisture. When the leaves are dry they are grey in color, due to the air enclosed by the scale, but whenever moisture is available the air is replaced by water and a deep green result appears. Water is absorbed over the whole surface of the plant which can stand serious desiccation but at first opportunity will reabsorb all the water which it has lost.

The best control for knocking out Spanish moss on trees is to use an arsenical, particularly arsenic of lead. The correct amount is six pounds to each 100 gallons of water. The concentration of the arsenic in the spray is not as important as the thorough wetting of all parts of the moss, so as to get the arsenic of lead well distributed.

Arsenic of lead should be used in place of calcium of arsenic, as the calcium arsenic seems to have a tendency to burn the leaves of trees, and the arsenic of lead will not do this.

The time of application seems to have little difference; it has been tried both in the wintertime and also in the summer, and good results were received from all. One point of *CAUTION* should be mentioned. Any time an arsenic type poison is used—*please keep grazing animals from the trees as this material will drop onto the blades of grass.* It is advisable if this material is applied to a tree in the pasture, that you keep those animals off for a few days until the arsenic has had a chance to penetrate into the soil and off of the leaf surface of the plant on which it fell.

Ball moss is so called because it forms a rosette shaped ball which is composed of from 20 to 60 individual plants. Ball moss, like Spanish moss is not dependent on its root system for nourishment. The roots hold fast, serving only to anchor it to the place on which it grows and do not enter the cambium layer of its host. It absorbs water and salts from the air and moisture. Many people believe that ball moss is responsible for the death of shade trees. If that be the case, injury results from the smothering of the buds of the host by the dense growth of the moss. For that reason, many have attempted to remove the moss from the tree by scraping the trees. It has been found that ball moss may also be killed by spraying the tree with an arsenic of lead at the rate of six pounds per 100 gallons of water. Generally one thorough spraying with arsenic of lead is sufficient to kill all the moss on the tree, whether it be Spanish moss or ball moss.

Insects

All type and varieties of insects infest trees from aphids to caterpillars to June bugs. In general, most of the insects infesting trees can be controlled by thorough application on a periodic basis of any of the chlorinated hydrocarbon insecticides or phosphate compounds. One of the best combinations would be a combination mixture of malathion and DDT. This is the insecticide that I use on my own shade trees at home and get excellent results spraying about every three weeks the entire foliage of a tree, whether it be an arborvite or a sycamore. The DDT will give a longer lasting effect than the malathion, and the malathion being a phosphate compound has a tendency to get to the aphids and other easily killed insects. I mix the two at the rate of four tablespoons per gallon of water (both the liquid DDT and the liquid malathion) and apply them with a pressure sprayer to get through coverage of the tree.

It is of basic importance, I think, to stress a preventative control, rather than an outright control after the insect has infested a tree. You will find that oftentimes it is much easier and more economical to control insects before they infest the tree than to try to knock them out after they have gotten on.

One of the prime examples of this, of course, is the tent caterpillar. This one webs up in specific areas in the tree and unless you use a high pressure spray to break through that fine web, you will not be able to get the insecticide into the area in which the insects are thriving, and you have trouble. Whereas, if an application of dieldrin-malathion is applied periodically, you will prevent the formation of the tent caterpillar. It is easier to keep them out than it is to get rid of them once they have infested it. This is true of all insects. As said, one of your best combinations would be DDT-malathion, sprayed onto the foliage—both top-side and bottom side of the leaves and thoroughly drenching the trunk and limbs.

Scale Insects

There are a number of scale insects that infest trees, and for those trees that go dormant in the wintertime it is advisable to spray the tree with an oil emulsion spray. *Do not* use this oil emulsion spray during the growing season as it will have a tendency to burn the leaf and cause defoliation.

If you have the presence of scale insects on trees during the growing season, use a light summer oil, or an insecticide with a light miscible oil in it—such as 50% emulsible concentrate of malathion. This will help to retard the spread of scale and hold it in check until the tree goes into dormancy. Then spray it with an oil emulsion spray.

For evergreens that do not go dormant, it is advisable to use the light miscible oil (such as is found in 50% emulsible concentrate of malathion). It will not only serve as an insecticide and knock out insects, but the light miscible oil itself will help to control the scale. Over a period of two or three applications this will knock it out.

Possible Causes of Withering, Scorching or Burning of Foliage

Many of the foliage and twig specimens from trees fail to show a parasite or pest of any kind. In such cases it is necessary to regard the leaf abnormalities as indications of some trouble occurring elsewhere in the plant. Usually there is not sufficient evidence about the specific case to do more than suggest a possible cause.

1. *Drying Wind.* During periods of high dry winds, moisture is removed from foliage faster than the roots can supply it. The result is scorched or withered foliage. Only protection from the wind can help in such cases.

2. *High Light Intensity.* Some plants cannot stand the bright sun of mid-summer in Texas. This is particularly true of shrubs and other plants which live naturally in forest shade, such as holly, magnolia, dogwood and azalea.

3. *Insufficient Soil Moisture.* The watering job must be done thoroughly in dry seasons. Merely sprinkling the ground around a plant until the surface is wet is inadequate. It is ordinarily helpful to build a circular dike of soil around a shrub or tree, creating a basin which can be filled with water 3 or 4 inches deep. This dike should be as large as the shade line at noon.

4. *Excessive Lime In The Soil.* Many Texas soils are highly alkaline, due to excessive lime. Many have a limestone or lime clay (caliche) subsoil. Rather few of our common ornamental and garden plants can tolerate this condition and will usually show yellow leaves and stunted growth. The excess lime cannot be corrected pemanently, but it is possible to keep plants growing reasonably well by temporary measures. Acidifying agents use-

105

ful for this are ammonium sulfate (applied at rates up to one pound per 10 square feet of soil surface), ferrous sulfate, also called copperas (at rates similar to those for ammonium sulfate) and sulfur (at rates up to one-half pound per square foot). These materials may be mixed with the soil in the root zone. Sulfur may be mixed with barnyard manure at rates up to 10 pounds per cubic yard and allowed to compost. This very acid compost is useful for mixing with alkaline soils before shrubs or annuals are planted, or for adding to the soil around the plants afterwards.

5. *Excessive Commercial Fertilizer*. Inexperienced gardeners often apply too much commercial fertilizer which results in foliage scorching and later death of the plants. A simple rule of thumb to remember is that a broadcast application of a high analysis fertilizer, converts to a little over a pound per 100 square feet. To go much above this rate at any one application incurs the risk of injuring the plants. Where excessive fertilizer has been applied, water the ground abundantly until the excess has been leached away from the root zone.

6. *Barnyard Manure Contaminated With Strong Fly Sprays*. Modern dairy practice includes strong measures to control flies. If manure from such establishments is used on plants, severe plant poisoning may result.

7. *Gas Injury*. Caused by the accumulation of commercial gas in the soil from leaking mains, etc. Gas companies are equipped to test for such leaks and they should be consulted. Injuries from gas are ordinarily found only in trees along curbs and parkings. A valued tree that has been injured by gas often may be saved by pumping compressed air into the soil around the roots to flush out the gas, followed by fertilization and heavy watering. Dying limbs should be removed.

8. *Fungal or Other Infection of the Parts of the Plant in Contact With the Soil (stems and roots)*. This can be sometimes verified by uncovering the bases of stems down to the point from which lateral roots issue. Decayed areas (cankers) or galls in that zone may account for above-ground symptoms. A true root rot, such as common cotton root rot, may cause rapid dying of the top of the plant.

Chapter 7

Turf and Lawn

St. Augustine Grass

St. Augustine grass, whose scientific name is Stenotaphrum secundatum, is a broadleaf perennial with stollens, runners, creeping on the surface. It is not as cold hardy as Bermuda grass, is best adapted east and south of Fort Worth, and is especially the ideal grass for lawns in the Texas Gulf Coast. The grass grows in shade and in open areas when adequate moisture and fertility are made available to it. St. Augustine remains green after a frost that kills Bermuda above the ground. St. Augustine grass forms a thick, dense turf—usually crowding out all other grasses and weeds if growing conditions are favorable. It should be cut at a height of between 1½ to 2 inches, and it grows best in fertile, well drained sandy loam soils, adequately supplied with ample organic matter. Due to its characteristics, the plant spreads from surface only. It must be propagated by sprigs or by sodding, *it cannot be propagated by seed*—as it does not produce vital seed.

St. Augustine grass as a turf grass is:

1. Susceptible to certain diseases, notably brown patch and leaf spot.
2. It is more susceptible to iron chlorosis, or iron starvation than Bermuda.
3. It is attacked by insects such as chinch bugs and leaf hoppers.
4. Needs more water for survival than Bermuda.
5. Will not survive at low temperatures as well as Bermuda.
6. Is a broadleaf, coarse textured grass.
7. St. Augustine does not produce live seed as previously stated, therefore must be established by planting sod or runners in place of seed.

St. Augustine grass is often confused with carpet grass, and often times is called carpet grass. The two are easily distinguished if the seed heads are examined. Seed heads of St. Augustine are single, short, flat, thick, with corky stems. The seed are sunken onto one side of the spike. Carpet grass seed heads are long, slender, drooping stems that fork at the end into two and occasionally three branches—somewhat like crab grass. Vegetatively the two grasses may be distinguished by the growth habit of the leaves. The leaves of St. Augustine arise from the collar at quarter angles, while those of carpet grass arise directly from the collar in a manner similar to most other grasses. Other differences between St. Augustine and carpet grass are:

1. St. Augustine grows in shade—carpet does not.
2. St. Augustine will not live in low, wet areas—carpet grass thrives in such areas.
3. St. Augustine must be established from plant materials since it produces no live seed, while carpet grass does produce live seed.

Carpet grass is not used generally as a turf grass and very few lawns of carpet grass are found in the state of Texas.

The Establishment of a New Lawn

Since there are a number of folks in Texas moving into new homes, there is a constant question being asked as to how to go about establishing a new lawn. Since there is a great deal of interest in this particular field, we felt it advisable to dedicate a section of our Gardener to the establishment of a lawn in hopes that it will be of help to a number of new home owners, and at the same time may give those that have already established the lawn some new ideas on how to go about taking care of the one they have.

There are three distinct steps necessary in the establishment of a new turf.

1. The preparation of the soil. This involves grading, drainage, the working in of organic matter into the top layers of the soil, supplying adequate plant food, and finally soil bed preparation.
2. The establishment of the grass.
3. The final step is the care and maintenance of he young grass as it develops.

Preparing the Soil

The soil is the very foundation of a lawn. As with any structure, including a building, the foundation is of greater importance than the structure itself. The better the foundation, the stronger and healthier the turf will be. The first step in preparing a new turf is to remove all debris—such as stones, lumber, trash and masonry work. In most instances the character of the soil needs to be changed considerably, normally this is due to the fact that the lot has been leveled, and some of the sub-soil may be on the top. In a lot of instances you have nothing but the heavy clay that has been spread and compacted in this area, and this is not desirable for the best production of a new turf. Sandy loam—high in organic matter—is considered most satisfactory for turf. In the event that a lot of the sub-soil clays have been brought to the surface and spread and packed as a surface soil, it may be advisable that additional fill dirt of a sandy loam nature be hauled in and mixed with the heavy clays in order to prepare a better consistency for the growth of St. Augustine or other grasses that will be seeded or sprigged.

In most all cases organic matter should be added. This organic matter can be in the form of peat moss, compost, well rotted manure, gin trash, decomposed sawdust (preferably hardwood), leaf mold or similar materials. Sand and organic material must be thoroughly mixed with the seed bed. This can be done either with a garden tractor, a rotary hoe, or mixing can be done by hand with a hoe or spade, which often times is very laborious and time consuming, but well worth the while.

After organic matter has been applied along with any top soil that is needed, these various compounds should be incorporated or mixed together. This can best be done by discing or plowing, and then it should be leveled. Grading for proper drainage is highly essential.

The area should be graded properly to provide excellent surface drainage, and the soil should slope gradually from the house, walks and driveways. As a general rule of thumb, a fall of one foot in every 40 to 50 feet is adequate for drainage, provided there are no pockets or holes left in the lawn. If a large part of the lawn area needs to be filled, such as a ditch or gully, a loam soil, high in organic matter should be used. If such soil is not readily available, sand with organic matter mixed in with it, or clay may be mixed and used. This should be plowed or spaded into the soil to supply the plant food nutrients needed for deep root development. Generally a fertilizer of a 1-1-1 (13-13-13) or a 1-2-1 (12-24-12) should be applied at the rate of 20 pounds per 1000 square feet. This will normally give the plants ample nutrients for a fast start, and rapid growth.

In the Gulf Coast and blacklands of Texas where there are tremendous amounts of calcium deposits, it may be advisable to add iron sulfate (commonly called copperas) at the same time the fertilizer is applied to make sure ample iron is available for the newly sprigged or sodded lawn. Generally 10 pounds of iron sulfate per 100 square feet will be ideal for the production of St. Augustine grass.

Establishing the Lawn Turf

Sprigging is essential for St. Augustine grass, as it does not reproduce seed. In general, lawns should be sprigged in the spring, though they may be sprigged almost any time during the growing season when adequate moisture is available. For a more rapid coverage of the lawn, larger blocks of St. Augustine grass sod should be used, and this is called sodding. Sodding is the laying of solid strips of sod, and because of the high cost involved, sodding is never recommended unless there is immediate need for complete, rapid coverage. Sprigging in the form of small blocks two by four inches square is the generally accepted principle of establishing St. Augustin grass. It should be sprigged on 12-inch centers. In other words, each block normally a two by two or two by four should be set 12 inches apart for the best results. Set in uniform rows on 12-inch centers, you will have rapid and uniform coverage of the lawn in a very short time.

Care of the Newly Established Lawn

New established turf areas should be watered and watered frequently. The watering should be light and frequent enough to prevent the surface from drying, because at this stage of the game the sprigs or sods have a rather shallow root system, and it is highly essential that frequent waterings be carried out. As the sprigs or sod begins to take root and grow, the frequency of watering should be reduced and the amount applied at any given time increased. This permits the development of a deep root system and ultimately reduces the amount of water needed.

Newly established lawns are likely to become weedy before the area is covered sufficiently with grass to choke the weeds out. Weeds should be controlled by frequent mowing. If this is not feasible, they should be controlled by spraying the weeds with a 2,4-D weed killer. Although this is more expensive than mowing perhaps, the use of chemicals such as 2,4-D weed killers will do an excellent job.

Lawns should be clipped frequently, even in the stage where they are beginning to spread and cover the barren soil. The height of course will depend upon the specie of grasses. St. Augustine grass should be mowed at a height of 2 to 2½ inches. It should be clipped frequently enough to prevent removing more than ¼ to ½ inch of growth at any one mowing. Never more than 1 to 1½ inches of growth should be allowed between clippings, and only the tips of the leaves should be clipped—never the entire leaf or stem. Frequency of mowing will have a tendency, for newly established lawns, to spread, rather than grow upward (it causes the rhizones or runners to extend outward—thereby covering the lawn much quicker). After the lawn grass has become well established it may be advisable to come back in on a monthly basis and top dress with a nitrogen fertilizer, such as Urea (45% nitrogen).

The rate of application should be five pounds per 1000 square feet for maximum growth of the turf without excessive mowing. As the lawn grows, keep it clipped, keep it well fertilized and keep it well watered. One mistake that a lot of folks make with a newly established lawn, is that they will sprinkle with a garden hose—and not sprinkle enough.

As the grass takes root, it should be watered thoroughly to a depth of about four to six inches at each watering. The frequency of watering can be cut down primarily, but the depth and the intensity of watering should be stepped up to make sure that ample moisture is available for the plants in their rapid growing state.

In well established lawns, watering is the maintenance practice that most often is done incorrectely. Lawns should never be watered until the grass shows a definite need for it. Grass suffering from a lack of moisture takes on a definite sheen, and the plants wilt and curl. When this occurs, the lawn should be soaked thoroughly to a depth of six inches or more.

Soaking the lawn until the top soil and the sub-soil moisture meet would be ideal. Apply water only as fast as the soil can absorb it, run off helps no one. Light sprinklings are never recommended except during excessively hot spells, following a prolonged period of heavy rainfall. Light daily sprinklings during this time reduces scalding of the leaf surface. Deep watering of six inches or more, encourages the development of a root system capable of utilizing more efficiently the nutrients available deep in the soil. Light frequent sprinklings produce shallow, weak root systems which encourage weed invasion. Shallow rooting does not allow utilization of plant food or moisture in the soil. The incidence of disease is more likely to be severe under such conditions. Light sprinklings continued over a long period may make the maintenance of a good lawn prohibitive. Water a lawn for healthy root system during excessively dry periods in the winter because the root system, you must remember, of most of our lawn grasses in the Gulf Coast are still alive, even though the top growth may not be green.

Fertilization Program for St. Augustine Lawn

In order to grow a beautiful healthy turf, one must fertilize in a way that maximum utilization from the fertilizer can be obtained. A lot of our lawn problems are caused by upsetting the balance between nitrogen, phosphorous and potash. An excess of one and the defiency of another causes trouble. One such example of this imbalance is seen in the presence and growth of clover in lawns. This designates an excess of phosphate in the soil. After extensive research on lawn grasses, here is the best recommended fertilization program for a beautiful lawn in Texas.

Month	Rate of Application	Product to Use
March	15-20 lbs. per 1,000 sq. ft.	balanced fertilizer
May	5 lbs. per 1,000 sq. ft.	Urea (45% N)
July	5 lbs. per 1,000 sq. ft.	Urea (45% N)
September	15-20 lbs. per 1,000 sq. ft.	balanced fertilizer

Apply fertilizer uniformly over turf when the grass is dry. *DO NOT APPLY WHEN GRASS BLADES ARE WET WITH MOISTURE.*

You should soak the lawn thoroughly after applying the fertilizer. The best time to water your lawn is during the day, not at night or late evening, because this in itself entices the fungus that causes brown patch and other fungi problems.

As has been stated previously, a complete balanced fertilizer should be applied in the early spring and fall. In between, every 60 days, the application of a nitrogen compound should also be applied. Quite frequently blotching or irregular growth of the grass results from improper application of fertilizer.

Fertilizers are utilized to supplement the soil supply of the essential plant food nutrients, therefore a definition of a fertilizer is a substance used for the purpose of supplying one or more of the elements essential for plant growth. The major reasons for using a fertilizer, thus can be stated as follows:

1. To promote growth and enhance the beauty of the turf.
2. To increase the plants' resistance to certain diseases and insects.
3. To increase resistance to winter and dry weather injury.

Therefore, one can readily see that the spring and fall applications of a balanced, complete, fertilizer is essential to keep the St. Augustine turf in a good healthy growing condition.

How Should You Use Fertilizer

To be most effective and obtain the end results desired, fertilizers must be applied properly. If they are improperly used, fertilizers can cause damage to plants. If fertilizer is placed near young plants it can stunt growth and in some instances cause a chemical burn or even kill the plant. If applied to the surface of wet leaves, fertilizer can severely scorch or burn the plant. In order to obtain the best results, one should follow some simple basic rules in the use of fertilizers on St. Augustine grass turf.

1. Apply the amount that is recommended, or that you know is desired from past experience. (It is the best policy to have a soil test made to determine accurately what the soil needs and what must be applied for maximum growth and beauty.)
2. Spread the fertilizer uniformly to avoid excessive amounts in certain spots and deficiencies in others.
3. Apply fertilizers when the grass is dry. Avoid getting on leaves of other plants, and it is a good idea to sprinkle the fertilizer in with a garden hose or a lawn sprinkler after the application has been made.
4. Avoid putting fertilizer in contact with seed or young plants, or young seedlings.

Fertilizer may be distributed by hand or with a fertilizer distributor. More uniformity can be obtained from the use of a fertilizer distributor than putting it out by hand. Where a small amount is to be utilized, such as five pounds of Urea per 1,000 square feet it would be advisable to apply this with a cyclone seeder, which is used quite frequently by farmers to apply small amounts of legume and grass seed over an acre of land. It is also advisable to distribute this fertilizer in two equal lots. Apply one lot lengthwise of the lawn, the other crosswise of the area, which will give you criss-crossing in order to insure uniform application.

It is a good idea to apply your fertilizer during the morning and turn around and water it into the soil.

Mowing St. Augustine Lawns

Height and frequency of mowing of a St. Augustine lawn are two major factors of great importance toward maintaining a beautiful turf. St. Augustine grass *should never* be mowed *below two inches*. And, it should be cut frequently enough that no great amount of clippings are left on the lawn.

Whether you use a hand mower, a power reel mower or a rotary power mower, it should be sharp enough to cut the grass blades cleanly without bruising or tearing the leaves. The cutting edge of the bed-knife of real type mowers and the reel blades should be sharp, and the reel should be set firmly against the bed-knife. Rotary mower blades require frequent sharpening. This can be done with a steel file.

Rotary Lawn Mowers

A rotary power lawn mower blade travels at speeds up to 150 miles per hour and is capable of throwing sticks, stones or other objects at comparable speeds. One can readily imagine what would happen if you were hit with one of these fast flying objects. This is one of the major disadvantages to the ownership of a power rotary lawn mower.

Power lawn mowers are now in the majority, both in town and among farm people. Along with their increased use has been a closely related increase in accidents involving both operators and bystanders. Most accidents, of course, have been due to carelessness or the lack of knowledge on the part of the individual. Therefore, from agricultural engineers who are in a position to know and understand why, here are a few of the suggestions on how to operate your power lawn mower safely.

1. Always disconnect the spark plug wire before working on the blade.
2. A clean sharp blade does a better cutting job and requires less power.
3. Never operate the power mower with the safety shield removed.
4. Make sure that all rocks and debris are removed from the area before close mowing is attempted.
5. Do not refill the gasoline tank when the engine is hot or running.
6. Run the mower as slowly as possible to do good work.
7. Keep the children and pets away from lawnmowers. These always fascinate youngsters, but they are in a position to get hurt if something should go wrong.
8. Always be certain of sure footing when mowing on steep slopes.
9. Never leave the engine running when the mower is unattended.
10. Make sure that the mower is steady and under control before starting the engine.
11. Always be aware of the hazards involved when you are using

a power mower and don't get caught napping, otherwise you might get hurt.

These precautions are not only true for the rotary mower but for the reel type mower as well.

Controlling Shady Effects on Grass

It is hard to maintain good turf under trees, particularly if the trees are the shallow-rooted type. Following are suggestions that may improve turf under trees:

(1) In the Coastal area of Texas and Louisiana use St. Augustine grass.

(2) Fertilize the grass frequently at twice normal rate. Use 4 pounds of balanced fertilizer per 100 square feet.

(3) Remove unnecessary trees.

(4) Prune the remaining trees heavily to remove dead or low branches. This will allow more light to fall on the grass.

(5) Fertilize the trees to keep them from competing for the grass nutrients. Punch holes around the tree two to four feet deep with a crowbar or a stick as far out as the branches reach. Put fertilizer in the holes.

(6) Remove fallen leaves and other debris frequently.

(7) Fertilize in the early spring to help the grass begin vigorous growth before leaf-shedding trees develop new leaves.

(8) When you water, wet the soil at least six inches deep.

Chemical Weed Control in Lawns

A weed has been described by agronomists as a plant out of place, and this especially applies to a plant growing in a St. Augustine grass lawn.

A vigorous turf is the best control for all weeds, and that is why we recommend proper fertilization of the lawn. This will assure less weeds and weed trouble than any other control measure one can carry out.

Normally weeds and weedy grasses, such as Dallis grass, are not a problem when a well adapted lawn grass is properly established, fertilized, mowed and watered correctly. A thin, weak stand of grass will be invaded by weeds. Killing weeds with chemicals will not keep them out unless it is followed by lawn management practices that encourages the grass to grow vigorously to compete with the weeds.

A number of weeds can be controlled by proper and frequent mowing. Mowing at the right height will help to control lawn weeds such as Pepper weed, Plantain, Buttercup, Johnson grass and Nightshade. Proper mowing heights are one to one and one-half inches for Bermuda grass, one and one-half inches for St. Augustine grass, and up to two inches for other grasses. The grass should be mowed often enough that not more than three-quarters to one inch of leaf tip is removed at any one clipping.

Proper fertilization eliminates many weeds such as Needle grass,

Sand burr (as some people call grass burr) which occurs mainly in Bermuda grass and other turf that is thin because of the lack of fertility and moisture. The controlling practice for the eradication of grass burrs is to fertilize.

However, when all methods of control have been utilized with the exception of chemical methods, then this of course must be tried. Chemicals should be applied when weeds are growing rapidly and before the seed are formed. Treatment usually will not be effective when applied to weeds that are maturing or growing slowly because of drouth or approaching the dormant season.

Chemicals to control up-right or semi-straight annual weeds (such as burr clover and etc.) should be applied when the weed plants are no taller than three inches. If the plants on which they are to be applied is greater than three inches, they first should be mowed and the chemical applied after three or four days regrowth.

The following chemicals have been tested and approved by scientists in reference to weed control. I will also list the weeds and other grasses and grass-like weeds that can be controlled by these various compounds.

1. *Endothal*—For easy to kill broadleaf weeds such as burr clover and henbit—use 3 to 4 tablespoons of Endothal per gallon of water.

   For grass type weeds such as Fescue grass—use six to seven tablespoons of Endothal per gallon of water. When these compounds are used it is advisable to use 1 teaspoon of liquid soap (such as a household detergent) or a commercial wetting agent —such as a spreader-sticker, to insure the mixture sticking to the leaves of these weeds. Apply the mixture as a broadcast spray or as a mop until the leaves and stems of the weeds are wet. For effective control, use the Endothal when the weeds are small. If they are more than three inches high, mow them closely and then treat after three or four days of regrowth. *ONE WORD OF CAUTION:* Endothal should not be applied to rye grass or blue grass for it is likely to kill them also. It is also toxic to all warm blooded animals when taken internally. Avoid prolonged contact with the skin. Keep the material out of the reach of children and small animals. Follow the directions of the manufacturer on the container label.

2. *Disodium Methylarsonate*—Prior to using this compound weedy grasses that are to be treated should be mowed three or four days before treatment. This material is especially successful in the control of Barnyard grass, Blue stem, Cow-foot grass and Dallis grass. The treated area should not be mowed or watered within 48 hours after the application of the chemical. For spot treatment—use seven tablespoons of wettable powder, containing approximately a 20% soluble arsenic, or seven tablespoons of wettable powder containing 12% soluble arsenic per gallon of

115

water. It is advisable also to mix a household detergent in with this material before it is applied. For an area spray application, use 10 to 14 ounces of the wettable powder, or one pint of the liquid formulation into four gallons of water per 100 square feet, including your wetting agent as described previously in this application.

One word of advice. This material will kill St. Augustine grass, but small spots killed by this treatment should be covered over by new growth within four the six weeks. Therefore, the best recommendation for the use of this material is to use it on a spot treatment basis such as the control of Dallis grass etc., and not on a broad scale over the entire lawn as you will completely destroy your lawn grass. Use it with discretion. One word of *CAUTION*—this is an arsenical compound which is poisonous. Avoid skin contact with the material and avoid breathing the spray mist. Keep the material out of the reach of children and domestic animals, and wait a few days after its application before letting children or pets play in the yard.

3. *Silvex*—This compound is more or less a trade name for herbicidal treatments for the control of broadleaf woods. You should use two tablespoons of Silvex per gallon of water, or per gallon of kerosene, with one teaspoon of spreader-sticker or liquid household detergent to cause it to stick. Apply the solution in the same manner as you would a 2,4-D herbicidal compound and follow the same directions in so far as precaution of this material is concerned, as it affects other broadleaf plants as well.

4. *2,4-D*—This is a herbicidal compound that has been used successfully in the control of various type broad leaves and is highly successful. However, one word of *CAUTION*—use only the Amine form of 2,4-D. The ester forms are more volatile and are more likely to damage desirable plants. Never apply 2,4-D under pressure, especially in close proximity to other broadleaf shrubs or plants, as a drifting mist can cause severe damage to desirable shrubs, trees and flowers. *Remember*, containers used to mix or carry 2,4-D solution should not be used to apply other materials to flowers, shrubs or trees—and this goes for the household sprayer. *DO NOT USE THE SPRAYER THAT YOU HAVE APPLIED 2,4-D WITH* to spray your trees or shrubs with as it will have enough residue of the 2,4-D left in the sprayer to cause detrimental damage to the tree or shrub that you spray. One of the best suggestions is to apply the 2,4-D solution with a mop or with a sprinkler can to thoroughly wet the leaves of weeds. Some weeds will start dying within 48 hours; other may require as much as two weeks to show the effects. Broadleaf annual weeds that are susceptible sometimes require additional treatment.

116

5. *Naphtha*—This is a petroleum type cleaning fluid, such as Varsol put out by Humble, or Philips 66 Cleaning Fluid put out by Phillips, or Gulf Solvent BT put out by Gulf Oil Company. This material should be applied as a coarse spray or mop to wet thoroughly the leaves and stems of weedy plants. Lawn grasses will be killed by Naphtha, but dead spots should cover over in a few weeks. Naphtha is an explosive since it is a petroleum product and will blister the skin covered by saturated clothing. Its limitations of course are strictly to grasses—such as Windmill grass and Texas winter grass. It is not considered a successful control measure for the control of broadleaf weeds such as burr clover and etc.

6. *Amine Methylarsonate*—This material also contains arsenic and is poisonous. You should observe the same precautions in reference to use of this compound as you do Disodium Methylarsonate.

In using this compound—take 12 to 14 tablespoons of liquid material to a gallon of water for spot treatment. It is suggested that you use this material only as spot treatment, instead of using it over the entire yard. Apply the mixture as a spray or mop to wet thoroughly the leaves and stems of the weeds. For area spray application—use 12 to 14 ounces in two to four gallons of water per 1000 square feet. To increase the effectiveness of this spray material you should use a household detergent or a commercial spreader-sticker agent at the rate of one teaspoon of liquid per gallon of water. As repeated once before, this material should be used only as a spot treatment on St. Augustine grass lawns.

7. *Ammonium Nitrate*—This is a commercial fertilizer, but it can also be used as a chemical weed control in lawns. Dissolve one pound of ammonium nitrate per gallon of water and allow the solution to settle a few minutes and strain it. Especially, this must be done if it is to be applied with a sprayer. Apply the solution broadcast with a sprinkler can or sprayer at the rate of four gallons per 1000 square feet. Spot treatment should be avoided since the nitrogen will cause green spots that are difficult to eliminate. It should be used on the entire lawn. Mow the plants closely three or four days before treatment is to begin. The solution is very corrosive. Sprayers or sprinkling cans should be rinsed out thoroughly. In some instances dry ammonium sulfate may be used as a substitute treatment in place of the liquid ammonium nitrate, although it is not as effective because coverage is not as good. The lawn should be mowed three or four days before treatment. Wet the plants thoroughly and apply 10 to 12 pounds of ammonium sulfate per 1000 square feet while the leaves are wet. This is very tricky to use on St. Augustine grass lawns because this treatment, if used according to the recommendations, can cause burn to the St. Augustine grass turf.

117

8. *Treatments for Non Turf Areas*—Oftentimes requests are made for the treatment to control weeds and grasses along drive ways, parking areas, fence lines and similar areas that are not turfed, nor will they ever be turfed. The recommendation to control such growth is used exclusively for that purpose and not as treatment on lawns or other turf areas.

To control Johnson grass and Bermuda grass—use one-half pound of sodium dalapon per gallon of water. Apply the solution as a coarse spray to wet thoroughly the leaves of the grass. Dalapon is slightly corrosive, and it kills most grasses. Do not saturate the root area of valuable flowers, shrubs and trees. You should wait five to seven weeks before planting areas treated with Dalapon during the growing season.

To control *poison ivy*, use four tablespoons of Silvex per gallon of water or kerosene. Spray the solution on the stems and leaves of the individual plants. This solution will damage lawn grass and will kill flowers, shrubs and trees.

Another product that will control poison ivy is Ammate. Dissolve Ammate into water and spray onto the foliage of the plant and this will control it very easily.

For ease and safeness of application, for controlling Bermuda grass and Johnson grass in close areas, next to living plants, it is advisable to use a naphtha type petroleum oil, such as Varsol, and apply the oil to wet thoroughly the stems and leaves of all plants. Repeat when regrowth occurs.

Listed Below Are a Number of Our Most Prevalent Weeds and Grasses and Grass-Like Weeds in This Area With a Specific Recommendation as to Compounds Best Recommended to Control It:

BROAD LEAF WEEDS—Chemical Treatment

Aster	2,4-D
Burr Clover, Black Medic & True Clover	Endothal, Ammonium Nitrate, 2,4-D
Crow Poison, Wild Onion & Wild Garlic	Silvex & Ammonium Nitrate
Dandelion	2,4-D
Dock	2,4-D
Dwarf Dandelion	2,4-D
Goathead	2,4-D, Endothal, & Naphtha
Lespedeza	Endothal, 2,4-D & Ammonium Nitrate
Morning Glory	2,4-D & Silvex

118

Oxalis	Endothal & Ammonium Nitrate
Pig Weed	2,4-D or Ammate
Poison Ivy	Dalapon & 2,4-D or Ammate
Ragweed	2,4-D
Sow Thistle	2,4-D
Sweet Clover	Endothal
Vetch	Endothal, 2,4-D & Ammonium Nitrate

GRASS AND GRASS-LIKE WEEDS—Chemical Control

Blue Grass	Endothal
Bahia Grass	Disodium Methylarsonate & Naphtha
Barnyard Grass	Disodium Methylarsonate, Amine Methylarsonate & Naphtha
Bermuda Grass	Dalapon & Naphtha
Carpet Grass	Disodium Methylarsonate & Naphtha
Crab Grass	Disodium Methylarsonate, Amine Methylarsonate & Naphtha
Crowfoot Grass	Disodium Methylarsonate & Naphtha
Dallis Grass	Disodium Methylarsonate, Amine Methylarsonate & Naphtha
Johnson Grass	Dalapon & Naphtha
Nut Grass	Dalapon, Fumigation with Methyl Bromide
Fescue Grass	Endothal
Rye Grass	Endothal
Sand Burr or Grass Burr	Disodium Methylarsonate, Amine Methylarsonate or Naphtha
Sedge	Disodium Methylarsonate
Texas Winter Grass	Naphtha & Disodium Methylarsonate
Windmill Grass	Naphtha

Controlling Dallis Grass

Dallis grass becomes a very bothersome pest in a number of our Bermuda grass and St. Augustine grass turf. Especially with its coarse texture and bunch type growth habit, some folks consider it a weed that invades lawn areas. It assumes a prostrate growth under normal mowing maintenance. When a lawn mower passes over the plants, the leaves and stems are depressed but not clipped off completely, as a result the round

119

bunches of Dallis grass make the St. Augustine grass turf very unsightly. Often times St. Augustine grass will compete very favorably with the Dallis grass if it is properly fertilized. However, in some instances, the Dallis grass has gained such a foothold that fertilization alone will not control it, therefore what is the answer?

Dallis grass is adapted through a wide range of soil types in the coastal prairie and thrives exceedingly well in high rainfall areas and in turf sites with high soil moisture content. Dallis grass begins flowering and producing seed in April and continues through October. Seed are produced abundantly and are the primary means of propagation in lawn areas, even though the seed vitality is low. Oil sprays, concentrated fertilizer water solutions and hand digging were methods to control Dallis grass before the introduction of Disodium Methylarsonate.

The chemicals which control Dallis grass are sold under the following trade names.

1. Weedone Liquid Crabgrass Killer
2. Artoz; Di-Met; Crab-E-Rad; and Weedone Crabgrass Killer
3. Clout
4. Ortho Crabgrass Killer; Artox; Crab-E-Rad; and Fert-itome Crabgrass Killer

Controlling Grass Around Fences and Sidewalks

One of the best and most effective materials to use for the control of grass and weeds around a fence, concrete sidewalk or driveways is *PROMETUNE*. This is a material made by Geigy Chemical Co. It acts as a soil sterilant to prevent grass and weeds from growing for at least a 12 months period. *Apply it with a low pressure sprayer at the rate of one quart mixed with one gallon of water.* Apply only to the area that you desire to keep the grass from growing. *DO NOT USE IN GARDEN BEDS OR VEGETABLE GARDENS.*

Controlling Grass With Petroleum Products

An easy and simple way to control St. Augustine grass, Dallis grass and Johnson grass growing on vacant lots, as well as under cyclone fence lines, and around concrete curbs, is to spray with a petroleum naphtha product such as Varsol, a trade name of a cleaning fluid made by Humble Oil and Refining Co. Put this material in a low pressure sprayer, adjust your nozzle to put out a very fine stream and apply it to the foliage or tips of the leaves of the grass. This will kill the grass back to the area where you have sprayed and will do no damage to your soil, trees or shrubs growing near by.

Lawn Aeration

Lawn aeration is strictly a method whereby the top soil and some of the sub-soil is renovated to enhance the movement of moisture, air and soil fertility for maximum production of the root systems under the soil.

Oftentimes soil becomes so compact that the roots cannot penetrate, and are stymied. Neither can the fertility or water or air penetrate. As a result, you are confronted with a stalemate, and the grass has a shallow root system. It is advisable to aerate the lawn for penetration of water and nutrients which will enhance the growth and depth of roots, thereby making a healthier St. Augustine grass turf. Aeration is strictly the removal of a plug of the soil, so that the soil itself can give as the roots protrude. This plug of soil is removed generally by the work of a soil aeration machine. To punch holes with a crow-bar does not answer the question because here you are punching a hole, but at the same time compacting the soil around the hole to a greater extreme than it was before. It certainly pays to aerate your soil, and its best to use a soil aerator or have it done commercially.

Putting the St. Augustine Turf to Bed During the Winter Months

In Texas it is a proven fact that it pays to give the St. Augustine turf a fall application of a complete balanced fertilizer—to put the St. Augustine grass turf to bed for the winter months. The basic reasons behind such a program are as follows:

1. To give the plant a reservoir of food supply to be stored up in the root system of the plant so that it can go through the winter without excessive damage.
2. To insure ample top growth so that it will act as a protection against extreme winter temperatures.
3. To have a reserve of food in the root system of the plant to enhance its growth and rapid recovery next spring.
4. To enable the root systems to become more resistant to brown patch diseases and winter damage due to freeze or frost.

This fall application of fertilizer should be made during the months of September or October, preferably during the later part of September or the first of October, to give the plants a chance to put on maximum growth and an opportunity to store the reserve in their root system before the first frost or freeze. A program to follow in putting on such an application should be as follows:

1. Prior to the application of fertilizer, grass should be mowed. Follow up the mowing with a complete application of a balanced fertilizer, one that has nitrogen, phosphorus and potash, to make sure that all three of the major elements are available if the plant should need them.
2. The proper application would range, probably, between 10 and 15 lbs. of balanced fertilizer per 1000 sq. ft. of lawn space.
3. Shortly after the application has been made, this material should be watered in—either with a garden hose or by sprinkler.
4. Since the onset of brown patch disease is most prevalent during the fall and winter months, it is advisable for the lawn owner to keep a close check as to the appearance of his grass, and if any signs of brown patch should appear, immediately take action. We

recommend applying Terraclor as a preventative control measure to prevent the outbreak of brown patch in St. Augustine grass turf. If such a program is followed, one will observe that the St. Augustine grass, even during the winter months on warm days, will revive itself and keep a semi-green turf the year around. He will also observe that his grass will have a much stronger root system and also put on faster green growth the following spring, once the soil begins to warm up.

Mulching of St. Augustine Grass Turf

It has become a common practice for gardeners to mulch or broadcast organic material on top of St. Augustine grass turf during the wintertime to:

1. Enhance the content of organic material in the soil for the turf grasses the next spring.
2. Achieve this process at a time when the turf is not in great use, as it is in the summertime.
3. Give some slight protection to the St. Augustine turf during the winter months.

However, of all of these reasons, the most important is the addition of organic matter to the soil for the benefit of the St. Augustine grass turf. Basically, two compounds are used in the Texas Gulf Coast that do a good job. One is animal manure, and the other is rice hulls, which are available in the Houston area. Both of these will be discussed to some extent, listing both advantages and their disadvantages.

Animal Manure

Excellent results are to be received from an even distribution of animal manure during the fall and winter months on a St. Augustine lawn. The material used should be well cured manure, not what we consider hot manure since it might have a tendency to scald or burn the foliage of the St. Augustine grass plant. It generally is applied on top of the turf. The biggest disadvantage in using animal manure to top dress a lawn in the fall and winter months is the problem of weeds. Oftentimes weed seed in the animal manure will produce a fresh crop of weeds. However, this can be easily handled in the spring if you will mow them. One cutting will be sufficient because the weeds themselves, after the organic matter works into the soil, down below the top level of the turf bed, cannot survive the congestion or competition of the St. Augustine grass turf.

If one has a weak or poor stand of St. Augustine grass, primarily from insufficient organic matter in the soil, it is advisable to add a top dressing of animal manure in the fall and winter. One must readily realize, however, that animal manure is very low in the essential elements necessary for mavimum production of St. Augustine grass growth. As an example: The following table will give you some idea as to the content of nitrogen, phosphorus and potash in different animal manures.

122

Kind of Animal Manure	% Nitrogen	% Phosphorus	% Potash
Rabbit	2.4	1.4	0.6
Poultry	1.1	0.8	0.5
Sheep	0.7	0.3	0.9
Cattle	0.7	0.3	0.4
Horse	0.7	0.3	0.6
Pig	0.5	0.3	0.5

From the above table one can readily recognize that additional plant food elements should be applied after the top dressing of animal manure has been evenly spread over the lawn. Generally 10 pounds of 10-20-10 per 1000 square feet should be ample for maximum growth. After the animal manure has been obtained (it should always be cured manure, not fresh), a liberal application of about two to three inches of this material spread evenly across the St. Augustine grass turf will be sufficient to accomplish the desired purpose. One should make sure that a uniform spread is obtained by raking across the area, filling in the low spots and knocking down the highs to obtain a uniform application of this material. The St. Augustine grass will have the ability to protrude through, and during the process of this material working its way down into the soil level, one should keep it damp. The time to do it, of course, is in the fall of the year and early spring so the grass will not be injured to any great extent. This is one way of working organic matter into the top level of the soil without disturbing the original turf, or without breaking up the soil and going in and adding organic matter and then having to replace the sod. Weeds oftentimes will germinate and come up prior to the time the St. Augustine grass will come bursting through with its surge of growth as is apparent during the early spring. As these weeds come up and begin to grow, it would be advisable to take a weed killer (such as those listed previously) and spray the weeds as they protrude. This way your weed problem can be completely whipped without mowing, and you will have 100% assurance that weeds will not become a problem in your lawn.

Rice Hulls

Since rice is a major crop in the Texas Gulf Coast, the availability of rice hulls is something to take into consideration for use as organic materials to be applied on St. Augustine grass turf in order to enhance the organic build-up. Rice hulls are rich in potash and can be used in either mulches or as compost. They decay, depending upon the variety, readily, and can even be spaded into the ground directly before the rainy season. However, in the Texas Gulf Coast a lot of folks have used rice hulls—some satisfactorily, others to their great disappointment. The major disadvantage in using rice hulls is that they are composed of a high content of silicon, which is the major component of sand, thus making them rather difficult to decompose.

This can be overcome by using the right kind of management. As has been explained previously, the decomposition process is carried out by micro-organisms that feed upon the cellulose material of the hull and convert it from organic matter into humus. This is the form that must go into the soil for the plants to receive benefits. The micro-organisms that feed on the rice hulls and decompose it primarily are great users of nitrogen. The big mistake that a lot of folks make when they utilize rice hulls as a mulch factor for their St. Augustine lawn, is that they fail to feed the micro-organisms to the extent that they will speed up the decomposition. Thus, the rice hull remains on the turf a greater length of time, doing untold damage to the St. Augustine grass stand.

Management Practices That Help Prevent Lawn Diseases

The following practices are only general guides to be used according to one's judgment. Their importance depends upon the kind and seriousness of disease. Not all of them are practical under all conditions; it will depend upon each individual case.

1. Select grass species best adapted to the soil, climatic and light conditions under which they will be grown. Normally in the southern half of Texas—St. Augustine is our best accepted grass.

2. Plant mixtures of recommended grass, normally this will not be an item to affect us here in this area because almost everyone uses St. Augustine grass for lawn turf. However, there are some folks that like to over seed in the winter with rye grass in order to give them a beautiful green lawn. This is applicable, provided one cuts the stubble of the rye grass in the early spring so not to interfere with the normal growth of the St. Augustine grass. Use Danish Rye grass, it's better than common.

3. Do not clip St. Augustine grass too closely to the ground. Normally 1½ inches above the ground line, is sufficient. Cutting it any shorter than this will interfere with the normal growth of the plant, and the grass will turn yellow.

4. Mow the lawn frequently enough in the fall to prevent the accumulation of a thick amount of grass before excessive rain sets in.

5. Mow the grass before it gets too tall. Not more than one-half of the leaf surface should be removed at any one time, as this is highly detrimental to the plant.

6. Apply enough fertilizer to keep grass vigorously growing, but avoid over-stimulating grass with nitrogen, which will cause excessive mowing and will not do the grass any good. Excessive amounts of nitrogen also open the doors for such diseases as brown patch. Apply lime if the soil test indicates that you need it.

7. Remove clippings if possible, especially on heavy fertilized

lawns or during periods when the grass is growing rapidly. Clippings provide nutrients for fungi and help maintain humidity long after sun has dried off surrounding uncovered areas. For this reason we advise that you mow the lawn frequently enough so that there are no huge patches of mowed grass left, as this will help to breed fungi and cause a disease problem.

8. Water early enough in the day to allow grass leaves time to dry out before night. Avoid frequent light waterings, especially during warm weather, and do not water at night or in late evening.

9. Do not water grass until it begins to wilt, then soak the soil to a depth of six inches or more, provided you have good surface drainage.

Look for Danger Signals in Your Lawn

Nothing adds so much to the appearance of a home as a beautiful well kept lawn. To have such a lawn requires constant care and supervision. A careful observer can detect and often correct most of his lawn problems before they become very serious. With this in mind let us take another trip over the lawn and observe it very carefully. Look for these things:

1. General yellowing and lack of vigor in the grass. This is very likely due to hunger. Carefully spread per 100 square feet two pounds of a good grade fertilizer like 10-20-10. Spread the fertilizer uniformly and water immediately.

    Even if the grass is green and vigorous it should have some plant food applied in fall so as to send it into the winter in a strong vigorous condition. If it looks good, feed it in the same manner with the same kind of fertilizer as suggested for the hungry grass, but reduce the rate to one pound per 100 square feet.

2. Sick spots, but not dead. This may be due to either one of these factors:

    (a) Low spots where water has stood during rainy weather. These low spots should be filled with good soil. Actually the ground level in these spots should be a little higher than the surrounding soil, so it will be level after the soil has settled.

    (b) High spots in the lawn where the mower cuts the grass to the ground level every time the grass is mowed. If this condition is not corrected, the grass will die. It must have many leaves to complete the operation of manufacturing the finished plant foods from the raw materials.

    Remove the turf if it is still strong and vigorous, so it can be put back in place. Then remove enough of the soil to leave it level after the spot is resodded. Keep watered until the new grass is well established.

3. Grass is very thin generally, but not necessarily any dead spots. This may be due to lack of time for newly sprigged areas to have covered over. If the grass is green and vigorous, it probably will cover over and form a good sod in due time. If greater speed in coverage of the soil is desired, additional sprigs may be added. Usually, however, if the lawn is properly fed and managed, and there are no large naked spots without plants, this extra sprigging is not necessary unless there is an erosion problem. In that case, a quick cover is highly desirable.

4. Dead Spots. There are many things that can kill the grass in spots. The thing most likely to cause this trouble is the brown spot fungus. It thrives during wet weather and is usually worse with the coming of fall cool weather. Those interested in keeping their lawns beautiful will want to be constantly on the look out for the very first small browning spots and treat immediately. In fact, some authorities suggest that the best thing to do is to go ahead and treat, as a preventive, before the disease strikes. Surely, it is easier to control any fungus outbreak before it builds up to the extent of killing the plants, than trying to control it after an outbreak has started.

Controlling Chlorosis in St. Augustine Grass

Chlorosis may be corrected by applying iron sulfate or iron chelates direct to the St. Augustine grass turf. This condition is recognized by the yellowing of the leaves. Actually, it is a bleaching condition—whereby the green color of the plant is bleached out. Chlorosis occurs on soils that are high in lime, such as characterized in the Texas Gulf Coast. When this condition is serious it ruins the appearance of the lawn.

In order to overcome it, the application of iron sulfate or iron chelate must be applied. Before these iron bearing materials are applied, the homeowner should be sure that the pale color of the grass is not due to a nitrogen deficiency; this can be quite confusing. A nitrogen deficiency is characterized by relatively small, thin, and yellowish-green leaves of the St. Augustine turf. Careful examination shows yellow to brown color at the tip of the leaf down to the midrib. If the roots are studied, it will show very little. Whereas, in a chlorosis condition, generally the entire leaf is bleached out, not just the tip end of it—back or sides toward the midrib, but the entire leaf, which is a true characteristic of chlorosis.

The most effective way to apply the iron compounds, either iron chelates or iron sulfate, is through the medium of a spray. Iron sulfate, commonly called copperas, may be applied at the rate of three ounces in five gallons of water per 1,000 square feet, 1½ ounces of home detergent—such as liquid Lux soap—should be added to insure good leaf coverage. Repeat applications will likely be necessary at four to six week intervals. Chelated iron compounds may be applied in a spray according to the manufacturers directions. The chelates are generally more effective in some cases and for slightly longer periods, but the cost is also greater.

Where chlorosis is not severe—10 pounds of iron sulfate, or one pound of chelated iron per 1,000 sq. ft., applied alone as a dust or in a mixture with fertilizer may correct the problem. If a sprayer is used to apply the iron compounds to the foliage of the grass, these sprayers should be cleaned thoroughly after they have been used because the iron bearing materials are highly corrosive and will cause damage to the sprayer. Do not use more than recommended in so far as the rate of application is concerned, as it may cause extreme damage to the grass. For instance—if higher dosages of the iron sulfate, applied as a foliage application, burning can result. If the application of more than 10 pounds of iron sulfate per 1,000 sq. ft. is utilized without watering real good, oftentimes detrimental effects will be observed in the grass. But, it will soon overcome it, with proper growing conditions and water.

Brown Patch in St. Augustine Grass

Brown patch is characterized by dead, brown, circular areas in turf that begin as small spots and enlarge rapidly. It is most prevalent in wet weather on dense turf when night temperatures remain 70° F and above.

St. Augustine grass is the most prevalent grass affected, also Bermuda grass. Avoid over watering, particularly in the late evening when this disease is serious, and if the disease prevails over a large area, as is quite common, the best compound to use is Terraclor.

This material should be used at the rate of one pound per 1,000 sq. ft. It is advisable also to treat the entire lawn instead of the affected areas. The main reason being the fungi, that causes brown patch, is prevalent in the soil and even though it may have shown through in specific spots, and you treat those, it will crop up somewhere else. Most people let brown patch (dead brown circular areas) appear before they start to do anything, then they treat it and expect the grass to come back. Normally by that time the grass has already died from the effects of the fungus, and it will be green growing season once again before those dead spots cover over. A preventive control measure for brown patch is much more effective than trying to control it after the characteristics of the disease show up. The one pound of Terraclor can be applied either by dusting on or mixing in water, and spraying on. Water well to carry the material into the crown zone where the fungus disease is located. But treat as soon as possible to protect the lawn, prior to the time the disease strikes. Normally one application of 75% Wettable Terraclor, at the rate of one pound per 1,000 sq. ft. or one quart of the 24% liquid Terraclor per 1,000 sq. ft. will give control for at least nine months. The amount of water used to carry on the 1 pound or 1 quart of Terraclor per 1,000 sq. ft. does not matter, coverage is most important. A Granule Terraclor is also available. Apply it by fertilizer spreader.

Dollar Spot in St. Augustine Grass

Dollar spot (some folks refer to it as brown spot) occurs quite frequently in St. Augustine grass, but is a separate fungus from the one causing brown patch. The fungus is most destructive during cool, wet weather, and it generally attacks in May and June, and stops during July and August—in the hot summer months, and starts again in September and runs through the entire fall.

Dollar spot may occur in any turf, regardless of management or soil fertility, but damage is usually greatest if there is a deficiency of nitrogen. The symptom of the disease is charactertized by the development of bleached spots the size of a silver dollar. Affected grass is killed and the lawn is left pitted; sometimes the diseased areas mereg and form large, irregular patches. At first, spots or diseased grass are dark and somewhat water soaked, then they turn brown and ultimately bleach nearly white. If the fungus is growing actively, a fine, white mycelium can be seen when dew is still on the grass. Sometimes only the upper most grass blades are affected and light colored blotches develop on them. Turf normally recovers quickly if treated with Terraclor at the same rate as recommended for brown patch.

Mushrooms

Mushrooms that grow individually or in clumps usually develop from buried organic matter, such as pieces of construction lumber, logs or tree stumps. Mushrooms with this growth habit are usually harmless to grasses, but are objectionable because they are unsightly and fruiting bodies occur repeatedly. They develop following prolonged wet weather and often disappear as soon as the soil begins to dry, or when the grass is mowed. Eliminate mushrooms that grow from buried lumber, logs or stumps by digging up the pieces of buried wood. If this is impractical, drench the area with a fungicide. The simplest way to drench is to punch holes six to eight inches apart and from six to eight inches deep in the ground, within and surrounding affected area. Use an iron rod or pipe for punching the holes. Pour a fungicide solution into the hole. One of the best fungicides to use is one that contains mercury. Mercury containing fungicides normally do an excellent job in controlling the mushrooms. Such Fungicides are Arasan and Cerasan.

Fairy Rings

Fairy rings are circles or arcs of dark green grass, surrounding areas of light colored or dead grass. During spring and fall the fruiting bodies being mushrooms, develop into the circle outlining the fairy ring. Unless the fungus is controlled, the ring enlarges each year and leaves alternate bands of green and discolored grass. The fungus that causes fairy rings begins growth at a particular point and continues to grow outward. It may spread from five to 24 inches annually. The rate of spread depends, of course, upon soil conditions, weather factors, temperature, moisture and fertility. The fungus is usually several inches below the ground, and forms a dense layer of threads that break down organic matter at the outer edge of the ring. Grass at the outer edge grows faster than the grass inside the ring and is a darker green. Dying or dead grass is inside the zone of stimulated growth. Fairy rings seldom occur in lawns that are adequately fertilized and treated with fungicides for the control of other diseases, such as brown patch.

CONTROL: The best control is to punch holes around the outside of the ring and pour into these holes a fungicide such as Terasan, Terraclor or Actidione.

Slime Mold

A group of fungi known as slim molds often covers grass with a dusty, bluish-grey, black or yellow mass. Slime molds are not parasitic on grass but are rather unsightly. They feed on dead organic matter. The most damage they do to grass plants is to shade and discolor the blades. Slime molds occur during wet weather; they disappear rapidly as soon as it becomes dry. The large masses can be readily broken up by sweeping with a broom, or by spraying with a strong stream of water from a garden hose. During prolonged damp weather, slime molds can be easily annoying, and it may be desirable to apply a garden fungicide, but normally the best treatment for this is to take the garden hose and thoroughly wash the blades of the grass. This will bring it under control.

Dog Urine Injury

Folks often see a leached out spot in the turf and think they have disease or insect damage. Actually it is nothing but affected areas caused by the deposit of dog urine. This particular chemical being high in salts, naturally interferes with the natural processes of plant growth, thus causing the grass normally to turn brown and straw colored and usually die. This oftentimes can be overcome by proper watering and fertility to stimulate growth and bring the affected area back. You might have a word with the dog, too.

Toxic, Compact Areas in the Lawn

In some lawns, there persists areas that are very difficult to keep the grass in a green, lush growing condition. This particular area, at first, appears as if it may have been affected with a disease. The plant will begin to wilt and gradually die. Upon closer examination and some digging in this particular area, one will normally find that two combination factors are causing the problem.

129

One, a toxic concentration of some type of soil condition that is objectionable from the standpoint of plant growth, primarily caliche or a dolometic limestone condition. In conjunction with this, the area was compacted when the home was built. With these two factors in mind, the grass has very little chance of thriving and growing as it should. Primarily it will show up in periods of less rainfall than it will during humid conditions. The grass never does take hold and grow when stimulated with fertilizer in these particular areas as it does elsewhere. To overcome such conditions, it is advisable to apply organic matter to this area. To break up the hard-pan caused by the compaction of this particular material, use a spading fork or spading tool, or soil aerator. It would be advisable to apply amounts of sufficient organic matter, whether it be barnyard fertilizer, rice hulls, or whatever it might be to this particular area so that it can be worked into the sub-soil strata, so the root system will have an opportunity to pass on through the compacted caliche or dolometic area, and set its roots into a more permeable type sub-soil. After one or two years of painstaking work in such immediate areas, one can overcome this detriment to the turf and cause it to grow as beautiful as in other areas of the lawn.

Fading-Out

Fading-out is a common summer disease of lawn grasses in all areas of Texas. It most often occurs on grasses that have suffered from lack of soil moisture in mid-summer. Fading-out is sometimes called melting out, "going out" or "grey leaf mold."

Irregularly shaped dead areas occur in the lawn. Isolated, scattered sprigs of living grass are usually found in the disease areas. Leaves die back from the tip end. Runners or stems of the grass may have small dead spots. These spots may or may not enlarge and girdle the stem. Roots may be rotten.

The disease is caused by a complex of Helminthosporium, Curvularia and Fusarium species of fungi. These soil molds are active following a heavy rain on grass that has previously been weakened by drought. There is an indication that soil nematodes may be associated with fading-out disease in some cases. Fading-out is controlled by proper management of the lawn. Proper watering, fertilizing, mowing and aeration are important.

In lawn areas that respond slowly to proper management practices in the summer, Zineb or Captan fungicide drenches may prove helpful. Use the above fungicides at the rate of two to four pounds per 100 gallons of water. Wet the grass with the solution to the soil line. Use a sprinkler can or hose on sprayer for small areas. Apply drench right after mowing. Also, drench the healthy grass beyond the disease area to a width of several feet.

Insect Free Lawns

Insect infested lawns can be a nuisance to people as well as pets. Chiggers, fleas and brown dog ticks are usually the culprits when a lawn is avoided instead of enjoyed. If proper measures are used, these pests can be eliminated with a minimum amount of work and expense.

For the control of chiggers, the specialists recommend the application of dusts or spray of chlordane, diazinon or lindane to infested grass and ground litter. An emulsion spray usually gives the best results. For treating small areas, use a compressed air or knapsack sprayer and apply two and one-half to three quarts of spray per 1,000 square feet. If dust is used, apply five percent Chlordane at 40 to 50 pounds per acre, or 2% Diazinon Granules at 30 to 45 pounds per acre (approximately one pound per 1,000 square feet).

Fleas usually enter the home on dogs, cats, rats and other animals. They deposit eggs loosely on their hosts, and these eggs fall onto the ground, into cracks in the floor, or similar places. Since fleas spend their early developmental stages in the soil, they often become a nuisance on the lawn and around out-buildings. These places should be treated with a 2½ percent Diazinon spray or with a 5 percent Malathion dust. Dogs should be dusted thoroughly with a five percent Malathion dust or dipped in one-half percent Malathion water solution. A commercially prepared 2 or 2½ percent Malathion solution is recommended for control or fleas in the home.

Diazinon has been approved for the control of fleas and chiggers in outdoor areas, and this material may be substituted for any of the previously listed chemicals. Brown dog ticks, which are resistant to chlorinated hydrocarbon insecticides, also can be controlled with Diazinon. This material can be purchased in a 25 percent wettable powder or in a 25 percent emulsifiable concentrate. Lawn pests can be controlled by mixing two quarts of emulsifiable concentrate with 25 gallons of water and applying this mixture at the rate of one gallon per 1,000 square feet of infested area. To mix smaller amounts of spray, use 2½ fluid ounces (five tablespoons) of emulsifiable concentrate to one gallon of water. The 25 percent wettable powder may be used at the rate of four pounds of powder to 25 gallons of water. For dog tick control only, spray the area of the lawn that the dog frequents. Ticks are not usually found in areas that are free of shrubbery. Spray should be applied under shrubbery and one grass growing next to buildings. Infested kennels and other quarters should be sprayed thoroughly. It may require two applications at ten day intervals to completely control the ticks. *Do not use this material on animals. Children and pets should be kept away from treated areas for several days after application.* To control fleas and ticks on a dog, dust the dog with a 5% Sevin dust or with a dog dusting powder containing Co-ral. Repeat only at 7 day intervals.

New Turf Grasses

Since so many problems exists with San Augustine; mainly Chinch bugs, Fade-out and Brown patch, researchers and Independent Plant breeders have been attempting to come forth with better quality turf grasses than San Augustine now affords. In recent years there have been many new turf grasses that introduced primarily for use on Golf Courses which have moved over into the individual lawn field. These grasses are Tifgreen 328, Tifway 419, Dwarf Tif, Blue Tif and many others. They are all hybrid bermudas. They must be propagated by Sprigs, Underground Root systems or Stolens as they produce no vital seeds.

Recently another introduction from Florida called Florida No-Mow has made its way on the scene and today is known to be adapted as far north as College Station, Texas and perhaps points beyond. We'll deal with each of these varieties in detail so that the individual homeowner can ascertain as to the variety best adapted for his use.

DWARF TIF—This was a selection found growing in the southern Florida and plant breeders estimate that it is a mutation of their major line of Tifway and Tifgreen. It's characterized by real dark green color, low growth—in fact it is estimated by some that this grass will perhaps never need mowing. It's above ground blades of grass perhaps will not reach any more than ½ inch in height. It spreads rapidly and gives a solid ground cover and when a solid turf is established no other vegetation, weeds etc. can impregnate it. However, it must have plenty of open sunlight and does not respond too well under dense shade.

TIFWAY 419—As one can imagine, this grass was perfected by the plant breeders to be used on the fairways of Golf Courses. It's a little higher growing grass than the Tifgreen 328 but is much higher than Dwarf Tif. It possesses a beautiful green color and grows extensively well into the fall months—much longer than common bermuda; however even though it does grow upright it must be kept low in order to maintain its color and quality. Therefore, it should be mowed at a height of no more than ½ inch and should be kept this way by mowing at least once a week or once every 10 days. It too loves a lot of open sunlight and will now spread and make a thick turf under the shade of trees.

TIFGREEN 328—This grass was perfected specifically to be used on putting greens of Golf Courses. In essence it looks a great deal like Tifway 419 except its growing characteristics upright are not as great as Tifway 419. It possesses about the same color, growth pattern and habitats as 419. It too likes sunshine and not a lot of shade.

All of these grasses possess and carries the major characteristics as the narrow leaf upright growing bermuda grass superior to common in all respects.

FLORIDA NO-MOW—As for this grass, it is the major grass that is adapted for limited sunlight. It will grow and produce a beautiful turf with only 30% filterated sun. It's characteristics are in between the Tifway and the Dwarf Tif and possesses all the charactertics of bermuda but it's primary advantage is the fact that it will grow in shade.

Now, in the establishment of any of these hybrid bermudas—there are a few points that should be remembered. They are not well adapted for sprigging in to an established San Augustine lawn as the two characteristics of the grass clash and therefore cannot compete with one another. These new tif grasses are better adapted for new lawns or one that has been taken out all the old grass and growth and started anew. They should be established with a good seed bed, by that I mean that the old lawn if taken up should be broken up with a tiller and organic matter added and leveled and then the sprigs should be applied and rolled in or cut in and then mulched and kept watered. With proper growing seasons, sunlight, temperature and water and fertility—if one puts down enough of the vegetative matter of these grasses, he should have good cover within 30 to 45 days. The major advantages of these new grasses over the San Augustine that we've been so accustomed too, is the fact that: One, its chinch bug resistant; Two, resistant to most of the fungus that attacks the other grasses; Three, it presents a narrow blade growth which gives you a better more manicured looking turf and a thicker turf which is more prone to crowd out weeds and other vegetative matter and maintains its color longer in the fall than San Augustine or bermuda and is drought tolerant—by this I mean it takes a lot less water to keep it green and growing than San Augustine and perhaps will take less fertility than San Augustine, as they do not grow as vigorously as the San Augustine does. But, as stated previously in this discussion, these grasses lend themselves better to a new homeowner establishing a lawn for the first time or for Golf Course or Industrial Use. There are many certified growers around the state carry all varieties and they are economical to establish. A little higher in cost than San Augustine, but with the added advantages mentioned are well worth it.

Chapter 8

Insects and Their Control

Insects

Identification and Their Control

Insects for the most part, are the scourge of mankind, and thus a continual battle between man and his ever present enemy goes on. It has been stated by a noted Entomologist that if this battle were not continuously waged, the balance of power would shift in the direction of insects and the world would become populated by insects. The pages of history fully well define this clear cut battle as in ancient times famines and plagues caused by heavy infestation of insects devoured crops and destroyed property. Even today, our modern civilization is plagued by the same situation. Mosquitoes spreading sleeping sickness; fever ticks destroying cattle; grasshoppers eating range lands; and army worms devouring crops. Without modern insecticides and distribution techniques, insects once again would plague the land, and man would be faced with the eternal problem of producing enough food and fiber to feed and clothe himself.

Insects belong to a group called Arthropoda. The members of this group are found in the seas and fresh water, on land or even flying freely. A group with remarkable differences of structure, and so abundant that all the other animals taken together are less than one-sixth as many as the Arthropods. Well known members of this group are the lobsters, crawfish and crab, scorpions, spiders, mites, ticks, the centipedes and millipedes; and last and most abundant of all, the insects.

Insects normally are identified by their external structure. Therefore bringing together all the facts, the following statements pertaining to insects are generally true. An adult insect is a bilaterally symmetrical animal, consisting of a series of segments one behind another. These segments are grouped into three regions, the head and front, followed in order by the thorax and the abdomen. The animal is covered by a skeleton, (shell like) in that it is on the outside of the body, but horny in its nature. Attached to the thorax are three pairs of jointed legs. A pair of antennae, mouth parts, and usually two pairs of wings are present. It breathes through air tubes. The reproductive organs open near the after end of the body.

This general classification is normally true but may vary according to the order and the species of the insect; however a basic understanding is a necessity in order to identify and recognize a control measure for insects. As an example, there are three basic control measures for insects:

1. Contact insecticides are recommended for the control of insects having no chewing mouth parts.

2. Stomach insecticides are generally recommended for the control of insects having chewing mouth parts.

3. Fumigation is a process whereby toxic gases are introduced through the air tubes of the insects to bring about complete control.

Oftentimes, one or more of these techniques may be used in combination to destroy the insect. One formulation—such as a contact insecticide—can be used to control those insects that have both chewing and sucking mouth parts. Therefore with these facts in mind a shortened summary of different insects are discussed in order that a positive identification can be made by the gardener followed by a complete recommendation for its control.

Ants

Ants are the most easily recognized of all insects. They are found in almost all climates and do damage to practically all crops. Three classes of ants always compose a colony. Males, queens and workers. Ants are nearly always recognized by the presence of petiole which is enlarged near or behind its middle, either being swollen or having a portion projecting upward, followed behind by a constriction where this segment joints the rest of the abdomen. This gives the insect a rather elongate, narrow portion between the thoracic and abdominal masses, enlarged at one of two places, according to the number of segments concerned. There are a number of different species of ants we are confronted with, namely the Argentine ant, cornfield ant, honey ant, black ant, red and carpenter ant, Texas leaf cutting ant and others. In general though, they can be divided into two distinct classes: Those infesting inside the home; those infesting outside the home.

Control—*Outside Ants*—Locate the colony and use one and one-half pounds of 10% Heptachlor granules per 1000 square feet, or three ounces per 100 square feet.

Application—Sprinkle the material mentioned above over the area infested. If mounds or colonies can be located, make a circular band application around mounds. Space these band applications at two to three feet intervals.

Control—*Inside Ants*—The most common species of ants that infest the home are the carpenter ant and sugar ant. For maximum control, treat the outside of the home around the foundation and in the flower beds with 10% Heptachlor granules. This will help to control the insect at its source. Inside the home, mix four to five tablespoonfuls of liquid Diazinon into one gallon of cleaning fluid and spray the woodwork.

Application—Use a small hand sprayer or a three gallon low pres-

135

sure sprayer and apply this mixture to base-boards, cupboards, etc. This mixture will also control roaches. CAUTION—avoid breathing the fumes from this insecticide during application. Do not apply to cooking utensils or food commodities and allow ample ventilation in the home during application for proper evaporation.

Imported Fire Ants

The imported fire ant was first imported to this country—supposedly from South America, and was first noticed near Mobile, Alabama, and is now located in 10, perhaps 11 southern states—including the Texas Gulf Coast. These ants are a menace to young vegetables and even young animals, often killing quail and other poultry. The workers are reddish to blackish-red—one-eighth to one-fourth inch, with two segmented pedicel. There may be 25,000 in an average mound, formed in the pastures, garden or lawn. This mound is generally 10 inches high and about 15 inches across. Whenever a fire ant injects its toxic poison into the tissue of a human, it forms a blister—thus it gets the name fire ant.

Control—Use 5% Dieldrin granules or a 10% Heptachlor granule. When the Dieldrin granules are used—apply one and one-half pounds per 1000 sq. ft. of surface area. When the Heptachlor granules are used— use one and one-fourth to one and one-half pounds of this material to 1000 sq. ft.

Application—Researchers have stated that it is best to apply the insecticide in the granular form in concentric circles around the mound. Oftentimes three concentric circles formed around the mound at proportionate distance apart from each other will give excellent control. As the ants make their way back and forth to the mound they have to cross the toxic barrier in order to reach their mound.

Aphids

Aphids or plant lice—This is one of the most important groups of insects from an economic standpoint as all its members are injurious, often very abundant, and a species, usually doing little harm, may at any time become a serious threat. Aphids are tiny, soft bodied insects, the largest being less than a third of an inch long, generally with long legs and antennae, and are of various colors: green, black, various shades of red and brown, white and grey being the most usual ones. Some are more or less completely concealed beneath long, white waxy thread, giving them a woolly appearance; others have a sort of dust or bloom, like that on a plum, coating their bodies. The majority are without any covering. They are sucking insects that sap the strength from vegetation and plants causing the leaves to curl and become discolored. They multiply at a tremendously fast rate and unless controlled can completely infest a plant within a matter of days. They are generally found on the underside of the leaves of the plants and oftentimes go unobserved by the gardener. They are often found on plants during cold weather.

Control—Both dust and sprays are effective, but since aphids are most generally found on the underside of the leaves of plants sprays are more effective. Use two tablespoonfuls of 25% Diazinon into one gallon of water.

Application—Thorough coverage is essential for maximum control. Apply the mixture with a low pressure sprayer and in order to obtain proper stickability it's advisable to apply in with the mixture a teaspoonful of Spreader-Sticker, or liquid soap, to cause the insecticide to cling to the leaf. Repeat the application within seven days.

Army Worm

The army worm is related to cut-worms. They are larvae of moths and caterpillars which work in armies, devouring everything in their path. There are many different varieties of army worms—such as the beet army worm, the fall army worm, the southern army worm, and the yellow striped army worm.

Control—Use 5% Dieldrin granules and sprinkle over the infested area. Also, a spray made from five pounds of 40% wettable Toxaphene in 100 gallons of water—applied to the area in which they are infesting will give excellent results. If a smaller amount of spray is desired, take three to five tablespoonfuls of 40% wettable Toxaphene in a gallon of water and thoroughly spray the area. 50% DDT can also be used.

Application—Make sure that the 5% Dieldrin granules, or the spray, is applied to all the areas in which the army worm is infesting.

Azalea Lace Bug

This is a major pest of azaleas wherever they grow. Nymphs and adults suck the sap out of the leaves, resulting in greyish, blotched, strippled, or blanched appearance of the upper surface. The injury is most unsightly and the plant vitality is greatly reduced. The small adult of this insect being only about one-eighth inch long has lacy wings with brown and black markings, light brown legs and antennae. The nymphs are nearly colorless at first, later black and spiny.

Control—Periodic applications of Diazinon.

Application—Use the liquid 25% Diazinon. Mix a spray consisting of three tablespoonfuls of this compound into a gallon of water and periodically spray the azalea plant.

ASP (Puss Caterpillar)

This insect is one of the stinging caterpillars that we have so much trouble with in the Texas Gulf Coast. They can be found on oak, elm,

137

plum, maple, rose, sycamore, and many other trees and shrubs, even on English ivy.

This insect is about an inch long in the larvae stage, covered with long, soft, reddish-yellow hairs, interspersed with stinging spines. If a puss caterpillar should fall upon a person's neck there may be severe irritation, if on the wrist—the whole arm may swell and the sting or poison from one of the stinging spines is very irritating. In the case of sensitive people, it can be very dangerous. Children are more seriously injured than adults.

The caterpillar is characterized by having its entire body, with the exception of the underportion, covered with urticating hairs or spines. It is about an inch long, may vary in color from a light grey to a yellow, and tapers toward the tail-end, slightly oval-shaped. The underside or belly is completely bare of hair.

Control—Toxaphene, DDT, Chlordane, Dieldrin, Diazinon.

Application—If 50% wettable DDT is used, use three tablespoonfuls per gallon of water. If 40% wettable Chlordane is used, use four to five tablespoonfuls per gallon. If the 25% Diazinon is used, use three to four tablespoonfuls of this material to a gallon of water. Make sure that thorough application of this material is applied to all the foliage of the shrubs or plant in which the caterpillar is infesting. A spray of any of these materials applied directly onto the caterpillar will not give control since the only susceptible spot on the caterpillar that can be victimized by the insecticide is on the underside of his body. Therefore, the insecticide must be applied to the foliage of the plant on which the caterpillar crawls, thus crawling across the leaf that has been coated with the insecticide, coming in contact with the chemical, the asp will absorb enough of it to kill him. Therefore, I would recommend that you add a spreader-sticker solution, or at least a teaspoonful of liquid detergent into the spray in order to facilitate sticking of the chemical onto the leaf surfaces of the plant.

Assassin Bug

This large family of bugs consists of carnivorous insects, some of which are small, and others are considerably more than one inch long. They possess a powerful short beak. Though generally beneficial and feeding on the blood of other insects, they may occassionally attack man—and in such cases produce rather painful wounds. Some of these blood sucking species transmit disease organisms. The group, its members preying almost entirely upon other insects should be regarded in general as beneficial.

Control—If a control is needed, 5% Dieldrin granules should be used.

Application—Apply this material on the ground where the assassin bug is located.

Azalea Bark Scale

Infestation of this insect shows up as a small, white cottony or woolly mass on the stems, especially in axles of the branches. Diazinon gives effective control if the spray is applied when nymphs are present, usually immediately after blooming season. Two or three applications, 10 days to two weeks apart will be required to assure adequate control. Once again, a preventive control measure of periodic sprayings of Diazinon, spaced every 10 to 14 days, on azaleas will prevent the infestation of any of these insects, including the greenhouse white fly.

Azalea Stem Borer

A beetle girdling tips of stems of azalea, and perhaps other plants in spring. It is slender, ½ inch long, with yellow head and thorax, the latter with 2 black spots, and grayish-yellow punctate wing covers. Twigs are girdled in 2 places, ½ inch apart, and a yellow egg is thrust through the bark halfway between. The tip dies and the yellow grub, legless, an inch long, bore down the twig and into the trunk, pushing out sawdust from holes near the ground. After 2 or 3 weeks it pupates, producing beetles in summer.

Control—Cut off and burn wilted twigs an inch or more below the girdled portion as soon as noticed. Periodic spraying with a Malathion solution will help in preventing and discouraging an infestation of the borer. Mix 4 Tablespoons of 25% Diazinon into 1 gallon of water and cover the plant. Repeat at 7 to 10 day intervals.

Bats

Even though this does not fit into the category of an insect, nevertheless, the application of an insecticide can be used to repel and kill bats. Since there are a number of folks who are vitally interested in this pest from the standpoint of rabies, we thought it advisable to give some information pertaining to this troublesome problem.

Bats are nocturnal animals leaving their roosting places at dusk to fly about in pursuit of night flying insects that provide the bulk of their food.

Bats are mammals, not birds, as so many people believe. Their wings are formed by thin leathery or membranous skin that stretches between the greatly elongated bones of the front legs and fingers. They are the only mammals thus equipped to fly. The ones found in this country are small, generally overaging three to five inches in body length, the wing-spread averages between 10 and 15 inches. They do not attack humans nor do they get themselves tangled in people's hair.

Originally bats roosted in natural shelters such as caves and hollow trees. Many still do, but others have found attics, spaces between building walls and unused areas in upper stories much to their liking. From the droppings and urine deposited about the roosts come a highly objectionable odor that is characteristic of bat roosting places. This odor persists for a long time after the roost are broken up and may serve to attract new colonies if preventive measures are not taken. The noises created by crawling bats are also disturbing to the householder. While they cause no actual damage to the structure, their presence in a dwelling is usually undesirable.

Control—Control can be based upon three primary preventive or control measures. One is repellents, two is fumigation and three is the application of an insecticide.

(1) Repellents—Bats dislike the odor of Naphthalene and Paradicholobenzene, two chemicals commonly used as moth and insect repellents. When the roost is located in attics or other closed spaces that can be reached easily, either of these materials can be used to drive them out. Three to five pounds of Naphthalene flakes will usually be sufficient to treat the average attic. Simply sprinkle the material liberally over the entire area. So objectionable is this material to bats that they will usually leave the roosts within a short time after it is introduced, even in broad daylight. Both of the chemicals dissipate rapidly on contact with the air; however, the applications may have to be repeated if no other control is practiced.

(2) Fumigation—In cases where the use of repellents and bat proofing will not suffice, it might be necessary to destroy the bats. Best results can be obtained by fumigation with gas. Calcuim cyanide is the material most generally used for this purpose, and operations involving space fumigation are dangerous and must never be attempted by an inexperienced person. Only trained professionals qualified to handle the material should be entrusted with the task.

The use of poisonous bait is impractical since bats feed primarily upon flying insects they catch in the air, therefore a poison bait is of no use.

(3) Chemical Control—Recent tests run by the Fish and Wildlife Service have found that one and one-half cups of 50% wettable DDT per gallon of water, sprayed on rafters, kills bats after two or three weeks exposure. Due to the breakdown of this chemical, the repeat application of this insecticide (about once a month) is highly essential in order to knock out the bat infestation.

Bagworm

Bagworms are caterpillars which carry their bag-like houses around with them. They are the larvae of moths, with wingless, almost legless females that practically never leave their bag. They are found from Massachusetts to Texas, more frequently on evergreens and conifers. The spindle shape bag—one to two inches long—is unbelievably tough silk, covered with bits of leaves and twigs from the host plant. A bag hanging on an arborvitae or cedar may look different from the one

140

that is hanging on a sycamore. Unless they are controlled, they can literally defoliate a tree and destroy it.

Control—When there is a light infestation one can pick the bags off of the tree and get partial control that way. However, for complete control, it is best to spray with either DDT, Malathion or dust the plants with Malathion. Toxaphene is also effective. Since thorough coverage is essential—a spray will likely give best control. If one uses the 50% wettable DDT—it should be used at the rate of three pounds per 100 gallons of water, *or* two tablespoons to a gallon of water.

Application—Since this insect generally infests the entire tree, it is of necessity that thorough coverage and saturation of the plant be obtained for maximum control. It is also wise to repeat the initial application within about a week to 10 days to make sure that any newly hatched eggs will be destroyed.

Bean Aphid

A common important, dull black species. It is very gregarious, congregating in large numbers on succulent plant parts, causing the foliage of the bean plants to wilt and turn yellow.

Control—Use 5% Malathion dust, or spray with Malathion.

Application—Use a duster and apply insecticide to top and bottom of leaves and stems of plants.

Beet Leaf Hopper

This insect is dangerous because it is a carrier of the virus that causes curly top disease in tomatoes. They fly in swarms. As they feed they introduce the curly top virus. They are the only known carrier of the disease, which makes the leaf vein warty, petals kinked, leaves rolled and brittle on the edge, plans stunted and finally killed.

Control—Dust the plants with 10% DDT, 5% Malathion, or 5% Sevin.

Application—Dust tomatoes with 5% Malathion dust, or 5% Sevin.

Blister Beetles

These beetles are rather long, three-fourths inch, slender, with prothorax narrower than the soft and flexible wing covers. The name comes from the cantharidian in their bodies, which will blister the skin if beetles are crushed. This powerful agent, obtained from the "Spanish Fly," a European blister beetle, was formerly used in much the same fashion as a mustard plaster and also as an aphrodisiac.

Control—Use 5% Malathion dust, *or* 25% wettable Malathion, using four to six tablespoonfuls of this material to a gallon of water. Thorough coverage is essential for maximum control. On ornamentals, spray with a general purpose insecticide containing DDT, Sevin, or Diazinon.

Borers In Trees
(Other than fruit trees)

Borers are grubs or caterpillars, larvae of beetles or moths, working in woody tissues of trees. Borers are particularly destructive to newly set trees and to those weakened by various causes, such as drought, sunscald, injuries, insect damage and chemical injuries.

Control—This is more of a preventive method than a control after infestation. To kill borers already in trees, use a commercial borer killer such as Borina.

Application—Use four tablespoonfuls of 18% Dieldrin to a gallon. Spray and repeat every two-three weeks. Saturate all limbs and foliage of trees until spray runs off.

Brown Dog Ticks

One of the biggest insect problems and also one of the most difficult to control. The reason being that a female tick, after engorging itself with blood, has the ability to go into a dormancy period for as long as 210 days. They hide in cracks of brick, under cedar shakes, boards, etc. With this type of cycle, female ticks are going into and out of hibernation constantly, thus a constant source of infestation is always a problem. One female tick can lay as many as 800 eggs, thus the infestation is one continuous problem. *There is no sure shot control.* However, the best control method to date is:

Control—Use a 25% Diazinon spray. This material can be purchased in a 25% wettable powder or in a 25% emulsifiable concentrate. Lawn pests can be controlled by mixing 2 quarts of the emulsifiable concentrate with 25 gallons of water and applying this mixture at the rate of one gallon per 100 sq. ft. of infested area. For best control repeat with a second application within 10 days. To mix smaller amounts of this spray, use two and one-half fluid ounces (five tablespoonfuls) of the concentrate to one gallon of watter. The 25% wettable powder may be used at the rate of four pounds of Diazinon to 25 gallons of water.

Application—Thorough coverage of the entire lawn, shrubbery Remove and pen all pets from the yard before spraying. Keep children beds, etc. is essential for maximum control. Spray should be applied underneath shrubbery and on grass growing next to buildings. Infested kennels and other quarts should be sprayed thoroughly. CAUTION: and pets off the grass, until the insecticide spray is thoroughly dry. It may also be advisable to sprinkle grass after spraying. Also spray the walls of the home as ticks may be hiding in a dormant stage, in the mortar of the brick, or underneath cedar shakes.

Cabbage Worm

This worm has numerous cross-striped black bands across its green body. Does tremendous damage to cabbage and other green leafy vegetables.

Control—Use 5% Malathion dust or 5% Sevin dust.

Application—Apply dust thoroughly to all sections of the plant. If 25% wettable Malathion is used, mix three tablespoonfuls to 1 gallon of water, *or* three pounds to 100 gallons.

Cabbage Aphid

This insect is a very small, whitish-green bug found in dense clusters on the underside of leaves, causing them to cup and curl. They are found on broccoli, cabbage, cauliflower, collards, turnips and radishes. Seedlings may be killed while other plants may be dwarfed. In the southern area, living young are produced throughout the winter.

Control—Use a 5% Malathion dust, or a Malathion spray. Apply the 50% Malathion at the rate of 4 tablespoonfuls of this material per gallon of water and thoroughly spray the plants.

Application—Thorough application, both on topside and underside of the foliage, of the affected plants is essential for maximum control. Apply the dust when there is a slight dew on the leaves so that it will stick. When applying the spray—it is advisable to use a spreader-sticker or a small amount of liquid detergent to cause it to stick to the slick leaves of the affected plant.

Cabbage Looper

This insect is a member of the caterpillar family, and is found throughout the country. It attacks all members of the cabbage family, such as broccoli, cabbage, turnips, tomatoes and even cotton. The looper winters as a green to a brown pupa wrapped in a cocoon, attached by on*e* side to a plant leaf and transforms in spring into a moth with mottled brownish fore-legs, a small silvery spot in the middle and a paler brown hind-leg. Wings expand to about one and one-half inches. The females lay many small round, greenish-white eggs on the upper surface of leaves. The larvae has a body tapering to the head, greenish with a thin white line above the spiracles, and two others down the back and three pairs of pull legs. After feeding from two to four weeks the pupa spins a cocoon. There are three to four generations a year.

Control—Any of the chlorinated hydrocarbons or phosphate compounds normally will do an excellent job. Toxaphene is readily recommended, except on cucurbits, and DDT also does an excellent job. When hard to kill loopers are run into, Endrin is the best control measure. One quart of six-pound Toxaphene into 50 gallons of water normally will do an excellent job in controlling this particular pest. On a smaller scale, use three to four tablespoonfuls of liquid six-pound Toxaphene for maximum control. One word of advice—the cabbage looper is extremely hard to kill once it gets into the adult stage; it is easier and much more economical to control when in the small larvae stage.

Carpenter Ants

These insects, nesting in wood, are oftentimes responsible for damage that is attributed to termites. It is the largest of our common ant, measuring from one-fourth to one-half inch long, dark brown to black. This insect infests homes, and especially is found around the bathroom fixtures and in the house itself. They also attack trees and enter through wounds and stubs of broken branches, causing damage in this particular area.

Control—Use 25% emulsible concentrate of Diazinon.

Application—When the Diazinon is used—mix at the rate of three to four tablespoonfuls to a gallon of water. Apply to the outside foundation of the house, underneath the house if it is up off the ground. And, on the inside—it is best to mix with a petroleum naphtha-type product such as Varsol, at the rate of three tablespoonfuls per gallon. Thoroughly apply to the interior surfaces, making sure that you keep it off of anything that is plastic—as this naphtha product will have a tendency to etch the plastic. If the 50% concentrate of Malathion is used—use four tablespoonfuls to a gallon of water for outside application, and four tablespoonfuls to a gallon of the naphtha product for inside application.

Chiggers or Red Bugs

Chiggers are microscopic, almost invisible insects that render a powerful toxic bite to humans, as well as livestock. They are more prevalent during the early spring and can be found in almost any green vegetation. It has been said by some scientists that the bite of the chigger breaks down the protein structure of the skin, and thereby you get the reddening, excessive swelling and painful sting of the red bug bite. They are normally found during the early spring and summer, in lush, green growth—especially where there has been excessive amounts of rainfall and humidity is high.

Dry, hot weather seems to render the red bug absolutely powerless.

Control—There are a number of different insecticides that can be used, either in the form of a dust or a spray. For instance: Chlordane, Diazinon, Dieldrin, Heptachlor and Malathion will do an excellent job in controlling the chigger. These materials should be applied to the lawn and turf, and in the area in which red bugs are infesting. The application of a 10% Chlordane dust, or a 5% Dieldrin granule, or a 10% Heptachlor granule, or a 5% Malathion dust to the lawn will give excellent control. For lawns and turf, when using 10% Chlordane—dust evenly—one to two ounces of this material per 100 square feet of surface space. Dieldrin, 5% granules—apply one and one-half pounds per 1000 square feet of surface area. For 10% Heptachlor—broadcast one and one-fourth to one and one-half ounces per 100 square feet, and when Malathion is used—apply at the rate of one to two ounces per 100 square feet. Also, 25% wettable Malathion can be used at the rate of three pounds of

25% wettable Malathion to 100 gallons of water, *or* two to three tablespoonfuls to a gallon of water and spray onto the turf.

Application—Thorough coverage must be obtained if any of these materials are to achieve maximum control.

Chrysanthemum Aphid

This insect is large, dark chocolate brown with short cornicles crusting on tender terminal shoots and on the under side of the leaves. The growth of the plant is stunted, the leaves curl and plants sometimes die.

Control—Spray or dust with Malathion. Use the 5% Malathion dust, or four tablespoons of 50% Malathion mixed with a gallon of water.

Application—Thoroughly cover all foliage of the plant for maximum control.

Chinch Bug

Chinch bugs are distributed throughout the United States but are especially injurious in the Texas Gulf Coast. One primarily that we are bothered with in this area is harmful to St. Augustine grass, causing yellow spots in turf, which turns brown, the grass dies.

This very small bug (1/16 of an inch long), black with white wings—which have a triangular black patch in the outer margins and red legs, gives off a distinctive vile odor when crushed. It hibernates as an adult in hedge rows, stubble and clumps of prairie grasses. When the days warm up to 70° the bugs fly to the grain fields and to the St. Augustine grass, feed by sucking sap, mate and lay eggs behind lower leaf sheaths of the plants, on the roots or on the ground. One female lays several hundred eggs at the rate of 15 to 20 a day. They hatch in two weeks into minute black-red nymphs, with a white band across the middle. They darken as they grow older, acquiring wings, and the black and white color at the last moult. As the grain ripens and dries up, they migrate, usually while still wingless, by crawling to a field of young corn or sorghum. There they mature, mate and lay eggs for a second generation on grass or corn. Adults fly to winter quarters for hibernation. In this particular area, the Southwest, there are generally three generations instead of two. In Florida and along the Texas Gulf Coast, the chinch bug feeds throughout life, for three or more generations. on St. Augustine grass lawns.

When they attack St. Augustine grass lawns, oftentimes they are not noticed by the average gardener and the grass begins to turn yellow and begins to die, you immediately think of brown patch or some other soil borne malady, which is not the case. After close examination one can find the small bugs feeding upon the reproductive parts of the plant and the root systems above ground, and sucking the life juices from the plant.

Control—Use 25% of emulsible concentrate of Diazinon, mixing one pint and 11 fluid ounces into 15 gallons of water or one quart to 20 gallons, or broadcast 2% Diazinon Granules according to directions.

Application—Prior to applying the insecticides to the infested area, it would be advisable to thoroughly wet the St. Augustine turf. Complete coverage of the entire lawn with the Diazinon spray would be beneficial as this would also control other lawn pests such as chiggers, ants, roaches, ticks etc. If a heavy rain should occur shortly after application, a repeat would be advisable within two or three days. Other insecticides that are effective against the chinch bug are Sevin, Ethiol, and Trithion. Apply according to manufacturer's directions.

Citrus Rust Mite

These pets cause russetting of fruit which makes it unacceptable to shippers of commercial fruit. However, it does not affect the quality of the fruit, the interior of it, but strictly the outside rind. The mites are almost microscopic in size and the damage only is visible. Populations increase sharply during and immediately after seasonal rainy periods. It has been said, I don't know how true it is, but researchers tell us in all likelihood some of the most acceptable fruits are those that have been affected by the Citrus Rust Mite. But from an appearance standpoint, it is not acceptable to the consuming public.

Control—To control the Citrus Rust Mite apply 50 to 80 pounds of dusting Sulfur per acre on the trees. Applications usually are required in March-May-August and October. The October application is used primarily for clean up purposes and is a good practice. Unfavorable weather conditions at the time and following applications may greatly affect the control of the Citrus Rust Mite. Wettable Sulfur and Lime-Sulfur sprays are sometimes used. Recent work indicates control is obtained by using Dithane Z-78, at the rate of one pound of Dithane Z-78 to 100 gallons of water, and thoroughly covering the citrus tree with this material during the months of May-August and October.

Citrus Whitefly

This is the most important economic species of whitefly, a native of Asia, introduced in Florida prior to 1885—when it was found on oranges. It appeared in California in 1907 and at later dates, but infestations have been fairly well eradicated, so it remains for the most part, a pest in the Gulf Coast states, where it is the most important citrus enemy or ranks only after purple scale. It injures through the consumption of sap and by the honeydew which encourages sooty mold all over fruit and foliage. It breeds in large numbers on Chinaberry trees. Besides these, and Citrus, preferred food plants are Umbrella trees, Cape jasmine (Gardenia), Privets, Japanese and wild persimmons, Lilac, Coffee, Prickly ash. Occasionally infested shrubs or vines

146

include Allamanda, Banana, Cerasius, Camellia, Choisya, Cherry laurel, Green Ash, Jessamine, Bear, Pomegrante, Smilax, Viburnum, Wild Olive, Ailanthus, Water Oak, Osage-Orange, Palmetto.

Small yellow eggs, looking like dust, hatch in 10 to 12 days, those from unfertilized females turning into males. The larvae are thin, translucent, scale-like; they lose legs and antennae after the first molt, about seven days after hatching. The second molt is in five or six days, the third after 10 to 12 days, after which the insect assumes the pupa or resting state, taking much less food, becoming thicker, the outline of the adult taking form, and finally the winged whitefly emerging through a T-shaped opening in the pupal skin.

Control—Oil emulsion sprays (use summer oils) control whiteflies fairly well if applied to kill larvae before they change to adults. Two sprays are recommended—May and September, are suggested, but for citrus the spray schedule should be directed toward all pests.

Common House Fly

This cosmopolitan insect is not only a household pest, but it is also a carrier of dysentery and a number of other organisms which cause serious human diseases. It is the most common fly in houses. The adult flies are about one-half inch long with reddish-brown eyes and transparent wings.

House flies are disease carriers, crawling over and feeding upon filth. The flies gather disease germs on their legs and bodies and take them into the digestive tract with their food. Later, in their visit to human food, the flies leave some of these organisms when they crawl over it, and the well known habit of disgorging some of their food and expelling fecal matter, both of which may contain the germs, is responsible also for contaminating food.

The common house fly is highly reproductive. It has been calculated that descendants of a single fly, which deposits her eggs in the middle of April, will number considerably over five trillion by the middle of September, if all the eggs hatched and lived to be adults, which reproduced in their turn. Fortunately, for mankind, this is not the case—many eggs failing to hatch and pupa never reaching maturity.

Control—It is essential to eliminate all unnecessary sources of attraction for flies and all waste materials that may serve as breeding places. Food should be protected so as to prevent contamination by house flies. Because house flies can travel several miles, a fly control program can be made only by organized, unanimous community efforts. Under the right conditions of light and moisture; manure, garbage and piles of fermenting grass and straw furnish the house fly with breeding places. These materials should be eliminated by either burning or burying. Others can be treated with chemicals to poison the fly larvae.

Insecticides that can be used to control the fly, one of the best is

Diazinon, and this is best utilized through the medium of a fly bait. There are a number of commercial fly baits on the market today with ingredients in them to attract the fly, and feeding upon this material the Diazinon will kill them. If one wishes to build his own fly bait—use bran and mix the Diazinon, either in the liquid or wettable form (and use syrup as an attractant), and scatter this material over the area where flies are present. This should do a good job in controlling them.

Corn Ear Worm

This insect is present everywhere corn is grown. The claim has been made that American farmers grow 2,000,000 acres of corn a year to feed the earworm. The larvae feed from the top, starting on fresh silk, then working down to the kernels, piling up masses of moist castings. Feeding on the silk prevents pollination, resulting in nubbins; feeding on the kernels introduces various mold fungi. Late seasons corn may be nearly 100% infested.

Control—Individual ear treatment is the most successful. *Mix three quarts of (two pounds of DDT technical to a gallon) with 2 gallons of white mineral oil (65 SAI viscosity) and enough water to make 25 gallons of spray.* For a smaller amount, mix one-fourth pint 50% emulsible DDT with three-fourths pint white mineral oil, add water to make one gallon.

Application—Use a small atomizer sprayer and apply only enough spray to wet the silks. This should be applied two or three days after silks appear, before they wilt.

Cotton Cushion Scale

This insect was introduced into the U.S.A. from Australia. The insect is reddish brown, but the female attaches a large compact, white fluted mass, holding from 600 to 800 bright red eggs. This white egg mass sticks out at an angle from the twig and is very easily recognized.

Control—Insect against insect has been tried and proven successful. In this case the Vedalia or Australian Lady Beetle will control the scale. This particular lady beetle is not known in this area and must be purchased and brought in, and distributed on the host plant. Since insecticides will kill this particular lady beetle, this solution of using the lady beetle is not necessary. Therefore, for best results—spray with 50% *Malathion concentrate.*

Application—Use four tablespoons of 50% Malathion into one gallon of water and thoroughly saturate the shrub infested. Repeat application every seven days until presence of all scale disappears.

Crawfish

Crawfish are a nuisance in a yard and make it very unsightly, also difficult to mow. Therefore, they should be controlled. They come under the same family or animal class as lobsters, crabs and sow bugs. Crawfish are almost miniature lobsters, having the same horny shell, head and thorax—united into one unjointed portion with the hind portion, the abdomen jointed and flexible. They have two big grasping pinchers or claws and behind these four pairs of walking legs. They are green to brown, three to six inches long, and molt frequently and periodically because the hard shell cannot grow. In autumn the female curls up her tail to form a basket and carries her eggs there until the next summer.

It seems strange to find such aquatic creatures as garden pests, but they live in burrows in wet soil. In places such as Houston and Galveston, along the Texas Gulf Coast where the surface is close to the water table, lawns are often dotted with Crawfish mounds, piles of mud three to four inches high, opening at the top like chimneys. The Crawfish crawl out of the burrows at night to eat cotton and other plants, as well as dead or live animal food.

Control—A number of ways can be exploited to control the Crawfish. One way is to use two and one-half tablespoons of cold tar cresote emulsion in one gallon of water, and pour a half cup into each Crawfish hole, or place two tablespoons of carbon bisulfide into each hole and cover with soil. An additional recommendation is to sprinkle 10% Heptachlor granules into each Crawfish run.

Crickets

Crickets are relatives of grasshoppers. They have chewing mouth parts and are noted for the chirping noise produced by the males when they rub together modified parts of their front wings. They feed mostly on plants, but become more of a nuisance than they are a problem to agriculture. There are many different varieties and kinds of crickets, but the one we are most confronted with in this area is the Field Cricket. They are present almost everywhere, they vary in color—black or brown, three-fifths to one inch long, and are indiscriminate feeders—feeding on plants in the garden, paper, food or clothing in the home. They may injure seedling cotton and cereal plants, cucumbers, legumes, tomatoes and strawberries.

Mole Crickets

This insect is known to be found in dark muddy places from Canada through Florida and into the south. These crickets are large— one and one-half inches long, brownish above, paler underneath, and covered with velvety hairs. Their front legs are greatly enlarged, adapted for burrowing and they terminate in four strong blade like teeth called dactyls. They live deep in the ground during the day, coming out at night to pulverize the garden bed and the plants growing in it. Most of the injury comes from the tunnels in the upper inch or two of soil, which cut off the roots of seedlings and injure lawns.

149

The Mole Cricket also eats pits in underground roots and stems, cuts stems off above ground and eat the seed. Use 10% Heptachlor granules as a dust—one and a half pounds per 100 square feet.

Control—A 10% Chlordane dust, *or* a 5% Dieldrin granule, *or* a 40% wettable Chlordane powder—applied as a spray—will do an excellent job in controlling the cricket. When the 10% Chlordane dust is used—apply it at the rate of one to two ounces per 100 square feet of surface area. Where the 5% Dieldrin granule is used—apply one and a half pounds of this material per 1000 square feet, or two to three ounces per 100 square feet. Where the 40% wettable Chlordane powder is used as a spray—use five pounds per 100 gallons of water of this material, *or* one to two tablespoons per gallon and apply.

Application—Application should be thorough over the general area in which crickets are located if control is to be obtained. Read manufacturer's directions for proper application.

Cut Worm

High in the ranks of "Gardening Headaches," this pest feeds on plants near the surface of the ground, cutting off succulent stems of tomatoes, beans, cabbage, flowers and other plants.

Control—Apply 50% DDT dust to the row where protection is desired, *or* mix one to two tablespoons of 50% wettable DDT per gallon of water and spray mixture directly onto row for maximum protection.

Application—Make sure the dust or spray covers the width of the row and around plants to obtain maximum protection. To carry out preventive control measures prior to planting seed or transplanting plants, broadcast 10% Heptachlor granules over the plot. Apply at the rate of one and a half pounds of 10% Heptachlor granules per 1000 square feet, *or* three ounces per 100 square feet. Use Heptachlor only where specified by manufacturer.

Eastern Tent Caterpillar

This insect is located from the apple growing section of the eastern United States west to the Rocky Mountains, and at the present time can be found in pear, plum, peach, pecan and walnut trees. The young larvae of the Easter Tent Caterpillars gather in the forks of limbs in the spring and early summer to spin their large webby nests. They leave it during the day to feed on foliage, but return at night or in rainy weather. They are hairy caterpillars, black with a white stripe down their back, brown and yellow lines along the side and a row of oval blue spots. When full grown, they are two to two and a half inches long, which requires four to six weeks, and are often seen racing down the side of houses or feeding on roses and other shrubs before spinning their dirty white cocoons on tree trunks or buildings. The moths are light reddish-brown with two diagonal strips across each forewing, emerge in about three weeks. The female lays a single egg column around a twig containing some 150 to 350 eggs, and covers this with a sticky substance which hardens and glistens like varnish. There is only one generation a year, and the periods of greatest abundance appears at about 10 year intervals.

Control—The best method to control the Eastern Tent Caterpillar is to use three pound of 50% wettable DDT per 100 gallons of water.

Application—Application should be applied so that the spray will penetrate through the web spun by the caterpillar, thus calling for a high pressure sprayer in order to spray completely the entire tree and to force the insecticide into the web spun by this insect. Once the webs begin to appear, action must be fast in order to safeguard further damage from this particular variety of insect.

Earwig

These insects are beetle like pests, easily recognized by the tail section that looks like forceps. For this reason, people have the mistaken notion that they sting like a scorpion. *SUCH IS NOT THE CASE.* They feed on decayed or living plant material and other insects. They work at night, living under bark, stones or other debris during the day. They are quite a pest in houses at night—crawling over everything, hiding under cushions, dishes, or clothing, into crevices of various sorts.

Control—Apply to the flower beds and areas around the home— 10% Heptachlor granules. Use at the rate of one and a half pounds per 1000 square feet, *or* three ounces to 100 square feet.

Application—Sprinkle the 10% Heptachlor granules on the infested area and moisten lightly with garden hose to diffuse granules into top soil. 2% Diazinon Granules are also effective.

Fig Beetle

This is a large, flat, broad beetle, over one inch long, usually green, sometimes copper to velvet in color, and is a notorious fruit pest found in Arizona, New Mexico and Texas. It prefers ripe peaches, but it also feeds on apricots, apples, grape, mushmelon, nectarine, pear, tomato and cactus. The larvae breed in the dung or manure of old corrals and the best control seems to be thorough cleaning of corrals and stack bottoms in late winter and early spring. After the insect reaches an adult stage very little control can be accomplished by the application of insecticides because they are so large and difficult to control. Therefore, it is easier to control the areas in which they breed rather than try to control them on the tree which they infest. However, for control on trees, mix 4-6 tablespoons of 80% Wettable Sevin and spray to thoroughly cover the entire tree.

151

Flat Headed Apple Tree Borer

This borer was formerly known as a pear borer, but was renamed because it more often infests apples. It also bores into ash trees and pecan trees from Maine to Texas. The borers are found in crotches and in rough bark of neglected trees, and attacks pecan trees at nearly every age, wherever they are grown. As a rule, injury is confined to trees that have already been weakened from some other cause—such as those injured by cultivation, cold, drouth, or sun scald, or retarded by transplanting. Borers usually work on the sunny side of a tree trunk. Injury results from the tunneling of the borer into the bark and sap wood of the tree. Trees two inches in diameter may be girdled and killed, and larger trees are weakened. The presence of one borer in a tree often leads to further attack. They disclose their burrows by pushing frass, similar to sawdust, from the cracks of the bark. Injured spots can be detected by the darker color and slight depression of the bark. The adult beetles are about one-half inch long, flattened and metallic in appearance; they lay their eggs in cracks in the bark or injured places in the sunny parts of the tree trunks. The larvae of this borer is readily recognized by the large flattened heads. The insect passes the winter in the borer stage and then pupate in the spring. The development of egg to adult usually requires about one year.

Control—These borers can be controlled with 2 sprays of Parathion. Use two pounds of 15% wettable powder to 100 gallons of water, or one-half pound of 50% wettable to 100 gallons of water, and spray at three week intervals. Be sure and observe all precautionary measures when applying Parathion, as it is highly toxic.

Fleas

A flea is a small, wingless insect, ranging from about one-twentieth to one-sixteenth inch long. They are related to flies in many ways, but are much modified for life on their host. They have piercing and sucking mouthparts, and the adult feeds entirely on mammals and birds. They do not remain on their host as continuously as do lice, but they visit their host more frequently than do bed bugs. Fleas are household pests, coming in on cats and dogs. Eggs dropped by the fleas fall to the floor, especially where the host animals are accustomed to sleep. The larvae feed under rugs and mattings, in floor cracks and similar places, and on reaching maturity attack any animal that they can reach, whether it be man or beast. Fleas are of major importance to man aside from their attacks on a person, because they carry the germs of the bubonic plaque.

Control—A 10% Chlordane dust, a 5% Malathion dust, 5% Sevin or the use of a 25% wettable powder of Malathion will control fleas. For inside the home—the best compound to use is Malathion—either as a dust or in the spray form. (On animals, such as dogs and cats, the best product to use is a 5% Malathion dust, or 5% Sevin dust—applied to the fur of

152

the animal and rubbed in. It will not have any detrimental effect on the dog.) Where the 25% wettable Malathion powder is used, take three pounds of this material to 100 gallons of water, *or* use two to three tablespoons per gallon, mix thoroughly and apply to the outside surfaces of the lawn and turf and flower beds.

Garden Springtail

Springtails are a group of small insects, less than one-fifth inch long, without wings, and almost no metamorphosis. They have chewing or piercing mouth parts and short antenna with few segments. They can jump incredible distances by means of a forked tail, which is folded forward under the abdomen when it rests. Oftentimes these insects are called Snow Fleas. In fact, Springtails are around us most all of the time, but they are so small we seldom notice them. The garden Springtail is a dark active species, found most often on young plants and seed beds and outdoor gardens. They have a soft round body, black to dark purple with yellow spots and a distinct head. They chew holes in thin leaves like spinach and make pits in cotyledon leaves of beans and cucumbers and may damage any small plant close to the ground.

Control—Put on a 5% Malathion or 5% Sevin dust, applied to the foliage of the plants that they are infesting.

Giant Cicada Killer

This large, stout wasp—which is about one and a half to two inches long, is characterized by black with yellow marks on the abdomen. It is without the slender waist typical of many wasps. Appearing in late summer, it makes its nest in the ground and provisions them with an adult dog day Cicadas. A sloping burrow may extend nearly 18 inches underground. In most instances this insect is considered to be beneficial as they feed upon other insects—eliminating some of the wasps and cicadas.

Control—Since this is considered a beneficial insect and does very little damage, no control is necessary. However, if one is needed, apply 5% Dieldrin granules or a 10% Heptachlor granules in the area in which the nests or burrows in the ground are located and lightly water.

Garden Centipede

This insect is called a centipede only because it looks something like one. Actually, it belongs to another class and has twelve pairs of legs in the adult form, fewer when young, no poison claws and no eyes. They live in damp places, rich in organic matter, leaf mold, manure piles or peaty soils. The Garden Centipede is small, one-fourth inch long, pure white, very active, it keeps its long antenna moving as it travels through the soil in cracks and tunnels left by decaying plant roots. It is an outdoor soil pest in warm climates, particularly injurious to asparagus in California, and is a greenhouse pest nearly everywhere. The msymphylid eat off fine roots and root hairs and scar underground parts of stems, so plants die or are stunted. Besides asparagus, which has its roots riddled with tunnels, the Garden Centipede seriously injures lettuce, radishes, tomatoes, cucumbers and many other ornamentals, including sweet peas.

Small, white eggs are laid in clusters of five to 20 about a foot deep in the soil anytime between April and September. The minute young hatch seven to 10 days later. At first they have only six pairs of legs, 10 body segments and very short antenna, but add another pair of legs and lengthen antenna at each moulting. When greenhouse soil is wet down and crops are started in the fall, they start feeding on the roots. In indoor gardens they are active in spring and are rarely seen on the surface of the soil, being strongly repelled by the light.

Control—Fumigation in greenhouses is about the only way that it can be controlled, using Ethylene dibromide or Methyl Bromide MC#2. However, since there are a number of chemical insecticides that do an excellent job, Lindane is suggested. Use three pounds of 25% wettable Lindane in 100 gallons of water, applied to 2200 square feet of area in the greenhouse. Also, 10% Heptachlor granules applied liberally on top of the soil and wet, will do an excellent job in controlling this particular garden pest.

Grape Leaf Hopper

This is a native leaf hopper occuring in all grape growing areas. Adults are slender—⅛ of an inch long, yellowish with red markings and they winter in weeds and refuse and fly to the vines when grape leaves are half grown, feeding for two or three weeks and inserting eggs into leaf tissues. Pale greenish nymphs start sucking in May and are full grown in three to five weeks. The grape is the principal host, but feeding may occur on such things as gooseberry, grasses, plums, grape and other vine leaves. Grapes turn brown and fall prematurely, interferring with proper ripening of the berries.

Control—This insect can best be controlled by spraying thoroughly with DDT immediately after blooming. Use it at the rate of one and a half pounds of 50% wettable DDT powder to 100 gallons of water, or two tablespoons per gallon if a smaller amount of mix is desired.

Grasshopers

Grasshoppers feed on grass and vegetation, in general, the amount of injury caused varying with their abundance.

Grasshoppers are moderately long insects, slightly deeper than wide, usually dark-mottled, with prominent jaws and eyes, and their antenna is always much shorter than the body. An ear (hearing organism) is located on each side of the first abdominal section. Their hindlegs are enlarged for jumping, and the abdomen of the female ends in four, hard, movable prongs—which function like a miniature post-hole digger when used for inserting her eggs an inch or so into the ground. Grasshoppers feed in the daytime in the sun. They are most numerous in states with an average rainfall of between 10 and 30 inches. They attack cultivated crops, range vegetation, destroying clothing and fabrics in houses, polluting water in wells and reservoirs, and presenting a hazard to motorists on highways. There are about 600 species in the United States, five of them doing 90% of the damage to crop plants.

Control—A number of different insecticides and baits will control the grasshopper. Those insecticides recognized to do the best job are a 10% Chlordane dust, 5% Dieldrin granules, 10% Heptachlor granules, and a 40% Chlordane wettable powder, or Toxaphene. When the dust of Chlordane (10% Chlordane) is used—apply at the rate of one to two ounces per 100 square feet of surface area. The 5% Dieldrin granules should be applied at the rate of one and a half pounds per 1000 square feet of surface area, and the 10% Heptachlor should also be applied at one and one-fourth to one and a half pounds per 1000 square feet of surface area. The 40% wettable Chlordane should be mixed at the rate of five pounds per 100 gallons of water, or one to two tablespoons per gallon of water.

Application—Apply the material in the general area where the grasshoppers are feeding, or to the plants. A barrier can be built around a field, in order to protect it from the ravages of the grasshopper, by spraying or dusting a swath wider than the grasshoppers can normally jump or fly. Thorough application of these insecticides on the foliage of the plants and the area in which they are feeding, must be consummated in order to obtain maximum control.

Greedy Scale

This is a common armored scale, attacking ornamentals throughout the country, mostly in greenhouses, but also outdoors in warm climates. The female is convex, elliptical to round, small, grey with dark brown patches near one edge. The scales are feeders on bark, sometimes leaves and fruits of many different types of trees. This is a very ferocious scale and unless controlled can do a great deal of damage to the tree or shrub that it infests.

Control—Spray the affected areas with a 25% emulsible concentrate of Diazinon.

Application—Mix four tablespoons of this material per gallon of water and thoroughly saturate the entire foliage and bark of the shrub affected. The light miscible oil in the 25% emulsible concentrate of Diazinon will bring the scale under control. One to two, perhaps three applications may be necessary before maximum control is received. It is also advisable, if the tree goes dormant in the winter months, to apply an oil emulsion spray at that time.

Greenhouse White Fly

Small gnat like insects that resemble fruit flies, that infest such plants as gardenias and citrus trees. Most noticeable symptoms of Greenhouse White Fly is when the black sooty fungus appears on the leaves. The fungus is due to this insect depositing a sugary media in which the fungus grows. This fungus can actually cover the leaf and suffocate it.

Control—Spray with 25% concentrate of Diazinon. Use three tablespoons of   mixed one one gallon of water, adding one teaspoon of Liquid Soap as a sticking agent.

Application—Make at least two applications at seven day intervals for maximum control. After the third application spray the shrub with the water hose. This will help to remove the fungus. To control the fungus growth on the leaf apply Consan 20 as directed on the label.

Harlequin Bug

This is the most important pest of cabbage and related crops in the southern half of the United States. Cabbage, cauliflower, collards, cress, mustard, Brussel sprouts, turnips, horseradish, and other flavored food plants are the major ones that they attack, but the bugs may wander over and eat beans, citrus, cherries, chrysanthemums, corn, egg plants, grapes, etc. The bugs are black with red markings, flat—3/8 of an inch long. They winter around old cabbage stalks and other garden refuse and lay distinctive eggs on the underside of the leaves of early garden crops. They look like tiny barrels with white hoops, and they stand on the end in double rows. They hatch in four to seven days, and the nymphs suck so much sap that the cabbage wilts, turns brown and dies, and whole crops may be lost.

Control—Dust the affected plants with a 5% Malathion dust. If this material is used on plants that are edible at the time, wait three to five days after dusting before consuming the vegetables, or dust the plants with a 5% Sevin dust.

Hickory Bark Beetle

This is the most injurious pest of hickory, found from Quebec to Georgia, Mississippi and Texas. Breeding normally is found in broken or weakened trees. They will attack and kill healthy trees in epidemics. The beetle is very small, dark brown, and the legless white grub with head is only about 1/4 inch long. The grubs mine in the sapwood and inner bark, sometimes girdling trunks and branches. Adults bore into the bases of leaf stems, terminal buds or green nuts. Infested trees lose their leaves in the summer, tops and branches sometimes die back. The bark is covered with small perforations, exit holes of the beetles. The larvae hide in the bark, pupate in the wood in the spring and the beetles emerge in the early summer and fly to living hickories, feeding on young twigs. The female bores through the bark to the sap wood and makes her longitudinal egg gallery, with eggs deposited in niches along the sides of the straight tunnel. Grubs burrow out at right angles.

Control—Most of the injury occurs during severely dry summers. Trees kept well watered are more resistant to injury. Spraying with DDT while beetles are feeding may give some control. Spray with three pounds of 50% wettable DDT mixed in 100 gallons of water, thoroughly covering the tree during the early part of the spring. One should cut and burn badly infested trees between October and May while the larvae are in their burrows. This will prevent beetles from invading other hickories. This is about the only control that can be accomplished with this insect.

Hickory Shuck Worms

The Hickory Shuck Worm frequently causes severe damage to pecans. In late summer and fall the shucks are tunneled out, as a result the nuts are slow to mature and the kernels do not mature properly. The shuck sticks to the nuts and fail to open, thus increasing the difficulty of the harvest. The adult shuck worm is a dark greyish-black moth with a wing spread of little over one-half inch. The larvae, which causes most of the damage to the shucks, is white with a light head and attains a length of about ⅜ inch at maturity.

Control—No economical chemical control for the shuck worm has been developed. Cultural methods will aid in reducing population. Plowing during July and August to turn under the infested shucks is relatively effective. The larvae are unable to mature in the decaying shucks and the adults cannot emerge from the soil. Care should be taken to cover completely the fallen shucks, but the depth of plowing should be regulated so as not to damage the root system of the tree.

Leaf Cutter Bee

The damage caused by this particular insect is unique in that you find the damage on the leaves of such plants as roses. It looks as if a seamstress had taken a pair of sharp edge scissors and cut a circle out of the leaf itself. It is hard to imagine that such an insect as the Leaf Cutter Bee could cause such damage. They are moderate size, stout bodied, solitary bees, nesting in wood or in hollow stems of woody plants. The bees are hairy, black or metallic blue, green or purple, with short elbowed antennae. The long legs are not equipped with pollen baskets, the pollen being carried on brushes on the abdomen. All members of this group are important pollinators, some are particularly useful with cultivated alfalfas and clover. The female cuts dime-size, very precise ovals and circles from margins of leaves, usually rose leaves. The ovals line the bottom and sides of her nest, the circles cap each cell after an egg has been laid inside. The nests are made either in broken ends of branches or in the pithy stem of plants such as dahlia. There is no control except to cut out wilted or dying shoots containing the nest, and because the bees are essentially useful—one should not begrudge them a few rose leaves. Actually, there is no control measure known, however, an application of Malathion might have a discouraging effect upon the bee. This is considered a beneficial insect and therefore no recommendation for a control is made.

Leaf Footed Bug

These insects are present in the South East and as far west as Arizona, and we have them in the Texas Gulf Coast. The bug is dark brown with a yellow band across the body, $\frac{3}{4}$ of an inch long, and with hind legs expanded like a leaf. It attacks pecans and many garden crops—potatoes, beans, cowpeas, and tomatoes being great favorites. It likes sunflowers and many of them swarm on Satsuma oranges and tangerines. They breed on thistle. Hand picking and spraying with a soap spray on a cloudy day or late afternoon has been recommended in the past.

Control—On potatoes use a 10% DDT dust. Sabadilla dust has been useful on bugs that are hard to kill, but in orchards spray with Malathion, preferably the 25% wettable Malathion—at the rate of four pounds mixed into 100 gallons of water. This should bring the insect under control.

Leaf Hoppers in Lawns and Gardens

Small winged-like insects that infest gardens and lawns. They are sucking insects that injure plants.

Control—Use Liquid Malathion or Diazinon.

Application—Use two-four tablespoons of either to gallon of water and thoroughly spray infested area.

Leaf Miners

Leaf Miners are insects which feed between the two surfaces of a leaf. They may be the larvae of flies, moths, saw-flies or beetles. They make blisters or blotched mines or serpentine tunnels, and because they are protected by a host plant, control has been very hard. Depending upon exact knowledge of the life history of each individual miner, there are a number of different varieties. Those that are most prominent in the Texas Gulf Coast are the Azalea Leaf Miner, the Chrysanthemum Leaf Miner, the Holly Leaf Miner, Eggplant Miner and the Sycamore Leaf Miner.

Control—Timing is of most importance when controlling the Leaf Miner. DDT applied at the beginning of emergence, with usually a second spray 10 days later—gives satisfactory control. Use two to three level tablespoons of 50% wettable DDT powder to a gallon of water and spray as soon as you see any apparent damage on the leaf surfaces of the affected plants. This will help to prevent further infestation. After the infestation of the leaf surface has taken place, a spray of

Lindane normally will do a better job than DDT, as it has a better impregnating characteristic that will help to control the Miner inside the leaf. Use four to five tablespoons of Lindane per gallon of water and thoroughly cover the foliage of the affected plant. 25% Diazinon concentrate can also be used.

Lesser Peach Tree Borer

This insect is nearly as important as the Peach Tree Borer, attacking such fruits as peach, plum and cherry in all the peach growing sections except the far West. The characteristic of this insect is noticed by the masses of gum, mixed with brown sawdust exuding from upper trunks and branches, especially at forks. White caterpillars with brown heads, 3/4 of an inch long, work in such gum masses. They pupate inside the burrows, but close to the openings which are covered with silk webs. Metallic blue-black, yellow marked moths emerge in May in the South, and lay eggs in bark crevices around crotches or crack wounds. They are very active on sunny days.

Control—DDT is apparently not effective, though it has been found to be good for the Peach Tree Borer. Fifteen percent Parathion at the rate of one and one-half to two pounds per 100 gallons of water or the same amount of 25% EPN wettable powder has given pretty good results where it has been tried. Some folks try to dig the borers out by hand. Keeping the trees properly fed and watered, helps to prevent further infestation. But one of the best treatments would be the use of Parathion. Use with caution as this is a very toxic compound.

"May" Beetle or June Bug

Familiar large, reddish-brown or black beetles, known also as May Beetles, June Bugs, or Daw Bugs. In the larvae stage they are called white grubs. Adults appear in April, May and June and fly at night, feeding on foliage of ash, pecan, elm, oaks, willow and other trees. During the day they remain hidden under grass and debris.

Control—Use 50% DDT or Toxaphene.

Application—Mix three pounds of 50% wettable DDT into 100 gallons of water, *or* two tablespoons of 50% wettable DDT to one gallon of water, and thoroughly spray the foliage of trees and shrubs. Use same formula for Toxaphene.

Melon Aphid

Also known as the Cotton Aphid, and considered one of our most destructive pests. The first sign of melon aphid infestation is the wilting or curling of leaves, accompanied by visits of ants, bees, wasps and flies to get the honeydew. The aphid is small, usually very dark green, but varying to yellow green, brown or black.

Control—Control is difficult after the leaves and tender tips start curling. Prompt and timely application of proper insecticide will give excellent control. Use 5% Malathion dust.

Application—Use a duster and apply thoroughly to top and bottom side of leaves of melons and cucumbers.

Millipedes

These insects are brown or grayish, worm-like, hard shelled, and many pairs of legs. They are generally one inch to one and one-fourth inches long when full grown. They are found under boards, flowerpots and other sheltered areas, or under decayed manure. They feed on roots, tubers, bulbs and also attack seed. They damage such crops as potatoes, carrots, beets, turnips, lettuce, cabbage and related crops.

Control—Apply 5% Dieldrin granules or 10% Heptachlor granules at the rate of one and one-fourth to one and one-half pounds per 1000 square feet of affected area. It is also suggested to lightly water this material.

Application—Apply these insecticides uniformly throughout the area, and also try to eliminate Millipede hiding places—such as boards and trash etc.

Mosquito Control

Mosquitoes are difficult to control since these pets do not feed on plants and shrubs, but rather must feed on warm blooded animals. They do not light and stay put for any length of time on any one given object. Therefore, to control these pests with a chemical, thorough saturation of all shrubs and plants is essential.

Control—Use 25% wettable Malathion and mix four lbs. into 100 gallons of water, or use 12% wettable BHC and use four lbs. to 100 gallons of water. For smaller amounts—use four tablespoons to one gallon.

Application—Use a power, or low pressure sprayer and thoroughly saturate the shrubs around the house. It is also a good idea to spray this insecticide around doors and window frames, and screens of the home. Recently many new insect traps have been developed that lure the mosquitoes to their death. Homeowners would be wise to investigate them.

Nematodes

Nematodes, sometimes called eel worms, include some of our most serious agricultural pests, but are a group of organisms little known to most gardeners.

This minute-like animal, usually slender and worm-like in shape, is too small to be seen by the naked eye. Out of thousands of different kinds of nematodes, 50 are known that injure plants. Some nematodes penetrate into the tissue, others feed from the outside. Roots, tubers, rhizomes and other structures that grow below ground are the parts of the plant most commonly injured, but there are also nematodes that invade the stems

160

and leaves and the buds. Some of the most important parasitic nematodes likely to cause injury to plants, fruits, vegetables and ornamentals that are ordinarily grown in home gardens are the Root Knot Nematode, the Stubby Root Nematode, and the Strawberry Dwarf Nematode.

(1) Root Knot Nematode, of which there are several varieties, are called hot weather parasites and are favored by short mild winters, long hot summers and light sandy soil. This nematode is the one most prevalent in soils along the Texas Gulf Coast, and causes the greatest problem.

The newly hatched young, or larvae, penetrate into the roots and other parts of the plant that grow below ground, and usually stimulate the development of galls. On some plants such as tomatoes and cucumbers, these galls may become large and conspicuous to the eye, while in others—such as sweet potatoes—they usually remain small and are not noticed.

The female parasite, after entering the root and becoming established in the root tissue of the plant, remains in this position throughout the rest of its life and gradually loses its slender form, becoming generally more or less pear shaped. Each female lays from 500 to 1000 eggs that usually accumulate in masses near the surface of the root. During the hot weather the complete cycle is passed in about 30 days. Nearly all of our common garden vegetables are susceptible to Root Knot Nematode. But some of them are more resistant than others.

Highly susceptible crops, likely to be injured severely by an invasion of the Root Knot Nematode, include all kinds of cucumbers, squash, muskmelons, tomatoes, beets, beans, lima beans, peas, parsley, carrots and okra.

Crops that are somewhat resistant or tolerant to this parasite, but by no means immune to it, include the cabbage, cauliflower, turnips, mustard, lettuce, endive, sweet corn, potatoes, sweet potatoes and onions.

At a number of our research stations throughout the nation efforts are being made to develop Root Knot resistant varieties of vegetables, but as yet, few are available. Alabama #1 is a root knot resistant pole bean of good quality; Fordhook 242 is less susceptible to root knot than most of the commonly grown varieties of lima beans. Strawberries, to a certain extent, are susceptible to Root Knot Nematode, but usually are not seriously damaged by it. Raspberries and blackberries are resistant, asparagus is resistant, but rhubarb is susceptible. Peach and fig trees are susceptible and may be severely injured.

Control—Different plants differ markedly in the degree of which they are injured by Root Knot Nematode invasion, and the presence of galls on the roots does not necessarily mean that the crop will be a complete failure. Unless acquired while the plants are small, a moderately severe infestation of the plant by this parasite may not seriously retard growth or reduce yields under good growing conditions, where ample fertility and moisture is available.

By incorporating into the soil, large quantities of organic matter, the severity of the infestation may be reduced, and growing conditions will be provided in which the plants are better able to grow, despite the disease. There are a number of fumigants on the market that will control the biggest portion of Root Knot Nematodes. These, of course, come in different formulations put out bl different commercial companies.

One can fumigate the soil using Methyl Bromide, which will completely eradicate all of the nematodes, as well as noxious weed seed and other parasitic insects in the soil. There is also a liquid fumigant called Garden Dowfume which can be applied to the soil and covered over, which will do an excellent job in eradicating nematodes.

There are also other type nemacides that contain an active ingredient either of dichloropropene, ethylene dibromide, or dibromochloropropane. These may be available as liquids, granules or capsules. As an example, Methyl Bromide is a gas, Vapam and Plantation Nematode Killer are a liquid, and Nema-Kill and Nemagon are granules.

Where these products are applied, it is of great importance that the person follow the directions on the manufacturer's label in so far as application is concerned for maximum benefit. Too much of anyone of these products could be toxic in some instances to the soil, while others can be applied around plants that are already growing, such as Nema-Kill and Nemagon, but to use in excess would be highly detrimental to the plant and oftentime result in death.

(2) STUBBY ROOT NEMATODE—Stubby Root Nematodes occur as far north as Maryland and Indiana, but the damage they inflict on crops is greatest in the Deep South. They are small creatures that feed at the root tips without entering tissue of the plant. Sometimes the root tip turns brown and sometimes there is little or no discoloration, but in either case the tips stop growing. Lateral roots form and the tips of these in turn may be attacked, eventually resulting in a small compact root system composed of numerous short, stubby branches. Deep lesions or dead roots do not occur, at least during the early stages of this disease, and swelling or galls do not develop. The plant, though, deprived of a normal functioning root system is stunted, shows symptoms of starvation, and wilts easily in the sun, even though the soil may have ample fertility and moisture. There are a number of crops affected severely by the Stubby Root Nematode. These include sweet corn, tomatoes, lima beans, cherries, celery, and others. Other crops that may be definitely injured, but on the whole, are more tolerant, are squash, beans, cucumbers, cabbage and cauliflower. Crops that seems to be resistant to this particular parasite are strawberries, lettuce and endive.

Control—In some sections of the South, soil where Bermuda grass grows is invariably infested with species of the Stubby Root Nematode, therefore it is advisable to keep this grass out of the garden . . . don't let Bermuda grass get started.

The soil population of this pest can be reduced substantially by dry tillage. In other words, by breaking the ground and rebreaking it and stirring it. Plow or spade the garden two or three weeks before planting and during the intervening period stir the soil once or twice just before planting. The 100% control measure for the eradication of this insect or parasite is to fumigate using Methyl Bromide. An over-all general coverage of this material, applied as a gas, will eradicate the Stubby Root Nematode. This is the only chemical that will get it.

(3) STRAWBERRY DWARF NEMATODE—This parasite lives in the buds of strawberry plants and feeds on the young developing leaves. However, at the present time this malady has not been discovered in the strawberry fields of Texas, but reaches basically along the eastern seaboard of Florida west to Louisiana.

It is a highly detrimental parasite that attacks the leaves of the strawberry plant causing them to unfold when they are small, rather distorted, crinkled and absolutely dark green. The parasite may be carried in the bud at the ends of the runners, and therefore it is imperative that you buy strawberry plants that are guaranteed to be free from such parasites when you order them from a nursery in that particular section of the country.

Applying Fumigants to the Soil to Control Nematodes

As has previously been mentioned, there are a number of active ingredients on the market by trade names that can be obtained to control nematodes, and undoubtedly other nemacides for home garden use will be placed on the market in the very near future . . . probably products that will be more successful than the ones we have at the present time.

Before a fumigant is applied, the land should be prepared to the consistency of a good seed bed. Roots of preceding vegetation should be removed if they have not had time to decay. The soil should be reasonably free of lumps, clods or trash, and should be moderately, but not excessively loose. A rotary tiller is the best thing to work the soil in order to get it ready for fumigation. Allow several days after working the soil with a rotary tiller so it will have a chance to settle and compact, so it will hold the fumigant in, once it is injected into the soil.

For light, sandy soil, such as those that might be found around the Waller County area, loosening by tilling the soil is neither practical nor desirable.

The soil temperature should be above 60° F., preferably between 60° F and 85° F, for best fumigation.

The land should be fairly moist, yet it should be dry enough to be tillable. Ample moisture is necessary if the fumigant is to be fully effective. As a rule of thumb, whether a gas, liquid or granules are used, the beds and soil should be prepared just ideal for planting purposes. This condition is perfectly ideal for fumigation.

Fumigants are applied by placing small quantities in the soil about six inches beneath the surface at intervals spaced 12 inches apart, this is one method. Another method is to open a row and apply the liquid fumigant into the row and cover over with soil immediately. A third method, is to inject a gas form of Methyl Bromide underneath a polyethylene tarp that has been chinched down on all four sides to make it airtight. The material is released under the polyethylene, being heavier than air, will penetrate into the soil killing nematodes and noxious weed seed.

Whenever one has nematodes, or thinks he has them, it is advisable to fumigate the soil prior to the planting of another crop. On plants that are already infested with nematodes, such as fig trees and so forth, it is advisable to attempt a semi-fumigation method by applying a granular form of fumigant around the soil of the drip line of the tree. It should be used as specified by the manufacturer on the label. Or use the Plantation Nematode Killer liquid by directions. This product is the only one on the market today that is effective against the namatode and the cut. It is safe to consume the produce also.

Use Nemagon or Nema-Kill as mentioned before, and use according to specification. Too much, will kill the tree, too little, will not accomplish the purpose.

After applying a given fumigant to the soil, an interval of time must elapse before it is safe to plant. Fumigants linger in cold wet soil, and in soil having a large amount of organic matter. For most soils under average conditions, and when fumigant is applied at the rate suggested, it is usually safe to plant after two to three weeks. When the soil is light and sandy and conditions are hot and dry, an interval of two weeks or less may be adequate. When the soil is heavy and conditions are cool and wet, an interval of four weeks, or even longer, may be necessary. After the fumigant has been applied the soil should remain undisturbed for one week, but thereafter the escape of gas can be hastened by proper tillage and turnage of the soil.

Precautions When Using Fumigants

All the fumigants that we have named are inflammable, and strict precautions should be taken to avoid igniting the fumes.

All soil fumigants are toxic to human beings and animals, but none are dangerous to the operator *when properly applied.*

Avoid any prolonged breathing of fumes, even though they may not be irritating or have a distinctive odor. Do not allow the liquids to remain in contact with the skin, wash off promptly, and leave exposed area open to air for a short time. If the liquid is spilled on clothing, including shoes or gloves, remove the garment without delay, usually it is not advisable to wear gloves when applying fumigants. Never, under any circumstances, take the risk of getting the material into the eyes or mouth.

Needle Scale

Needle Scale is a small sucking insect that literally sucks the sap out of the Arborvitae, thus lowering its vitality and ultimately causing death. Oftentimes this pest is not recognized because it cannot be seen with the naked eye, and goes unobserved by the gardener until its damage has been inflicted.

Normally, a spray of light miscible oil, especially a dormant oil during the wintertime, when the sun isn't shining so brightly, will bring the Needle Scale under control. In the summertime, if there is an invasion of this scale, it is advisable to apply a light summer oil to prevent possible phytotoxic burn on the foliage of the Arborvitae. I suggest that you see your supply dealer for full details and rates of application. Different formulations of the material dictate the proportions to use safely.

Obscure Scale of Pecans

Obscure Scale is a pest of great importance, particularly in the Gulf Coast section of Texas. The tiny insect under a scale covering sucks the sap from the limbs and branches, causing them to lose their leaves and die back from the tips. The tree is so devitalized by the feeding of this insect that it is made vulnerable to attack by wood borers. The scale covering over a full grown female is about one-eighth inch long and is usually dark grey and closely resembles the bark of a tree. The infested limbs appear to have had wood ashes sprinkled over them. The winter is passed by the female scale under their coverings on the bark. Eggs laid in the Spring hatch into tiny salmon colored crawlers which move about for a short time, then settle down and insert their beaks into the sap wood. While they are feeding, the scale covering develops, which is made up of secreted wax and cast skins. The females never move again from the spot that they have selected, but the adult males develop wings and emerge from the scale covering to mate with the females. There is only one generation produced each year.

In all likelihood, more pecan trees are killed by this one insect than any other, and it is generally due to the fact that the gardener does not recognize the Obscure Scale on the limbs until it is too late.

Control—It is advisable to treat during the dormant season with an oil emulsion spray. A single spray application, using three and one-half gallons of 97% miscible dormant oil per 100 gallons of water, during the months of December, January, February or March will keep this pest under control. Under no circumstances should this material be applied during the growing season as it will kill the tree. Therefore it is highly essential that the application for the control of Obscure Scale be put on during the dormant season.

Onion Thrips

This insect is probably the most widely distributed thrip found in the world. It is found in all the onion growing sections, attacking nearly all garden plants, many field crops and weeds. Injury to the onion shows first as whitish blotches, then blasting and distortion of leaf tips, followed by withering, browning and falling over on the ground. Other plants affected by the Onion Thrip are roses and carnations, and the Onion Thrips also transmit the spotted virus to tomatoes and many flowers. The insect itself is variable in color, ranging from pale yellow to dark brown, one twenty-fifth of an inch long, wings are uniform dusty grey without fans, and larvae are creamy white, and the pupation of this insect takes place in the soil.

Control—Use a 5% Malathion dust or spray with 25% Diazinon.

Application—Take a 5% Malathion dust and dust the plants thoroughly, or take 25% Diazinon and mix at the rate of three or four tablespoons to a gallon and thoroughly spray the plants that are affected.

Orange Dog

This is a common and destructive pest attacking citrus in Florida and the Texas Gulf Coast. It is called Dog because one end of the caterpillar looks like the nose of a dog. Two black spots on the thorax serves as eyes. It is about two and one-half inches long, dark brown with blotches of light yellow. When disturbed—orange-red horn-like processes are protruded and a strong odor given off. The dogs feed on the foliage, often defoliating young trees in two or three days. This is a member of the caterpillar family and most of the chlorinated hydrocarbons will do a fair job in controlling them.

Control—Spray the infected plants with 50% wettable DDT or a general all-purpose insecticide.

Application—If the 50% wettable DDT is used—use at the rate of three pounds per 100 gallons of water, or three tablespoons per gallon. If the 25% wettable Malathion is used—use it at the rate of three pounds per 100 gallons of waters, three tablespoons per gallon, making sure that thorough coverage is applied to top and bottom side of all leaves and foliage of the citrus tree affected. Repeat application within 10 to 14 days if complete control is not obtainable with the first spray.

Pea Weevil

This is a seed weevil present throughout the entire country. The weevils are short, chunky, one-fifth inch long, brown, flecked with white, black, and gray patches. The larvae is white with a small brown head, the female lays her eggs on the outside of a pea pod, and the larvae bores through the wall of the pod into one of the young peas, growing inside for five or six weeks, consuming the contents. It pupates inside the pea and the adult emerges in one to three weeks. Several larvae may enter a pea, but only one survives. There is no continuous breeding in storage as with bean weevils. Weevils may remain in the storage seed a year or two before emerging, but usually they come out soon after pupation and hibernate in any protected area.

Control—In home gardens dusting with Rotenone or DDT weekly from the time the peas start to blossom will generally do a good job. After they start to bear it is best to switch to a 5% Malathion dust from the standpoint of toxicity to keep the peas free from weevils. One should also destroy vines immediately after harvest.

Peach Tree Borer

This is the most important enemy of peach trees. It also attacks plum, wild and cultivated cherry, apricot and other ornamental shrubs. The first sign of injury is usually a mass of gum and brown frass at the base of the trunk, indicating that the white, brown-headed worm is in the bark—anywhere from two to three inches below the ground to 10 inches above.

They winter as larvae of all sizes in the burrows, finish feeding in the spring when they are about one inch in length, and pupate in brown-silk cocoons in the soil near the base of the tree. Just before the moth emerges the pupa is forced out of the cocoon.

Preventative Control—Treat between October 20 and November 15, when the soil is dry and soil temperature is 55° F. or above. Remove weeds and loosen and level soil about one foot from the tree trunk. The material to use is Paradichloro-Benzene crystals, commonly called PDB. Place crystals in a narrow, circular band—preferably in a groove about 2 inches from the trunk. Place several shovels of clean soil over the crystals and mound the earth into a cone-shaped pile about 6 inches high around the base of the tree. In placing the first few shovels of soil, avoid pushing any of the material against the tree since the crystals coming in contact with the tree will cause injury. Compact the soil with the back of the shovel, remove earth mounds in the early spring. For two and three year old trees use one-half ounce of the PDB crystals, for four and five year old trees—use three-fourths ounce, and for fully mature trees use one ounce of this material. One can spray the trunks of the trees with 4-5 tablespoons of 18% Dieldrin during mid-June and mid-August.

Application—*REMEMBER*—is essential that this material be applied between *October 20 and November 15* for maximum control of the Peach Tree Borer.

THE PECAN NUT CASEBEARER

The pecan nut casebearer is the major insect pest attacking pecans in Texas. Casebearers can be successfully controlled if insecticides are applied in the proper manner and at the correct time. The following practices are of primary importance in carrying out an effective control program:

1. Proper timing of the spray application.
2. Adequate coverage.
3. Use of adequate spray equipment.

167

Insecticides must be applied at about the time the eggs are hatching or before the young worms have entered the nuts. Proper coverage is essential in order to deposit an insecticidal residue on the nut cluster and on the stem a few inches below the cluster. Good equipment is essential to force a sufficient volume of spray through the foliage, directly on the twigs and nut clusters in all areas of the tree. Inadequate coverage, more than any other factor, is responsible for poor control of the pecan nut casebearer. Since the insect feeds over a small area, the insecticide must be uniformly distributed.

In carrying out a successful casebearer control program, it is very important to know and understand the life history. Casebearers overwinter as small worms inside tiny silken cocoons called hibernacula which are usually attached to a bud. In the spring, the larvae emerge from their hibernacula, feed for a short time on the buds and then tunnel in the developing shoots until they reach maturity. Pupation usually occurs in these burrows in the shoots, and the moths emerge in late April and May. The presence of wilted shoots which have been tunneled out is a good indication that control measures will be required for the next generation of larvae in the nuts. About 9 days are required for development of the pupal stage.

Two or three days after the adults emerge, females deposit eggs on the tips of the nuts. The bluish-white eggs are deposited singly. In a few hours, small red spots appear in the egg. These spots increase in size until the egg is pinkish to reddish. The worms which hatch from these eggs are known as *first generation casebearer larvae*. The period of egg laying usually coincides with the completion of pollination at which time the tips of the tiny nuts turn brown. This is the period during which the nut clusters should be carefully examined for eggs to determine when the control program should be started. The exact time of egg laying will vary from one season to the next. Also, the time of egg laying may vary from one location to the next during the same year even though the locations are only a few miles apart. Consequently, the most effective means for determining the best time to spray is by checking and observing the developmental stage of the casebearer.

Casebearer eggs hatch in four or five days. When the small worms hatch, most of them leave the tips of the twigs and migrate to the buds below the nut cluster to feed. After two or three days' feeding, the worms leave the buds and enter the base of the nut. From the time the eggs are deposited, about six to eight days pass before the nuts are attacked. Depending upon environmental conditions, four to five days are required for the eggs to hatch, the young worms feed on the buds for two to three days. One larvae of the first generation frequently destroys an entire nut cluster. The length of the larval period is about twenty-five days. To obtain good control, insecticides should be applied during the interval when eggs are hatching or when the young worms are feeding on the buds.

Ordinarily, only one application of spray is required to control the casebearer. If heavy rains occur shortly after treatment, benefit may result from another application. Generally, growers tend to spray too early and much of the effectiveness of the insecticide is lost before the insects appear. If several days are required to spray large orchards, it may be necessary to start the operation before the optimum time. Therefore, if possible, select one of the recommended insecticides which has a long residual effect. When the larvae reach maturity they pupate in the hollowed out nuts and emerge as moths. The female moths deposit eggs of the *second generation* which appear about *six weeks* after the first generation eggs are laid. At this time the nuts are nearly half grown and the eggs are usually deposited in grooves near the tip and base of the nuts or on buds below the nut clusters. The eggs hatch in about five days and the larvae feed in the leaf axis below the nuts for a short time. Then the larvae migrate to the nut cluster, enter at the base of a nut and hollow out the inside. Less injury is produced by this generation because the nuts are larger and each larva requires only one or two nuts to complete its development. To control second generation casebearers an application of an insecticide may be given if trees in the vicinity were not sprayed to control first generation larvae or if poor control of the first generation was obtained.

A *third generation* usually follows, but the shells of the nuts have become hard and only a few of them are penetrated by the larvae. Instead, they feed on the shucks. A number of third generation larvae construct hibernacula while the remainder pupate and appear as adults, emerging during late August, September and October. These adults deposit eggs which hatch into *fourth generation larvae.* If nuts are available, their shucks constitute the principal food of the larvae of this generation until they prepare for winter. In the absence of nuts, the larvae feed on buds and leaf stems. Overwintering cocoons or hibernacula are constructed by the very small larvae by the middle of November.

Insecticide and Amount to Use To 100 Gallons of Water	Safety Restrictions
1. DDT—3 lbs. of 50% wettable powder	Do not graze livestock in treated groves. Do not apply after shuck split.
2. Parathion—2 lbs. of 15% wettable powder	Do not apply within 15 days of harvest or after shucks open. Do not allow animals to graze in treated groves until *15 days* after application.

3. Malathion—3 lbs. of 25% wettable powder	Do not allow animals to graze in treated groves until 5 *days* after application.
4. Toxaphene—5 lbs. of 40% wettable powder	Do not allow dairy animals to graze in treated groves. Remove beef cattle for 3 *days*.
5. Nicotine sulfate—1 pint of 40% plus 2 qts. of summer oil	Remove cattle from groves during spraying operation. No other limitations.

Pecan Phylloxera

This insect characterizes itself by swelling or galls occasionally appearing on leaves, leaf stalks, succulent shoots, or nuts of the current season's growth. The galls are caused by small insects known as Phylloxera, which are closely related to aphids. One or more species are found in practically all sections of the pecan belt, but only one has been reported as doing serious damage.

The attack of this insect causes the twig to become malformed, weakened and finally to die. Sometimes an entire limb may die. The insects pass the winter in an egg stage in protected places on the branches. The young appear in the early spring about the time the buds unfold; they insert their beaks into the new growth, and the gall forms which soon envelopes the insect. The insect matures within the gall and lays a large number of eggs, the young insects that hatch from these eggs develop into wing forms and usually late in May or early in June the gall splits open and releases the insects.

Control—Timing is of great importance in the control of this insect. Any number of compounds will control it—BHC, Lindane, Toxaphene, Malathion, Dieldrin will all do an excellent job in controlling this insect, if it is applied in time.

Application—Apply the spray during the delayed dormant period until the buds show one to two inches of new growth before the galls appear. Control must be a preventive one, as after the gall appears there is no insecticide that will impregnate through the gall and reach the small insect. On leaf galls, it is advisable to rake all the leaves and burn them during the fall, and apply one of these sprays mentioned above just at the time the buds begin to form. As a matter of simplicity, listed below are the various compounds and the rate of mix to be applied to pecan trees and other shade trees for the control of the Pecan Phylloxera.

2 pounds of BHC (containing 10%-12% gammar isomer) to 100 gallons of water

1¼ pounds of Lindane to 100 gallons of water

3   pounds of 25% wettable Malathion to 100 gallons of water
3   pounds of 50% wettable DDT to 100 gallons of water
½   gallon of 6-pound Toxaphene to 100 gallons of water
½   gallon of 2-1 mix Toxaphene-DDT to 100 gallons of water
½   gallon of 18% liquid Dieldrin to 100 gallons of water
1   pound of 50% wettable Dieldrin to 100 gallons of water

Pecan Weevil or Hickory Nut Weevil

This insect is found wherever pecans or hickory trees are grown, sometimes causing loss of 80% of the pecan crop. The dark brown adults, three eighths inch long, attack newly formed pecans, causing them to shrivel and drop. Early maturing varieties such as Mahan, Stuart, and Money-Maker are most commonly infested.

The female has a beak longer than its body, and with it she punctures the nuts and places the eggs (usually three to a nut) in the kernel as soon as the water stage has passed. The larvae emerge from the nuts in late fall, go down three to nine inches deep in the soil and stay there one to two years, then pupate in September or October, transforming to the adult in three weeks. They remain in the soil until the next July or August when they come out to feed on nuts. Thus the life cycle takes from two to three years.

Control—DDT is very effective, spray susceptible varieties, such as those named, with 6 pounds of 50% wettable DDT powder to 100 gallons of water.

Application—Make the first application in late July or early August when at least 6 weevils can be jarred from the tree onto a sheet spread underneath. Normally the latter part of July is the ideal time to start spraying. Toxaphene is also effective and does not increase mites as rapidly as DDT does. Use 6 pounds of 40% wettable Toxaphene powder to 100 gallons of water. Use spray equipment, with sufficient power to thoroughly cover the tree from top to bottom with either one of these sprays.

Pepper Weevil

This insect originally came from Mexico, but is now of great importance in the states of California, Arizona, New Mexico, Texas, Georgia and Florida. Small white grubs feed inside the buds of bell, sweet and chili peppers, causing the buds and most of the pods to drop off. Adults are reddish brown to black with a brassy lustre. They have curved beaks one-eighth inch long.

Control—There are several generations each year and dusting with a 5% DDT dust every 7 to 10 days until the pods mature is effective.

Application—In the event the DDT would be too toxic as far as a residual effect is concerned, I would recommend dusting with a 5% Malathion dust for good control. In Texas and along the Gulf Coast a 20% Toxaphene dust is satisfactory.

Pill Bugs or Sow Bugs

These pests are related to the crawfish. They have flat, oval, gray to brown segmented bodies about one-half inch long, and seven pairs of legs. Pill bugs breathe by means of gills and prefer damp, protected places. They are found as scavengers on rotting plant parts, under flower-pots, or decayed boards, or in manure, and they are quite injurious to seedlings; eating roots, girdling young stems.

Control—Use 10% Heptachlor or 5% Dieldrin granules.

Application—Apply either material at the rate of one and one-half lbs. per 1000 square feet of affected area, or one-fourth lb. to 100 square feet.

Pine Top Moth

This insect is found from Massachusetts, west to Texas, and is injurious to almost all two and three needle pines. The moth that lays the eggs, is small—about one-half inch wing spread, reddish-brown with silver grey markings. They lay yellow, flattened, circular eggs in needles, buds or shoots. The larvae, yellow to pale brown, three-eighths inch long, mine or bore into needles, then into buds, spinning a web around the needles—often covered with pitch and then burrow into twigs of new growth to pupate. Young pines are seriously deformed and occasionally die. Loblolly Pine is most often injured.

Control—The best control is to cut off infested tips in late fall or winter and spray the tree with Lindane or BHC. You should start this early in the spring in order to control it and continue to spray it every 14 to 21 days in order to prevent further recurrence of the Pine Tip Moth. Mix one pound of BHC or Lindane (the wettable powder form) into about 25 gallons of water for maximum control.

Plum Curculio

This insect is a major pest of stone fruits, mainly plums, peach, cherry, apricot, prune, nectarine and many others. The adult is dark brown with a greyish patch on the back, four definite humps on the wing covers, and a long curved snout which projects forward and downward in an arc one-third of the length of the body. It resembles a Boll Weevil very closely. The beetles themselves feed on leaves and petals. They injure young fruits by feeding and laying eggs in small circular excavations—marked by a crescent shaped slot underneath. Feeding punctures may result in warts or scars, sometimes misshapen, knotty fruits. But, in the Gulf Coast area, the primary injury is due to the eggs that are laid in the fruit, which form worms, and thus wormy fruit. After the eggs are laid in the fruit, they hatch within a week into grey-white legless grubs with brown heads and curved bodies. They feed in the flesh of the fruit for two weeks or more, by which time the fruit has probably fallen to the ground, although some species of peaches

172

remain on the tree until ripe. The larvae leave the fruit and go into the ground to pupate. The adults emerge in about a month.

Control—A timely application of either Dieldrin, Sevin or Diazinon to the fruit trees is the best recommendation.

Application—For maximum control, a spray consisting of either Dieldrin or Malathion applied to fruit trees (such as plum and peaches) must be applied when about two-thirds or 75% of the blossoms have fallen. If one waits until after this time, considerable damage will result. Use one-half pound of 50% wettable Dieldrin to 100 gallons of water or if the 25% wettable Malathion is used—use three pounds of this material to 100 gallons of water to obtain maximum results. Thorough coverage of all portions of the tree must be obtained for maximum control. It would also be advisable to repeat this application within 10 to 14 days after the first spray application, if maximum control is to be obtained.

Soil Treatment for Plum Curculio Control in Peach Orchards

Experiments indicate that soil treatment may eventually replace tree spraying to control the Plum Curculio in peach orchards, according to the U.S.D.A. Orchard tests conducted by research workers at Fort Valley, Georgia proved several insecticides capable of giving good control of the pest. Aldrin, Dieldrin or Heptachlor was spread in the spring on the ground under trees at the rate of two pounds per acre, this two pound designating actual material itself and not in the formulated stage.

For instance: This would be equivalent to 20 pounds of 10% Heptachlor granules and mixed with the top layer of soil. This treatment controlled the plum curculio by killing the pest before it could emerge from the ground. Similar results were obtained with all three chemicals.

In one orchard—two pounds of actual Dieldrin per acre, incorporated in the soil, prevented the development of adults from most of the larvae, which over a period of three years were placed in the soil under the spread of peach trees.

In a cooperative experiment with a Georgia peach grower, 64 pounds of 25% Aldrin was mixed with each ton of fertilizer and spread under several thousand trees in March, 1958. Each tree was treated with two and one-third pounds of the mixture. The material was broadcast by hand and disc into the ground. No wormy peaches were found when the orchard was harvested in 1958. In 1959 they found wormy fruit in only one small area. In contrast, the peaches in a neighbor's orchard was ruined by the plum curculio.

Even though this has not been tested and proven in Texas, it is worth a try, and it might simplify the method of controlling the plum curculio, plus the fact that it could become much more advantageous.

Potato Bug

The Colorado potato beetle is hard shelled, very broad—three-eighths by one-fourth inch, very convex with 10 longitudinal black lines and

173

with black spots on the thorax. Both the beetle and larvae completely ravage potato foliage, often destroying whole fields. Although the potato is preferred, the beetles may go to other members of the nightshade family—such as egg plant, tomato and peppers.

Control—Use 5% Malathion dust, or 10% DDT dust.

Application—Thoroughly cover the foliage of the plants. Keep foliage covered during periods of rapid growth.

Red Spider, or Southern Red Mite

This particular insect is injurious to Holly, Azaleas and other shrubs in the North, but here in the South—Camellia, Azaleas, Oaks and other ornamentals are infested. The mites feed on the leaf surface, rasping the epidermis of the leaf, the leaves turn grey or brown—as feeding continues. Adult females are nearly black. Males and nymphs are light red, both have spiny hairs curving backward. Red eggs are laid on leaf surfaces and heavily infested leaves look as if they have been dusted with red pepper. There are many generations, but in the South most damage is in the fall or spring, with low population in the mid-summer —due to the extensive hot temperature.

One method a home gardener can use to detect presence of red spider mites is to take a piece of white paper and beat a portion of branch or twig against the paper. The red mites will fall off on the white paper where they can be detected with the naked eye.

Control—Spray with Diazinon.

Application—The best recommended procedure is to take 25% liquid Diazinon, mix four tablespoonfuls per gallon of water, and thoroughly saturate the foliage of the affected plant. The Diazinon will help control the spider mite, and the light miscible oil that is used as a carrier for this insecticide will help control scale insects.

Red Band Leaf Roller

A native insect found in Texas that infests Chrysanthemum, Geranium, Roses and many shrubs. The larvae is slender, greenish and pupates in a half cocoon on trees, or other objects. On ornamentals they roll and tie the leaves on terminal growth. Due to this characteristic this makes the insect very difficult to control. By rolling up in the leaves they build themselves a natural protection against the penetration of an insecticide when it is applied. Therefore, insecticides should be used that have a long residual effect and more than one application should be used for maximum results.

Control—Use three to four tablespoonfuls of 18% liquid Dieldrin to one gallon of water. Add to this mixture one teaspoonful of "spreader-sticker" or liquid soap, to enhance the insecticide sticking to the leaves. Wet the plant or shrub until the liquid drips off. Repeat every seven to 10 days until all signs of insects disappears.

174

Roaches

These insects are known by a variety of common names; such as, cockroaches, roaches, water bugs, and black beetles. Cockroaches are generally brown or dark colored although some are green. They are broad or flattened, with the head bent under the body so that the mouth opens backwards and the eyes look downwards. The antennae are long, slender, and of many segments. Wings are usually developed in the adults and the hinder pair fold once. The mouth parts are strong, the legs long, and in many species bear many spines. Cockroaches are usually active at night, hiding in dark places, such as cracks and crevices during day light and running very rapidly when disturbed. This household pest consumes food and food materials, gnaw on woolen goods, leather and anything that has paste on it. Besides eating, they leave a disagreeable "roachy" odor, which spoils food where they have been. They breed rather fast and when abundant become very troublesome.

Control—To attempt to control exclusively inside the home oftentimes becomes a troublesome problem. This is due to the fact that they are continually infesting the premises by invading from the outside, thus it becomes advisable in a complete roach control program to spray a 10 to 20 foot barrier around the house. The best material to use is liquid Diazinon. Mix one pint of this material to 10 to 15 gallons of water and apply as a spray completely around the outside of the home. For maximum results inside the home use four tablespoonfuls of liquid Diazinon to one gallon of cleaning fluid or solvent and spray this material wherever roaches are infesting. This can be applied with a low pressure sprayer, hand sprayer, or even painted on with a paint brush. Apply to base boards, cabinets, etc. Do not apply where cooking utensils or food stuffs are stored, unless they are removed. Avoid inhaling the fumes from the mixture—keep away from open flames and provide open ventilation in the home when applying.

Application—Repeat as often as necessary to prevent or to control the build-up of a roach infestation.

Rhinoceros Beetle

This is a member of a group of very large beetles, with a projection like a rhinoceros, and is generally found in the Great Southwest. The male is very dark brown, practically black, very broad, over an inch long with a horn curving back from its head like a rhinoceros. The female is similar but a small tubercle instead of a horn. The larvae, looking like large white grubs, attack lilacs and sometimes other shrubs just under the surface of the ground, girdling it and killing them. They are also found near ash trees. The beetles come out at dusk, but life histories and control measures are not very clear.

Control—One of the best control measures is to find their burrows underneath the ground where they attack plant roots. Apply 10% Heptachlor granules to the affected areas and water in thoroughly. This should bring the insect under control.

Salt Marsh Caterpillar

This insect is generally distributed throughout the Texas Gulf Coast and is one of the woolly type caterpillars. The caterpillars are very hairy, grey when young, then black with yellow, broken lines, and cinnamon-red hair—up to two inches long. At times, usually in late summer, they may be as bad as Army Worms—eating everything in sight, including beans, vegetables, flowers, rice, etc.

Control—Dusting or spraying with DDT or Toxaphene generally gives excellent control. Malathion also works quite well. If a dust is applied—use the 5% Malathion dust in the area where they are invading, or if a spray is applied—use a 50% wettable DDT. The Toxaphene can be applied in the form of a dust or spray.

Application—Follow the manufacturers directions. If a 50% DDT spray is used—apply three pounds of 50% wettable DDT to 100 gallons of water, or three tablespoonfuls per gallon.

San Jose Scale

This scale probably came from China and was first discovered in San Jose, California in 1880, and is now present in every state in the Union. It is particularly injurious to fruit trees, often causing death if left unchecked. Such fruit trees include apple, pear, peach, plum, etc. The female is yellowish, covered with a grey, circular, waxy scale— 1/16 inch in diameter, elevated in the center into a nipple, surrounded by yellow rings. Young scales are small and nearly black.

Control—Spray during the growing season with 25% emulsible concentrate of Diazinon. During the dormant season spray with an oil emulsion spray.

Application—During the summer months, in order to prevent excessive burning from the use of a dormant oil spray, one must use a 25% emulsible concentrate of Diazinon, or a light summer oil, mixed according to the directions of the manufacturer, and applied to the foliage, limbs, and trunk. During the dormant season, it is advisable to use an oil dormant spray to get maximum control. Use one gallon of Oil Emulsion Concentrate mixed with 25 gallons of water.

Shot Hole Borer

This insect is also known as a Fruit Tree Bark Beetle. It makes small holes, like shot holes, in the bark of healthy twigs of fruit trees, and in branches and trunks of weakened trees—attacking such things as peach, plum and pear. On stone fruits the shot holes are usually covered with gum. If beetles are abundant, the foliage yellows, wilts and the tree may die. The pinkish-white grub, about one-eighth inch long, winters in the inner-bark. The galleries are winding, sawdust filled, leading out from a shorter central gallery. The black, blunt beetles, one-tenth inch long, emerge in early summer and the females fly to unhealthy trees to excavate an egg gallery in the branch or twig, depositing the eggs on each side of this. There may be one to three generations, depending upon the climate.

Control—This borer usually attacks dead or weakened trunks and branches; all dead or dying trees and branches should be removed and burned. The vigor of remaining trees should be increased by proper fertilization, drainage and the control of other borer and scale insects. The best control is to keep the tree in a good healthy condition.

Silverfish

This is a household pest found in many parts of the world. It is silvery-grey in color, usually less than one-half inch long, very active and hard to catch. Beside the two long cerci at the hindend of the body, it has a similar filament giving the insect the appearance of having three tails. It prefers dark and damp places and feeds on material containing starch, such as wheat flour, sizing on wallpaper and rayon. It often loosens wallpaper by feeding on the starch in the paste used in applying the paper to the wall. It prefers temperatures of about 80° F., but is often found in much cooler places.

Control—DDT or Diazinon applied in the form of a spray or dust will give excellent control of silverfish.

Application—Applied in cracks and places where dust deposits are not objectionable, will give excellent control of the silverfish. A 10% DDT dust is recommended. If a spray is more feasible to apply, then take the 25% Diazinon and use three tablespoonfuls of this material to any liquid carrying agent. This could be water or a cleaning fluid. Apply with a low pressure sprayer.

Slugs

Slugs are essentially the same as snails in general structure, except they have no external shell or hump. The mantle being a smoother area occupying a forward fourth or third of the back. Slugs range in length from one-fourth inch to eight or 10 inches long, depending upon the species and the age of the individual. They vary in color from whitish-grey to various shades of grey to black, usually more or less mottled with darker shades. Most snails and slugs have a definite mouth which is equipped with a horny file which they rasp away the substance to be eaten.

Control—Slugs and snails can be controlled with a bait containing Methaldehyde, plus either Calcium Arsenate or Sodium Fluosilicate. You can buy bait containing these materials or you can prepare it yourself.

Bait Mix: Bait mix *should consist of one ounce of Methaldehyde and either two ounces of Calcium Arsenate or one ounce of Fluosilicate with two pounds of wheat bran, cornmeal or similar materials.*

For small gardens apply one pound of bait per 1,000 square feet. For larger areas—use 40 to 50 pounds per acre. Moisten the bait with water just before applying it. You can also obtain bait pellets and their use is preferred for large scale operations. Methaldehyde will attract slugs and snails from their hiding places. Therefore where the bait is not likely to be found by domestic animals or children, it may be placed in piles about the size of a 50¢ piece every few feet near the plants where slugs are feeding. Under dry conditions the Fluosilicate will kill the pests, but under moist conditions, such as you have along the Texas Gulf Coast, one or the other poisons is necessary in the bait for satisfactory kill.

PRECAUTION—Methaldehyde, Calcium Arsenate and Fluosilicate are poisons, but with care they may be handled safely. When mixing the bait, wear rubber or leather gloves to protect your hands, wash your hands and all utensils and tools properly and thoroughly after mixing or apply baits. Store baits in closed containers in a place where they cannot be mistaken for food, and where children, pets or farm animals cannot reach them. See that the containers are properly labeled. Since Methaldehyde is difficult to obtain and can only be bought in large quantities, it is more feasible to buy a prepared bait.

Snails

Snails are usually some shade of grey, but their shells vary from nearly white through brown, to nearly black, and they are often ornamented with stripes or mottling of contrasting colors. The body of a snail consists of a head, neck, the hump, tail and foot. The head bears two pairs of tentacles or feelers, a large pair of bulbs upon which the eyes are borne, and a small pair below which are used for smelling. The mouth is in the center of the head below the lower pair of tentacles.

Snails or slugs are mainly nocturnal, but they come out of their hiding place and feed in the evening or on dark days. Their favorite hiding places are under old decaying boards or logs, or under wood boardwalks, in cellars, creameries and spring houses, and rock piles along hedge rows, and beneath damp refuse. Snails are less particular in this respect than slugs as they have the power when confront with unfavorable living conditions of sealing the opening of the shell with a mucous sheet which soon hardens to a leathery texture. The snails then become dormant and some may exist this way as long as four years. When conditions again become favorable the door of the shell is washed away and the snail resumes its normal activity.

Control—Sprinkle 5% Dieldrin granules around plants.

Spiders

Spiders generally have an unwarranted reputation for being, as a whole, poisonous and harmful. On the contrary, they are decidedly beneficial because of the number of destructive insects they consume. The Black Widow spider appears to be the only dangerous North American spider. The Black Widow spider is small, nearly black, but with rather long legs and smooth body. On the underside of the body is an orange-red marking of variable form—but usually shaped like an hour-glass.

Control—Use a 10% Chlordane dust or a 40% Chlordane powder and spray. Where the Chlordane dust is used—apply at the rate of one to two ounces per 100 square feet of surface area around the spider's den. Where the wettable 40% Chlordane is used—mix at the rate of two tablespoonfuls per gallon of water and thoroughly saturate the area where spiders are located. This will also help give control on scorpions.

Southern Pine Beetle

This insect is a small native bark beetle, most injurious pest of pines in its range into Texas and Oklahoma. It kills healthy trees as well as attacking weakened and felled specimens. The adults are brown or black, one-eighth inch long, makes winding or S shaped galleries in the inner bark. There can normally be five generations a season, with epidemics when rainfall is below normal.

Control—Normally these pests are kept under control by a host of natural insects, but in case they do become a problem, the best control measure is to spray the pine tree periodically with BHC or Lindane, which will also help control the Terminal Bud Moth. One can use the wettable powder BHC or the emulsible concentrate of Lindane. Mix according to the manufacturer's directions, into the specified amount of water and thoroughly saturate the affected tree. This should bring it under control.

Spittle Bug

Spittle bugs are sucking insects and they are not true bugs but rather closely related to leaf hoppers and are sometimes called Frog Hoppers. The adults are drab brown, grey or black, sometimes marked with yellow, and they look rather like short robust leaf hoppers. They hop away but do not fly very much, they insert eggs in plant stems or in between stem and leaf sheaths in grasses. The remarkable thing about the Spittle Bug is the frothy mass, children oftentimes call it spit, which envelops the nymphs.

This spittle is a combination of a fluid voided from the glands of the insect, which cover the nymph. The greenish nymph is soon hidden under a mound of snow white foam protected from sun and preying insects. Many Spittle Bugs are relatively harmless, but several are in-

179

jurious to plants. Spittle Bugs normally do not cause sufficient damage to make spraying necessary. If they do become abundant in an orchard they may be controlled with one application of Parathion or Malathion.

Control—Recommended that three pounds of 25% wettable Malathion to 100 gallons of water be used. If one is spraying a pecan orchard for the control of Pecan Scab or for Pecan Nut Casebearer, there would be no need to incorporate an insecticide other than the one already recommended for the Pecan Nut Casebearer, as this would bring it under control. Thorough application with 200 to 300 pounds of pressure is necessary in order to get uniform application over a large tree. On smaller shrubs less pressure would be necessary.

Spotted Cucumber Beetle

This adult beetle is greenish-yellow, rather slender, with 12 black spots, a black head, one-fourth inch long, and feeds on a vast number of flowers and vegetables besides cucumber. The larvae of the cucumber beetle feeds on roots of the plants and bore into underground parts of stems. They are sometimes called overflow worms, or bud worms, or drill worms—because they bore out the crown of the plant and kill the bud.

Control—Spray the plants with 25% Malathion. Use four pounds of 25% Malathion to 100 gallons of water, or dust with a 5% Sevin dust.

Application—Early and regular applications of these insecticides will give excellent results.

Squash Bug

This insect is found throughout the country, attacking all vine crops with preference for squash and pumpkin. The adult is dark brown, sometimes mottled with grey or light brown, hard shelled, five-eighths inch long. It gives off such a disagreeable odor when crushed it is commonly called a Stink Bug. But, true stink bugs belong to a related family. During the feeding process the squash bug apparently inject a toxic substance into the vine, causing a wilting known as Anasa Wilt of cucurbits, closely resembling Bacterial Wilt. After wilting, the vines turn black and crisp; small plants are killed; larger vines have several runners affected.

Control—Dust the vines with 5% Malathion, 20% Sabadilla dust, or with a 5% Sevin dust.

Application—Thorough coverage of all foliage and vines with these insecticides are essential for maximum control.

Squash Vine Borer

The squash vine borer winters as a larvae or a a pupa inside of a silk-lined, dark cocoon, an inch or two below the soil level. The moth, wasp-like, with copper-green fore-wings and orange and black abdomen, one to one and one-half inches across the wings, appears when vine crops start to run. It glues small, oval, flat, brown eggs singly on stems and leaf stalks. Young borers hatch in about a week, tunnel into the stem to feed, and the first sign of their presence being sudden wilting of the vine and masses of greenish-yellow excrement protruding from holes in the stem. The borer, a white, wrinkled, caterpillar with brown head, up to one inch long, can be seen by splitting the stem with a knife.

Control—The control is difficult, as after the borer gets inside the vine, about the only way to get him out is to slit the vine, using a razor blade, killing the borer inside of his habitat, then mounding the dirt up over the slit vine so that it will be protected and will take root. A preventative control measure to prevent infestation of the squash vine by the borer, is to apply 5% Malathion dust to the vegetative parts of the plant.

Application—For best results, use a garden-type, or pump-type duster—using enough dust to lightly, but thoroughly, cover the foliage and this will sift down around the stems.

Stink Bugs

A large oval, bright green bug, five-eighths inch long, *bad smelling*. It is a special pest of beans, causing pods to fall, distorting seeds; and of peaches—which are "cat faced" by the feeding punctures. It also causes discoloration on tomatoes.

Control—Dust or spray with Malathion.

Application—Dust foliage and fruit with a 5% Malathion dust. If a spray is used—take two to four tablespoonfuls of 25% wettable Malathion to one gallon of water.

Sweet Potato Weevil

The sweet potato weevil occurs in Texas in all the major sweet potato producing areas of this state. The adult weevil is about one-fourth inch long and resembles a large ant. The head, snout, and wing covers are dark metallic blue, the body and legs are reddish-orange, and the adults have well developed wings and are capable of limited flight. The adult weevils damage sweet potato plants by feeding and egg deposition cavities. The larvae which feed in both vine and the potato do the most injury.

Control—Control or eradication of this pest depends upon strict adherance to the recommended procedures and constant care by the grower to prevent reinfestation. The principle of control is to deny the weevil the host plant on which to feed. Strict sanitary, cultural and storage practices are required. The use of insecticides to destroy weevil population helps to a certain extent. In areas where sweet potatoes are grown, where weevil infestations are light and where planting zones can be establised, the weevil can be eradicated, if it is deprived of its food for about a year. If weevils are found on ones property, no sweet potatoes should be bedded, grown or stored within a zone extending one-half to one mile from the point of infestation. Also, it would be advisable to clean up the premises on which sweet potatoes have been stored. The place where the potatoes were stored should be thoroughly cleaned and the debris burned. Storages and store houses should be dusted with 10% DDT dust at the rate of one pound to each 1600 square feet of surface area. A spray may be used consisting of eight pounds of 50% wettable DDT powder to 100 gallons of water, applied at the rate of one and one-half gallons to each 1000 square feet. This treatment will eradicate any remaining weevils, then the failure to plant or bed sweet potatoes within an aera of one-half to one mile of that area for one year will completely eliminate the sweet potato weevil.

Tarnish Plant Bug

This particular insect is found throughout the country, and is injurious to more than fifty plants. Such plants include beans, beets, cabbage, turnip, potatoes, and occasionally citrus. The adult is small—one-fourth inch long, flattened, oval, irregularly mottled with white, yellow and black splotches, giving a generally tarnished appearance, but with a clear yellow triangle marked with a black dot on the lower third of each side. Adults hibernate among weeds, under stones, leaves or bark, flying early in the spring to feed on fruit tree buds, then migrating to other plants to lay eggs in leaves or flowers. The cycle takes about three to four weeks, and there are three to five generations a season.

Control—The tarnish plant bug has been very hard to control. Most efforts being put on removing weeds and trash in the fall to prevent over-wintering. Both DDT and Malathion, in the form of a dust, give pretty good control.

Application—A 5% Malathion dust generally gives excellent control for this particular insect, as well as the spray of 50% wettable DDT. Where the 5% Malathion dust is applied, make sure to get thorough coverage of all areas of the plant infested. If the 50% wettable DDT is applied—use three tablespoonfuls of this material to a gallon of water and thoroughly saturate the area that is infested.

Tea Scale

This is a most important Camellia insect in the Deep South, especially in Texas. Although the scales are on under side of foliage, infested Camellias can be told at a distance by yellowish blotches on the upper leaf surface, generally unhealthy appearance of the whole plant, and premature dropping of the leaves. Bloom is normally decreased, cuttings may dies before roots develop. The scale is as serious on Chinese holly as on Camellias, and many times infests ferns, palms, orchard figs and a few other plants.

The female is at first thin, light, yellow, later hard brown, elongated oval or boat shaped, 1/16 inch long, with a residue from the first moult attached at one end. Yellow eggs, 10 to 16, are held under the shell. The male is soft, white, narrow and with a ridge down the middle. Both scales are held in a conspicuous tangle of white cottony threads, often the entire undersurface of the leaf is white and dotted with small brown female shells. The eggs will hatch in from seven to 21 days, depending upon the weather conditions. Flat yellow crawlers move to new growth, attach themselves after two or three days, secreting first a thin white covering, later many white threads. The first moult normally takes place within 18 to 36 days, the second moult a week later, and egg laying starts 41 to 65 days after birth. There are many overlapping broods, so that crawlers and young nymphs are present on foliage at any time between March and November.

Control—Spray the Camellia plants, or affected plants, thoroughly in the spring after blooming, with a white oil emulsion—using six level tablespoonfuls per gallon, hitting the underside of leaves with great force. A second application may be required in the spring or in September. Parathion is effective and safer than oil on the plants, but is very dangerous to the operator, and should not be used if one has not used Parathion before. Malathion can be substituted in place of the oil spraying throughout the growing season—with four to five tablespoonfuls of Malathion per gallon of water.

Termites

Termites are not ants although they are often called white ants. The best way to tell termites from ants is to look at the waist. Ants are deeply constricted, while termites have a broad joining between the thorax and the abdomen. They have chewing mouth-parts, and they live in galleries in wood or in the ground, except when the winged forms are swarming. Termites are social insects like ants and have a well developed caste system. The food of termites is wood or cellulose in some form. They have a protozoa in their intestines to enable them to digest the cellulose.

Some species live in dry wood above the ground, but the species that are of major importance to the gardener and the home owner are the Subterranean termites. These work on wood or in the ground and build covered runways to reach wood above the ground. Subterranean termites sometimes injure living trees and shrubs, being more harmful in warm climates.

Control—Control Subterranean termites by blocking them off from the soil—usually where they obtain their water supply. To do that, foundations must be made impervious to their attack. Masonry walls must be free of voids and expansion joints must be filled with coal-tar pitch. After such structural modifications are made, as are necessary to block the entry of termites, the soil next to the foundation walls and piers must be poisoned to kill termites already present in it and to set up a toxic barrier to prevent others from entering.

There are a number of chemicals that will control the termite, these primarily being DDT, Chlordane and Dieldrin. They can be applied in a trench dug around the foundation as previously described, or injected into the soil under pressure. Recently, Dieldrin has been recommended as being one of the most effective compounds against termites. It can be applied in a trench around the home in the form of a 5% Dieldrin granule, or you can take the 50% wettable or 18% liquid Dieldrin and mix with water and spray or pour into the trench, or have it forced into the soil around the foundation under pressure.

Application—As stated previously, one of the best compounds to use is Dieldrin. Take the 50% wettable Dieldrin powder and mix two pounds of this material to 100 gallons of water and thoroughly saturate the soil around the foundation of the home. 40% wettable Chlordane mixed with water at the rate of three pounds per 100 gallons should also be of excellent control. But in order to get 100% control measure of termites, one must remember that this chemical barrier must be placed all the way around the foundation of the building in order to cut the termites off from reaching the building itself.

Texas Citrus Spider Mites

These mites are small and their damage is confined mainly to the leaves of the tree. Heavy infestations cause mottling of the leaves, giving them a greyish appearance, and may cause some defoliation of trees where heavy infestation exists.

Control—A spray containing 2% of actual oil emulsion or miscible oil will control this mite, as will two pounds of 15% wettable aramite per 100 gallons of water. Dusting sulfur is of some benefit and oil sprays should not be used after September because it will damage the fruit.

Texas Leaf Cutting Ant

This is a native, confined to southern and eastern Texas and western Louisiana, interesting for its habit of cutting leaves from plants. These are macerated, fertilized in the nest, and in this compost the ants grow a fungus for food—a method comparable to man's culture of mushrooms. The workers vary from 1/16 to ½ inch long, are brown with spines on the head and thorax, two segmented pedicel. Their enormous nests can be 10 to 20 feet deep, with numerous craters. They invade homes, steal seed, ravage garden and field crops, and destroy young pine seedlings, and they are also quite a nuisance around creep feeders in pastures. They are easily recognized by their nests, and also by the paths they cut through forest and through pasture land, transporting food to their nests.

Control—One of the most economical and easy ways to control the Texas Leaf Cutting Ant is to use Methyl Bromide, applied into the den. They also can be controlled by the use of Heptachlor or Dieldrin granules, sprinkled in concentric circles around the nest.

Application—If Methyl Bromide is used, obtain this product, which comes in its manufactured form, in one pound cans, using an applicator to inject this gas, which is heavier than air, into the den. All openings need not be covered as the gas will have a tendency to be carried downward and will pentrate through the entire nest. Normally one to two pounds of this material, applied to the den, which may be ten to twenty feet wide, will give excellent control for not only the ants but also the eggs.

As to the application of 10% Heptachlor granules or the 5% Dieldrin granules, take this granular material and form concentric circles outside the nest itself. Space the concentric circles three to six feet apart all the way around, making three applications. This should give excellent control of these ants as they cross the barrier going back to the nest.

Tomato Horn Worm

This is an awe inspiring caterpillar, three or four inches long with seven oblique white stripes and a red horn projecting at the rear. It feeds on tomato, tobacco, eggplant, pepper, potato and weeds.

Control—Dust plants with 5% Malathion, 10% Chlordane, Lindane, or with a 10% DDT.

Application—Thorough coverage of all foliage of the plants is essential. Constant coverage of the foliage with the insecticide at all times is essential to prevent reinfestation by this pest.

Tomato Russett Mite

This small insect feeds on tomatoes, potatoes, petunias and other type hosts. The typical injury caused by this insect is the bronzing or russetting of the surface of stems and leaves, with the feeding starting at the base of the main stalk. Leaves turn brown three to four weeks later, and fruit is attacked only in severe cases, but loss of foliage results in sunburned fruit.

Control—A 5% Malathion dust will control this insect. Also sulphur dust will wipe it out very easily.

Tree Borers

There are a great many borers affecting shade or fruit trees, ornamental shrubs, annuals and perennials. Borers are particularly destructive to newly set trees and to those weakened from various causes—such as disease or drouth. Some of the factors predisposing trees to borer attack are as follows:

1. Drouth seems to be the primary factor in making trees susceptible to borer attack.
2. Sun scald is important with newly transplanted trees, and also on established trees suddenly exposed to the sun—by removal of another tree, hedge or building.
3. Injuries from hurricanes, storms, fires, etc., provide easy entrance for borers.
4. Defoliation by leaf cutting insects produce a weakened condition, highly inviting to borers.
5. Construction activities, where the change of grades, lowering or raising of water table, mechanical injuries from equipment, etc.
6. Chemical injuries from leaking gas in the soil, and chlorides applied to roads to lay dust or to melt snow and ice in winter (of course we are not interested in this section), or fumes from factories are conducive to poor health and borer attack in trees.

As has been stated previously a number of times, the best control measure is a preventative one, plus a program carried out for the maximum promotion of good health and vigor in the tree. This of course can be handled by adequate watering, insect control and fertilization practices.

Spraying trees and shrubs with an anti-desiccant also helps to prevent borer attack. Spraying the trunks and branches of trees and shrubs with a Dieldrin solution is effective in preventing egg laying by many borers. In this case you can use either the liquid Dieldrin or the wettable 50% Dieldrin. The recommended rate is three tablespoonfuls of either of these compounds into one gallon of water. As has been stated previously, it is easier to keep borers out of trees than it is to get them out once they have infested the tree.

After the tree has been infested, there are a few compounds that can be used to a good advantage. Fumigants are helpful. For instance: you can squirt a few drops of carbon bisulfied from a machine oil can, and plug up the hole with putty or gun. This will kill the borer.

An old time remedy that has been used successfully on shade trees; *but not on fruit trees*, is to dig or punch holes around the base of the tree (around the drip line) and into each hole drop a teaspoonful of moth ball crystals, then fill the holes up with water. This seems to act as a systemic type insecticide, the root system picking up the chemical, carry it into the sap stream, and in coming in contact with the borer will help kill it.

Once again—*PREVENTIVE CONTROL BY KEEPING THE TREE HEALTHY AND SPRAYING IT PERIODICALLY WITH A RECOMMENDED INSECTICIDE IS MUCH EASIER THAN TO TRY TO CONTROL THE BORER AFTER IT ONCE INVADES THE TREE.*

Twig Girdler

The Twig Girdler girdles twigs and branches, weakening them so that they fall off or die on the tree. This insect is active during the late summer and early fall and many twigs may be found on the ground under a severely infested tree. The Twig Girdler is a greyish-brown beetle, one-half to five-eighths inch in length with a broad grey band over the wing covers. Its head is reddish-brown and bears a pair of long antennae—which is characteristic of this insect, making it easy to identify. The antennae often times are much longer than the insect itself. This insect over-winters as a partially grown larvae in a twig on the tree or on the ground. It develops rapidly in the spring —feeding on the twig. Following pupation the adult emerges in late August or early September. The female systematically girdles twigs and deposits eggs in the severed portion since the larvae is unable to develop in healthy sap wood. The eggs hatch in a few weeks into larvae which remain small until the following spring when they complete development, pupate and emerge as adults in late summer and fall. There is only one generation annually, and some individuals require two years to mature.

Control—Infestations can be reduced considerable by removing the girdled branches from the trees and burning them. The insect, as we stated previously, deposits its eggs in the severed portion, thus destroying the branch, you cut down on infestation of future generations.

The tree should be sprayed with five pounds of 40% wettable Chlordane powder per 100 gallons of water when the first injured branches are observed in late August or early September. Two, perhaps three, applications at two-week intervals may be required for most effective control.

Application—Thorough coverage of the Chlordane on the limbs and twigs of the tree is essential for maximum control.

Velvet Ant

This ant is rather large and is characterized by a red velvety color, with one black, dark band at the tip end of the tail. Most species of this insect live in the nests of bees and wasps in the ground, some of them parasitize ants. Both male and female are generally covered rather densely with hair, often long, and usually of two or three contrasting colors—such as black—with a red cross band of white, yellow and black. The females have a very powerful sting. In a lot of instances they are considered as a beneficial insect, however, in others, they get into beehives and cause considerable damage.

Control—Locate the area in which the Velvet Ants are feeding and use 5% Dieldrin granules or 10% Heptachlor granules.

Application—Thorough coverage in the area in which the Velvet

Ant is feeding, around beehives and such, with these materials will generally bring them under control.

Walnut Caterpillar

This insect pest is generally about two inches long, dull black, reddish when young, covered with long white hair. The moths are dark buff with four brown transversed lines on the four wings. Eggs are layed in masses on the underside of leaves, and the larvae feed in colonies—crawling to the tree trunk to moult and going back to feed again. Masses of Walnut Caterpillars can do extensive damage to a tree.

Control—Use any of the chlorinated hydrocarbons as a spray and apply to the foliage of the trees in which they are infesting.

Application—Use three pounds of 50% wettable DDT to 100 gallons of water and apply with a pressure sprayer to all the leaf surface of the tree. Also, a 25% wettable Malathion can be used at the rate of three to four pounds to 100 gallons of water, or three to four tablespoonfuls to a gallon. Thorough coverage of the entire tree is a necessity.

Walking Sticks

This insect belongs to the family Phasmidae. The bodies of these insects are usually long and stick-like, owing largely to their long, slender body segments. Their legs and antennae are also generally long, the insects are slow moving, and the 15 to 20 kinds found in the United States are brown or green in color, wingless, with only wing stubs, thus adding to their twig-like appearance.

Walking Sticks feed on foliage, although not often sufficiently abundant, they may entirely strip the leaves from many acres of forest trees or shade trees on the lawn. Their eggs are laid in the fall, usually being dropped singly wherever the insect happens to be, and falling to the ground with a sound like rain. The remain until the following spring, or in some cases until the second spring, before hatching. In the case of infestations accessible for economic spraying, as in recreation areas or on home plots, spraying with DDT—will prevent further injury.

Control—Mix 3 pounds of wettable DDT into 100 gallons of water and spray wherever the insects are located.

Wasps—Dirt Dobbers—Bumblebees

These winged insects are a problem due to their toxic sting. Often times a sting from such an insect on a person who is super sensitive to the toxin can lead to death. Wasps and Yellow Jackets are most dangerous, especially to children.

Control—Use wettable powders of Chlordane, DDT, or Dieldrin.

Application—It's the best policy to locate these insects' nests and apply the insecticide at night when the pests are less active. Spray the nest and also the surrounding areas. Use three-four tablespoons of 50% wettable DDT—40% wettable Chlordane—50% wettable Dieldrin to one gallon of water. Or use any good insecticide put up in aerosol can and one good treatment will automatically knock out all the insects.

White Marked Tussock Moth

This insect pest is primarily a city pest, feeding on many deciduous shade trees such as elm, sycamore, willow, Chinese tallows and others, but they also infest fruit trees, but not on evergreens.

Foliage is skeletonized and the fruit scarred by conspicuous hairy caterpillars 1½ inches long—with red heads, two pencil like tufts of long black hair projecting like horns, with a third tuft at the rear. A black stripe down the middle of the back, bordered with a wide yellow line, four white brushes or tussocks of hair on the front segments of the abdomen.

Control—Any of the chlorinated hydrocarbons and also the organic phosphate compounds—such as Malathion, will control the White Marked Tussock Moth. Use three pounds of 50%DDT, or four to five pounds of 25% wettable Malathion per 100 gallons of water to control this insect. Also three pounds of 50% Toxaphene per 100 gallons of water will control the insect.

Application—Thorough application at first sign of the insect on a tree is necessary for 100% control.

White Grub

Larvae of the June Bug or May Beetle. Oftentimes found in St. Augustine lawns where they cut the roots of the grass and cause the grass to die.

Control—Use 10% Heptachlor granules at the rate of one and one-half pounds per 1,000 square feet, or three ounces per 100 square feet.

Application—Sprinkle granules lightly over the area and water in.

Wireworm

These insects are the larvae of the Click Beetle. They are usually found more extensive in land recently taken over in sod, but in some sections—wire worms are found in soil continuously under cultivation. They eat seed, resulting in almost a total loss of the planting of corn, peas and other grain.

Control—Use 10% Heptachlor granules in rows or broadcast over entire plot prior to planting.

Application—Use one and one-half pounds of 10% Heptachlor granules over 1,000 square feet when broadcasting prior to planting. Distribute in rows prior to planting. Use one-fourth pound of 10%

Heptachlor granules per 100 linear feet of row in 12-inch band, centered over furrow.

Helpful or Beneficial Insects

A great number of people are prone to think that all insects are harmful to either food, crops, shrubs, flowers, and are disadvantageous to mankind. Such is not the case. Scientists think that about one-tenth of all the insects in the world today actually may be helpful to man's economy. Assistance received from this small group of beneficial or helpful insects could mean the difference between balance of power and are essential to our over-all survival. There is no way of putting a dollar and cents valuation upon the benefit derived from such insects, but it runs into the millions of dollars. At least 50 of our important food crops are dependent upon pollinating insects—such as the bees, and for setting fruit, and as a result . . . seed.

Insect pests could ruin crops and vegetation if it weren't for the balanced power maintained by beneficial insects that capture and feed upon them, and also parasitic insects that help to check insect pests.

These scavengers or beneficial insects should receive our thanks for helping to keep the earth clean and sanitary. Some insects help aerate, fertilize, and condition the soil. There are also insects that make shellac, and others make dyes; the silk worm is the only producer of true silk, and only bees make honey and beeswax. Other benefits from insects are providing food for fish and animals, aiding in scientific research (even the common house fly fits in this category), and producing certain medicinal substances.

Knowing which insect to control and the one to leave alone is very important. Therefore, we wish to give a brief summary of those beneficial insects that are likely to be found in the Texas Gulf Coast that are helpful to you and me.

Honey Bee

This insect is recognized by practically all gardeners and is commended for the tremendously important job that they perform in the garden, especially in fruit orchards and legume fields for pollination.

Our greatest advantage in bees in Texas is helping to set a beautiful seed crop of clover. Of course, this is the source from which most of the honey bees derive the nectar that makes the wonderful honey that we all consume.

Bumble Bee

In some instances the bumble bee, where he stings a person, is considered a non-beneficial insect—but this is not true. Their greatest beneficial aspect is as pollinators once again. Collecting nectar from the flowering portions of plants and inadvertently carrying pollen from one flower to another, thus assuring setting of a crop.

The only time a bumble bee should be destroyed is when it is likely to cause painful injury through stings.

Carpenter Bee

This insect is dark bluish-green and less than one-half inch long. It nests normally in the pith of various woody shrubs, especially the rose, and for this reason a lot of folks are tempted to destroy it. Of course, if it does infest the pith of a rose it is a harmful insect and should be controlled.

But, these bees also act as pollinators of various crops and are a beneficial insect, unless they start doing damage to the rose plant.

Normally they are easily detected on a rose by the opening into the stem itself, and when the cut stem shows a hole in the pith, this is a definite sign that it is caused by the carpenter bee. Slitting the stem lengthwise usually reveals a half dozen or so yellowish curved maggots in the cavity, which is the larvae developing stage of the carpenter bee. They are very difficult to control once they infest the pith of the stalk of a rose plant. The best thing is to cut the stalk down and destroy it.

Braconid Wasp

These wasps belong to the Braconidae family and are characterized by being small with a short abdomen. Their greatest benefit to mankind is the fact that they attack aphids. They also lay their eggs for future generations in many caterpillars, and the larvae emerge simultaneously. They can kill literally thousands of aphids on plants in a very short time, and therefore should not be destroyed at all.

Lady Beetle

These insects are also called Lady Bird Beetles and Lady Bugs. They are small, one-sixth to one-fourth inch long, red or sometimes tan with black spots, or black with red spots. They are easily recognized by most folks in the gardening business and are recognized to be helpful insects. They are known to be ferocious eaters of aphids or plant lice. The life cycle of this insect takes 12 days in warm weather, 20 to 35 days in cool weather. As a full grown larvae—Lady Beetles consume about 25 aphids a day, and when they change to beetles the daily quota goes to 50. In an average season the aphid population may be reduced enough so that spraying is not necessary, thus saving the gardener money.

Praying Mantis

These insects are easily identified and belong to the grasshopper family. They eat other insects, capturing their prey with marvelous front legs, long and muscular, fitted with grooves and spines for grasping and holding. They get their name from the position they take as they wait for an insect—the position is normally in an attitude of prayer.

Baby Mantis, looking ridiculously like their older folks, except for wings, are cannibals from the day that they are born. They start with aphids, or perhaps one another, going on to larger insects as they grow. A full grown praying mantis is not afraid to strike at a frog or lizard or a hornet. There are about 20 known species in the North American Continent, and we have about three to four of them in this immediate area.

Dragon Fly

The dragon fly is found more predominantly in marshy wet places than on dry land, and around fresh water especially. They are large insects and youngsters often times call them Snake Doctors. They feed on many insects captured in flight, such as mosquitos and etc., and they are seen basically around fresh water more than anywhere else.

Ant Lion

The Ant Lion is another of our graceful flying insects that captures a number of insects in the air. The adult is very graceful, the larvae is the doodle bug, and digs a pit—partially burying itself in the bottom, waiting for ant victims. The pupa rests in the sand cocoon until it emerges as an adult moth, characterized by two pair of wings and a long slender abdomen.

Aphid Lion

These insects, when fully grown, measure about 3/8 inch in length. They have a lace wing larvae, and they feed on aphids or plant lice, as well as other insects, and often times go unobserved by the gardener.

One unusual characteristic of this insect is that they use a stake to leave their egg on the leaf, and this in itself prevents other insects from consuming the larvae when they hatch out.

Digger Wasp

This insect, when fully grown, is about three-fourths inch in length, has all the natural characteristics of belonging to the wasp family. It is a nest builder—either in the earth or in dead wood. They feed upon insects by paralyzing them first with their venomous sting, and then the larvae feed upon the insect. Often times the insect, that is devoured, is of harmful nature.

Glossary of Terms

The technical names of most insecticides and fungicides have very little meaning to the average gardener. In order to facilitate better understanding of the various terms, it is advisable to list a number of terms used in connection with the manufacturer's distribution and use of agricultural chemicals.

In order to keep it brief and to the point, we have concised the definitions and used a non-scientific language in order to facilitate easier understanding. The following terms are used at your local feed, seed and fertilizer store. In order for you to be better acquainted with various formulations and so forth of insecticides, fungicides, and rodenticides; we list the following:

1. AEROSOL SPRAYS—A fine spray which leaves particles of a pesticide chemical suspended in the air. So far as quantity is concerned, these are the most expensive for the amount of insecticide purchased. The reason, of course, is in the cost of manufacturing the aerosol cans and the small quantity of insecticides required to build an aerosol spray.

2. ACTIVE INGREDIENTS—Any ingredient in a pesticide which has pesticidal action.

3. PESTICIDE—Any chemical compound effective in killing or controlling pests.

4. BASIC MANUFACTURER—A chemical processing company which produces active pesticide chemicals, and generally sold to formulators for the formulation of insecticides sold under various brand names. As an example: Hercules Powder Company is a basic manufacturer of Toxaphene, yet various insecticide companies throughout the United States and the world utilize Toxaphene in their brand name products.

5. CARRIER—An inert material mixed with an active pesticide chemical to make an insecticidal dust or spray material.

6. CONTROL—A prevention or reduction of crop or property loss due to insect, plant disease, weed, or rodent attack.

7. DEFOLIANT—A chemical which causes leaves or foliage to drop from plants to make harvesting easier. This is of great concern to the cotton industry, as generally where mechanical picking is carried out, a defoliant is applied to the plant, causing it to shed its leaves. As a result the bolls open, thus facilitating rapid, clean picking by mechanical cotton pickers.

8. DESICCANT—A chemical which artificially speeds the drying of plant tissue to make harvesting easier. Here again, this one is used primarily in the cotton industry in order to facilitate the drying of the stalk, making it more readily available for stripping of cotton by mechanical machines.

9. DILUENT—An inert agent used to dilute an active insecticide chemical—such as the addition of water to, say for instance a DDT solution, reduce it in strength.

10. DUST—An active pesticide chemical mixed with suitable carriers, diluents and other inert material into an insecticidal dust.

11. ENTOMOLOGIST—A scientist who studies insects, and makes a career of bugs and their control.

193

12. FORMULATOR—A manufacturer who obtains active pesticide chemicals from a basic manufacturer and mixes the active pesticide chemical with carriers, diluents and other materials to produce a usable pesticide material.

13. FORMULATION—A mixture of an active pesticide chemical with carriers, diluents and other materials into a pesticide material. For example: A 5% emulsible Malathion would be a formulation.

14. FUNGICIDE—An active chemical or a formulation used to prevent or cure plant diseases caused by fungi. An example would be Terraclor—a fungicide which is used to control the Brown Patch fungus in St. Augustine grass.

15. HERBICIDE—An active chemical or formulation used to kill unwanted vegetation, primarily and principally a weed. An example would be 2, 4-D weed killer.

16. INERT INGREDIENTS—Any ingredient in a formulation which has no pesticide action. Example would be the finely ground clay particles—known as dust, mixed with a pesticide chemical to formulate a pesticide, such as 10% DDT dust. It is strictly a carrier or an inert material that is used to carry the active material on to the plant and has no killing power whatsoever.

17. INSECTICIDE—An active chemical or formulation used to kill unwanted insects. Such chemicals would be Chlordane, DDT, Malathion, etc., all are insecticides. Anything to kill insects.

18. PESTICIDE RESIDUE—The deposits of a pesticide chemical which may remain in or on a surface after the application of a pesticide, and of great interest to all farmers and vegetable folks who must utilize pesticide chemicals on edible products. The Food and Drug Administration has set a level of tolerance in so far as the application of certain chemicals on specific crops.

19. PLANT REGULATOR—A chemical which exhilarates, retards or otherwise alters the behavior of plants. A good example of this is gibberellic acid.

20. PLANT PATHOLOGIST—A scientist who studies plant diseases and makes diagnosis of those diseases on particular plants, shrubs and etc.

21. RESIDUE TOLERANCE—This is the amount of pesticide chemical residue which may legally remain in or on a crop (food crop) when the crop enters interstate commerce. The residue tolerance is established by the Food and Drug Administration to assure consumers of complete safety in respect to use of pesticides in food production.

22. RODENTICIDE—An active chemical or formulation used to kill unwanted rodents. Such things would be rat poisons, mole poisons and etc.

23. SPRAYS—A mixture of an active pesticide chemical with carriers, diluents and other materials into a liquid material which can be sprayed.

24. WETTABLE POWDER—A mixture of an active pesticide chemical into a powder which can be used either as a dust or can be dissolved in water and used as a spray. Most of these are designated by a "W" on the bag, or the identification as wettable. Such as 50% wettable DDT.

Twelve Simple Suggestions for Spray and Dust Safety

Today's agricultural chemicals are made to provide a maximum amount of safety, both to the growers and to consumers. Like all tools, however, care must be used in handling them. The following twelve simple rules are published by the National Agricultural Chemical Association in the interest of maximum safety in the use of sprays and dusts for the control of pests and fungus.

1. ALWAYS read the label before using sprays or dusts. Note warnings and cautions each time before opening container.

2. Keep sprays and dusts out of the reach of children, pets and irresponsible people. They should be stored outside of the home and away from food and feed.

3. Always store sprays and dusts in original containers, and keep them tightly closed. NEVER keep them in anything but the original container.

4. Avoid inhaling sprays or dusts, and when directed on the label— wear protective clothing and masks.

5. Never smoke while spraying or dusting.

6. Do not spill sprays or dusts on the skin or clothes. If they are spilled, remove contaminated clothing immediately and wash thoroughly.

7. Wash hands and face and change to clean clothing after spraying or dusting. Also, wash clothing each time before reuse.

8. Cover food and water containers when treating around livestock or in the kitchen, or wherever food might be kept. Do not contaminate fish ponds.

9. Use separate equipment for applying hormone type herbicides in order to avoid accidental injury to susceptible plants.

10. Always dispose of empty containers so that they hold no hazard to humans, animals or valuable plants.

11. Observe label directions and cautions to keep residues on edible portions of plants within the limits permitted by law.

12. If symptoms of illness occur during or shortly after spraying or dusting—call a physician or get the patient to a hospital immediately.

Sprays and dusts are effective farming and gardening tools if you follow these simple rules.

To the average household gardener the use of insecticides has become a complicated procedure. There are various strengths, various concentrations, various types of materials, and by the time the gardener reads the various labels on different products, he becomes so confused that often times he throws up his hands in complete disgust. Not knowing which way to turn, afraid that he will apply too much material and kill his plants, run the danger of injuring himself, and etc., that he decides to give up and let the insects have it.

Controlling insects on shrubs, flower plants, vegetables and etc., is a constant battle, and one must be ready at all times with a spray gun or the duster in order that the flowers, shrubs and vegetables will perform to the maximum of their ability. With dust, one has very little trouble because it is already formulated. All you have to do is apply it with a dusting gun. But, when it comes to spray mixtures, various concentrations of materials, carriers and etc., make it quite complicated. However, let's try to make it as simple as possible.

Making Up Spray Mixtures

Measurements must be exact, so keep with your spray materials a set of plastic measuring spoons, a glass measuring cup marked in ounces, then remember your household measurements:

> 3 level teaspoonfuls—equal 1 level tablespoon
> 2 tablespoons—equal 1 fluid ounce
> 16 tablespoons—equal 1 cup or 8 fluid ounces
> 2 cups—equal 1 pint
> 4 cups—equal 1 quart
> 16 cups—(4 quarts)—equal 1 gallon

Thus by a little figuring you can save a lot of time in measuring. If directions call for one and two-thirds tablespoons—you can be exact by measuring one tablespoon and two teaspoons. But, if you need eight tablespoons—it is a lot quicker to measure out one-half cup. If you are making up a dormant oil spray at 1 to 15 dilution—put in one cup of oil and add water to make one gallon. But, if you want a summer spray of one to 50 dilution—you add three gallons (that is 48 cupfuls of water to 1 cup of oil). The actual dilution is in 1 to 49, but that is near enough in such a great dilution.

If directions in a bulletin or publication calls for one pint in 100 gallons—just figure that that means one pint in 800 pints, or a 1-800 dilution; one quart to 100 gallons is a 1-400 dilution. The following table will help in transposing figures for any amount of spray that you wish.

DILUTION TABLE FOR SPRAYS

Desired Amount of Finished Spray	Amount of Concentrated Spray for Dilution			
	1-200	1-400	1-600	1-800
1 quart	1 tsp.	½ tsp.	1/3 tsp.	½ tsp.
1 gallon	4 tsp.	2 tsp.	1½ tsp.	1 tsp.
5 gallons	6 tbsp.	3 tsp.	2¼ tbsp.	1½ tbsp.
50 gallons	1 quart	1 pint	1½ cups	1 cup
100 gallons	2 quarts	1 quart	1½ pints	1 pint

When it comes to mixing sprays with dry materials, directions are usually given in pounds of chemical per 100 gallons of water. For instance: three pounds of 50% wettable DDT to 100 gallons of water. Transplanting pounds to tablespoons for small amounts of spray is difficult because of the difference in the weight of the various compounds. For instance: One ounce of lead of arsenic is 5½ tablespoons; where one ounce of calomel is only 1¾ tablespoonfuls. Wettable sulfur is about 3 tablespoonfuls to an ounce, and hydrated lime 4 to 5 tablespoons to an ounce, whereas 50% wettable DDT is about 6 tablespoons to an ounce. Measurements also vary according to whether the material is fluffed up or packed down hard. In purchasing dry materials for garden use, read the label to see how many pounds are recommended to 100 gallons of water, and then figure how many grams or ounces that means for one gallon. Then weight that amount out and see how many tablespoons it fills and mark it one the package for frequent use in the days ahead. Remember that 453.6 grams equal one pound, and that 28.35 grams equal one ounce.

In making sprays, the usual method is to make a slurry by adding water very slowly to the dry material, stirring constantly. But, some chemicals work better sprinkled on top of a pail of water. Directions on the package will generally tell you as to the best method to mix it. Some compounds work better if a spreader-sticker or other commercial compound is used in order to get the dry mix to stick to, oftentimes, on oily type leaf surface.

DILUTION CHART FOR MIXING SPRAYS

Insecticides	100 gals.	5 gals.	1 gal.
Aldrin 25% Emulsion Concentrate	1½ pt.	1 oz.	1 tsp.
Aldrin 25% Wettable Powder	1¾ qt.	1½ oz.	2 tsp.
Armite 25% Emulsion Concentrate	1 qt.	1½ oz.	2 tsp.
Armite 15% Wettable Powder	3 lb.	2 oz.	1 tbl.
Chlordane 40% Emulsion Concentrate	1 qt.	1½ oz.	2 tsp.
Chlordane 40% Wettable Powder	2 lb.	1½ oz.	2 tsp.
DDT 25% Emulsion Concentrate	2 qt.	3 oz.	4 tsp.
DDT 50% Wettable Powder	2 lb.	1½ oz.	2 tsp.
Dieldrin 20% Emulsion Concentrate	1 pt.	1 oz.	1 tsp.
Dieldrin 25% Wettable Powder	1 lb.	1 oz.	1 tsp.
Emulsifier (Soap) Use with Nicotine Sulphate	4 lb.	2 oz.	1 in. cu.
Lead Arsenate	3 lb.	2½ oz.	2 tbl.
Lime Sulfur, Dormant Spray	9 gal.	3 pt.	1½ cups
Lindane 25% Emulsion Concentrate	1 pt.	1 oz.	2 tsp.
Lindane 25% Wettable Powder	1 lb.	1 oz.	2 tsp.
Malathion 50% Emulsion Concentrate	1 pt.	1 oz.	2 tsp.
Malathion 25% Wettable Powder	2 lb.	1½ oz.	2 tbl.
Miscible Oils (3½% for Dormant Spray)	3½ gal.	1½ pt.	9 tbl.
Miscible Oils (1½% for Summer Spray)	1½ gal.	½ pt.	3 tbl.

Nicotine Sulphate	1 pt.	1 oz.	1 tsp.
Toxaphene 60% Emulsion Concentrate	3 pt.	2½ oz.	1 tbl.
Toxaphene 40% Wettable Powder	5 lb.	4 oz.	2 tbl.
Wettable Sulfur (325 mesh)	7 lb.	1/3 lb.	3 tbl.

Pesticide Tolerances

On ornamentals, flowers, lawns and trees tolerance level means absolutely nothing, because the *tolerance is established for animals and humans that would consume the plants on which the insecticide has been applied.* The only precaution that must be taken in the application of such insecticide with these type plants is to the applicator himself from the standpoint of safe application.

More and more emphasis is being placed on the restrictions and the use of chemical insecticides, both on crops, livestock and also vegetables and fruits. This has all come about by the crack-down of the Food & Drug Administration through the U. S. Department of Health and Welfare. Therefore, it is becoming increasingly important that a person who uses insecticides around the home, on the vegetable garden, must of necessity acquaint himself with the various insecticides that can be used and how they must be used for safe control.

Since the advent of the crack-down by the FDA and the U. S. Health and Welfare Agency, the word *TOLERANCE* has come to mean a great deal to the general public. What is tolerance? The tolerance is simply the amount of a pesticide which scientists have determined may safely remain as a residue on a food crop without injury to the consumer. The tolerance is specific for the pesticide and the crop. It is set by regulation. The Food & Drug Administration first considers evidence of safety and the amount of residue which will remain if the product is used according to the directions on the label. The FDA then sets a "tolerance" which will be safe and which can be met if the directions are followed.

If a tolerance is not necessary for protection of the consumer, the Food & Drug Administration may exempt a particular use from requirements for a tolerance. A limited number of pesticide chemicals have been officially declared safe and do not require either a tolerance or exemption. Except for these products, no amount of residue of a particular chemical on a specified crop is permissible if (1) there is no tolerance or exemption, (2) the tolerance is zero. However, the absence of a published tolerance or exemption does not necessarily imply that a pesticide chemical may not be used. Some pesticide uses for example, certain dormant sprays and soil treatments do not result in residues of the chemical on the harvested crop. Uses which do not leave residue do not require tolerances or exemptions and do not have to be passed upon by the Food & Drug Administration.

This is of great importance to the commercial producer who is producing vegetables and fruits for the consuming public. Nevertheless, it is just as important to the individual home owner who is using pesticides to control insects on his own homegrown vegetables, because what will apply for one will also apply for the other. As far as I know, your pesticide manufacturers live by this tolerance level and give explicit instructions on the use of a particular insecticide or pesticide on a given crop, with detailed information on the application and the concentration of the same on the label.

Therefore, the following restrictions should be adhered to:

Restriction 1. Do not apply DDT or Toxaphene to beet, broccoli, brussels sprouts, carrot, kohlrabi, leaf lettuce, rutabaga, or turnip after first appearance of leaves, stems, or heads that are to be eaten, marketed, or fed to poultry, dairy animals, or animals being finished for slaughter.

Restriction 2. Do not use Parathion, TEPP, Phosdrin, or Demeton in the home garden. These insecticides are extremely poisonous and should be applied only by a trained operator who will enforce the precautions prescribed by the manufacturers and assume full responsibility for safety.

Restriction 3. Do not feed plants treated with DDT or Toxaphene to dairy animals or animals being finished for slaughter.

Restriction 4. Do not apply Chlordane to leafy vegetables past the seedling stage of growth, or after the appearance of foliage that is to be eaten, marketed, or fed to dairy or meat animals.

Restriction 5. Do not use Lindane in fields to be planted later to potatoes or other root crops, as it may adversely affect their flavor.

Restriction 6. Aerosols that are effective for use on plants usually contain the poison gas, methyl chloride. Regardless of the insecticide in these aerosols, they should be applied only by a trained operator who will enforce the precautions prescribed by the manufacturers and assume full responsibility for safety.

Restriction 7. Do not apply DDT or Toxaphene to cabbage or to head lettuce after the heads begin to form if any of the outer leaves are to be left on them at harvest. DDT and Toxaphene may be applied up to seven days before harvest if all outer leaves are stripped from the heads at harvest.

What Is a Combination Dust and Spray?

Combinations of dusts and sprays are not named as such by the manufacturer. These mixtures are sold under various trade names and all brands contain a mixture of two or more insecticides. For example, one mixture may contain DDT plus Malathion, while another will contain DDT, Malathion plus Lindane. One commercial mixture contains DDT, Lindane, Malathion and Tedion. DDT will control a large variety of beetles and worms, but will not control aphids, scales, spider mites and similar pests. Malathion will control some worms, beetles and many of the sucking insects such as aphids, scales and some species of spider

199

mites. Lindane will control a wide variety of pests but it works best on sucking insects. Tedion is a new insecticide and is rather specific for controlling red spiders.

Don't expect the following recommendations to work one hundred percent in every case. Improper spray equipment could be a limiting factor.

In controlling several pests around the home, it is not necessary to use a combination spray or dust in every instance. One certain insecticide will do the job as well as two or three mixed together. If an insect is attacking flowers, trees or shrubs and feeding on the foliage, the combination insecticides will generally give good results. It is best to recommend that the home owner use these mixtures in those cases where you are not sure what insect is involved.

The best control is generally obtained with sprays. It is difficult to get dust to adhere to some of the slick-leaved ornamental plants. Dusts are handy to use and will give satisfactory results if only a few small plants are to be treated.

1. LAWN PESTS:

   Ants, chiggers, white grubs, sod webworms and termites—(Chlordane, Heptachlor or Dieldrin). Fleas—Treat infested areas with Malathion or Diazinon.

2. FLOWERS AND SHRUBS:

   A. Insects feeding on leaves, flowers, and stems, such as cucumber beetles, grasshoppers, aphids, bed bugs, leafhoppers, red spiders, ants, bagworms, white flies, mealybugs, scale, leaf rollers, thrips and many others. (Combination sprays or combinations dusts are recommended)

   B. Soil insects, such as wireworms, white grubs, cutworms, rootworms, mole crickets. (Chlordane, Heptachlor, Lindane or Dieldrin)

   C. Snails, sowbugs, millipedes, earwigs, cutworms, grasshoppers. (Commercially prepared baits or combination sprays or dusts to control all pests except snails)

3. SHADE TREES

   A. Chewing Insects—Webworms and tent worms—worms feeding in the open. Beetles, leaf rollers and leaf skeletonizers. (Combination sprays)

   B. Sucking Insects—Aphids, plant bugs, lace bugs, red spiders, scales. (Combination sprays, Lindane, Malathion, Diazinon— use oil in dormant season for scales. Other insecticides mentioned will control the young scale, but will not control the adults which have the protective covering over their bodies)

   C. Wood Borers—Once borers become established in the tree, they are very difficult to control. Two common groups of borers which attack trees are the round headed (long-horned beetles) and flatheaded borers. The larvae of round headed borers make galleries beneath the bark and also tunnel into the heart-wood. Flatheaded borers tunnel beneath the bark making long, shallow, winding galleries packed with frass. See section on Tree Borers in this chapter.

Controlling Plant Pests Around the Home

In controlling ornamental pests there are five basic principles:
1. Good equipment for applying the insecticide.
2. Select the proper insecticide.
3. Apply the insecticide in the proper manner.
4. Start control measures before serious damage occurs.
5. Repeat applications must be made in 7 to 10 days to control certain pests such as scales, white flies and red spiders.

It is desirable to know as many ornamental pests as possible and in some instances it is essential to have this information on hand. The main points you need to know are how the insect is causing damage and the part of plant it is feeding on.

There are several brands of combination dusts and sprays on the market and any of these combinations will generally give good control of a large variety of sucking and chewing insects. These insecticides are packaged in small containers designed for home use and all directions for applying the insecticides can be found on the label.

Chapter 9

Plant Diseases and Their Control

First you'll find mention of diseases that are common to specific plants—all arranged alphabetically. Then there is a section on diseases common to most plants.

Azalea Diseases

FLOWER SPOT (PETAL BLIGHT)—Whitish spots on open flowers; all flowers on the plant may suddenly wilt. Later the small black scleortia form on dried blighted flowers. Petals only are attacked.

Spray open flowers with Dithane Z-78 or Zineb at least three times in a week, starting when plants are coming into bloom.

LEAF GALL—Distorted leaf and bud growth with whitish thickened areas.

Removal and burning of affected parts is usually sufficient to control this malady, but in severe cases spray twice with a Bordeaux mixture at intervals of about 10 to 14 days.

CHLOROSIS—The symptom of this disease is yellowing, primarily of the young foliage near the tips of the branches. Later, leaves on the older portion of the plant may become yellowed. Leaves are pale with the veins dark green, and severe chlorosis eventually causes lack of vigor, production and yield of flower unit, and can cause death to the plants.

Proper applications of iron bearing compounds such as iron chelates or iron sulfate to the soil around the feeder roots of the plant generally brings about a rapid recovery. But, only a temporary one, as there is no known complete 100% cure of this malady, in so far as a permanent cure. As the leaves begin to turn yellow, once again repeat the application—let the plant tell you when it needs iron.

COTTON ROOT ROT—Plants attacked by cotton root rot generally die suddenly after first symptoms of wilting. When pulled from the soil the bark of the azaleas, especially the root system, is decayed and frequently brownish, and woolly strands of fungus are on the surface. In affected plants the whole root system decays and the plants slip out of the soil with little pulling effort.

After a plant has been affected with cotton root rot there is little that can be done. However, if such should occur in azalea beds, the best thing to do is to fumigate the bed using Methyl Bromide in order to destroy the fungus that causes cotton root rot, or plant varieties that are resistant to this particular malady. A new product has recently moved onto the market scene, it is Plantation Nematode and Root Rot Cure. If applied in time, it will control the fungus. Follow manufacturer's directions.

Bean Mosaic

Bean mosaics are a group of diseases, growers are likely to overlook. These virus diseases are very common on fall beans in all areas of Texas.

A mosaic virus disease may infect every bean plant in a field. It reduces yield, quality and selling price. The disease rarely kills a plant. Often it produces no conspicuous symptoms.

Damage by common bean mosaic results in stunting of the plant. Irregular light and dark green areas occur in the leaves. Leaves may be crinkled and puckered. Sometimes leaves are longer and narrower and display a downward cupping. Pods may be rough and shiny and be seriously deformed.

Aphids carry the viruses that cause the mosaic diseases. They spread the virus by feeding on infected plants and then on healthy plants. Sweetclover, crimson clover, red clover and gladiola are hosts of some of the bean viruses. Normal looking bean seed may also carry the viruses. A few of the less common bean viruses are spread in the fields by cultivation, roguing, or picking.

Some bean virus diseases are controlled by growing mosaic-resistant varieties. Others are reduced by destroying nearby hosts. Avoid planting beans near clovers or gladiolus. Always obtain good, disease-free bean seed from a reputable dealer.

Cabbage Diseases

BLACK ROT—The characteristics of this disease is a blackened leaf vein near the margin of the leaves, stems show a blackened ring when cut across, leaves turn yellow and drop, and the plants may eventually die. If this disease should persist, one of the best recommendations is to rotate with crops other than the cabbage family for two or three years. Discard and destroy all plants as the disease occurs in the seed bed where cabbage sets are being grown.

As a chemical control measure, it would be advisable to soak the cabbage seeds for 20 minutes in bichloride of mercury—at one part per 1000 parts of water, rinse the seed in clear water, dry surface, and plant the seed at once.

CABBAGE YELLOWS—This disease causes the plants to appear yellow and stunted. The disease first attacks one side of the plant, then the other. The lower leaves die and drop off. The disease is caused by a fungus in the soil, and as a control it is best to plant seed in a disease free soil, if possible, or fumigate the soil with Methyl Bromide. There are a few resistant varieties to this particular disease, mainly Marion Market and Globe.

DOWNEY MILDEW—This disease is characterized by moldy spots on the seedling leaves. Spots are formed on older leaves, heads and seed stalks of cabbage. About the best control measure for this malady is to locate the seed bed in a new place each year and plant seed far enough apart so that seedlings will not be crowded. You should spray or dust the seed beds weekly with Spergon. For those who are trying to grow cabbage from seed, transplant only the healthy seedlings into the garden.

Camellia Diseases

CANKER AND DIE BACK—Dead twigs and small branches are the symptoms of this disease and canker like areas on larger branches and main trunk. Pale spots on leaves and grey blotches on bark may be an early infection. Prune all dead wood.

In addition to pruning all dead wood remove infected wood and cankers and paint the wound with asphalt emulsion, thinned with a 4% Lysol. Spray the bark twice a year with one-half tablespoon of 50% copper compound, plus one-half teaspoon of Casco glue in one gallon of water.

LEAF SPOT—This disease is characterized by brown spots on the leaf. The leaf my die back gradually from the tip end. Small black specks in the dead areas of the leaf is also apparent.

Preventive control is by far the best, for after this disease has taken hold there is very little hope for a cure. A preventive control of spraying the plant frequently with either copper or Zineb, which is commonly called Dithane Z-78, generally will keep the plant from taking this disease. Also, destroy all fallen leaves and replace with well rotted compost or manure. Consan 20 will also give good control.

LEAF GALL—This disease is apparent when the leaves are swollen, misshapen and covered with a powdery substance. Affected leaves should be hand-picked and burned.

Heavy infestation can be controlled with an application of Bordeaux mixture. Follow the directions on the container for mixing.

Cedar and Arborvitae Twig Blight

Twig blight is a common disease for cedar, arborvitae, juniper and cypress. The fungus disease is more apt to be a problem in areas of higher rainfall or during seasons of above average rainfall. It occurs in epidemic form in coniferous nurseries and in ornmental plantings in the eastern half of the United States.

Tips of branches turn brown with progressive dying back. A whole branch or even a young tree may be killed. Trees over five years are not apt to be killed. A large amount of young nursery stock can be blighted in a very short time.

Microscopic fungus seed (spores) are produced in quantity on diseased twigs and branches. Spores ooze out in little tendrils in moist weather to be spread by wind and rain. Germinating spores gain entrance through healthy wood as well as through wounds. Wetting foliage with the lawn sprinkler encourages the spread of the disease.

Prune off and burn dying branches during the dormant season. Make the pruning cut several inches below the diseased area. Avoid leaving branch stubs when pruning. In nurseries the diseased seedlings should be removed and burned as soon as possible.

Spray with a fixed copper or Bordeaux mixture fungicide after pruning. Make three applications at three week intervals through the winter or spring. More applications may be necessary if above average rainfall occurs. When landscaping, buy healthy trees and shrubs.

Fig Diseases

FIG RUST—Fig rust is a fungus disease which attacks the foliage. Rusty brown spots occur on the leaves with pustules containing yellowish spores on the underside. Often the leaves shrivel and fall, and an under-size, poor quality fruit is produced.

The disease can be controlled by spraying the newly developed leaves with a Bordeaux mixture. Applications should start in early June and continue at intervals of three or four weeks as long as new leaves are forming. Both the lower and the top sides of the leaves should be sprayed.

ROOT-ROT NEMATODE—The root-rot nematode is common in fig trees. This pest devitalizes the tree and stunts its growth. No resistant rootstocks are available. If the plants are watered adequately and fertilized, growth will be satisfactory despite the nematode. Treat infested trees with Plantation Nematode Killer.

COTTON ROOT ROT—This disease often attacks the fig and does a great damage south and west of San Antonio. The symptoms are similar to those of most root rots in that the tree wilts suddenly and dies. A yearly application of Plantation Nematode and Root Rot Cure will control it.

SOURING DISEASE—Souring is a disease caused by several bacteria and yeasts. Souring organisms are introduced by insects, primarily the dried-fruit beetle, which almost invariably is found in full ripened fruits with open eyes. The only practical remedies known are planting varieties such as Celeste and Kadota which have eyes that prevent the entry of the insects, harvesting the fruit before it is fully mature and destroying the fallen fruits which have soured. Several insecticides are reported to have controlled the dried-fruit beetles, but it is not known whether the fruit retains enough of the insecticide to be damaging to humans.

However, if one intends to use an insecticide to control the dried-fruit beetle, the best insecticide to use is Malathion spray since it has been recommended to be used on green leafy vegetables—with only about a seven-day waiting period prior to consumption. There is no reason why this would not also work just as good on figs as on green leafy vegetables such as turnip greens.

Grape Diseases

BLACK ROT IN GRAPEVINES—Black rot disease is quite prevalent during wet seasons and affects the vines, leaves and fruits of the grapevine. The disease appears in the leaves as reddish-brown dead spots, and in half grown fruit as pale spots which turn brown, enlarge and soon involve the entire berry. Later, the infected berries become shriveled, black mummys which may fall to the ground, all remain in clusters. All infected vines should be pruned out and the fallen mummied fruit and leaves, as well as pruning trimmings in which the fungus may over-winter should be raked together and burned.

Control—When new shoots are about three to six inches long it is advisable to apply a Bordeaux mixture to the vine. This Bordeaux mixture is commonly referred to as an 8-8-100 Bordeaux mixture. *Or,* you could use two pounds of Dithane Z-78 to 100 gallons of water. Completely cover the entire vine for maximum control.

Hibiscus Diseases

BUD DROP—This malady is characterized by the abnormal dropping of buds.

There is no chemical control to correct this malady. The best thing to do is to avoid extremes of dry soil, extra vigorous growth, too much shade and cool weather. Any one of these factors will influence bud drop in hibiscus. Or apply Medina around plant.

SOUTHERN BLIGHT—Symptoms of this disease is generally small, seed-like structures that are found along with a whitish fungus growth at the base of the infected plants. Plants may wilt and die within a few days, and if the soil is dried out it may be necessary to pull the plant to make a complete diagnosis. Positive diagnosis can be made this way. Place suspected plant parts in a plastic bag, tie the end of the bag securely, after having placed two or three moist paper towels inside the bag with the specimen. After six to 14 days, typical white bodies, about the size of mustard seed, will have formed among the white fungus growth. The fungus grows mostly in the top one or two inches of the soil where there is sufficient oxygen. This disease is more damaging following a period of drouth. A soil temperature of 85° F. or higher is necessary for the disease to develop.

Irish Potato Diseases

SCAB—This disease is characterized by roundish or irregular rough, corky areas that occur on the surface of the tubers. Injury does not extend far into the potato, but scabby potatoes have objectionable appearance and of course have very little sales value.

A person should always rotate his crop, never grow two crops on the same land in consecutive years. It is always wise to use certified seed when planting Irish potatoes, and it is also advisable to soak the seed tubers, before cutting, in corrosive sublimate—using one ounce to eight gallons of water. Soak them for about 90 minutes. This disease is most prevalent in soils that are high in lime—therefore you should used acid forming commercial fertilizers when scab has been bad.

I would suggest, when growing potatoes in scab infested land, to use an acid forming fertilzer. Avoid, by all means, using barnyard manures in areas where scab is known to infest the soil. In some instances sucessful work has been done whereby Terraclor has been used in badly infested soil. Apply according to manufacturers recommendation.

EARLY BLIGHT—This disease is characterized by small brownish spots, often with a faint concentric ring found on the lower leaves first. Several spots may run together to kill a portion of the leaf. For a control —dust with Zineb, or Dithane Z-78, or Bordeaux mixture—using two quarts of Nabam, plus one pound of zinc sulfate in 100 gallons of water. Apply weekly if needed, and during rainy or foggy weather—sprays or dusts should be applied more frequently than in dry weather. Sprays are better than dusts when applied properly. If you use Zineb, be sure and use it according to the manufacturers recommendations.

Ligustrum Diseases
(for Privet, Magnolia, Gardenia, Holly)

LEAF SPOT—Many people notice leaf spots on Magnolia, Ligustrum, Euonymous, Gardenia, Holly, Photinia and other broadleaf evergreens, especially in areas of high rainfall. These fungal leaf spots may be of different sizes and colors. They lower the esthetic value of trees and shrubs; however, the plants are damaged little since the damage is on one year old leaves that are about ready to naturally fall from the tree or shrub. Several different fungi or molds may cause these leaf spots.

If the value of the shrub or shade tree is high enough to justify the cost, a preventive spray program is effective in reducing the damage by leaf spots. Use two tablespoons of Captan or two tablespoons of Zineb per gallon of water. Add a spreader-sticker to the spray. A combination of Zineb and Captan may be more effective. Zineb or Captan may be used with safety during any part of the year. It is more important to have plants protected during times of above average rainfall or high humidity.

With bacterial leaf spots, it may be necessary to spray with a fixed or insoluble copper such as copper A compound or tri-basic copper sulfate. Bordeaux mixture may also be used. Use fixed copper or Bordeaux with care since they may damage leaves to some extent. The use of a spreader-sticker and avoiding hot weather will tend to lessen the spray damage.

Leaf spots may occur during the growing season. Continued premature loss of leaves may weaken a tree or shrub so that it is more susceptible to other troubles. A good spray program plus proper fertilization and watering will help improve health of trees and shrubs. Avoid wetting foliage while watering as this tends to spread leaf spots.

ANTHRACNOSE—The symptoms of this disease is that the leaves dry out and cling to the stem. The twigs are blighted and cankers are formed at the base of the main stem. Cankers may be spotted with pinkish pustules. Bark or wood of diseased portions become brown and the bark on the cankers become split, exposing the wood. Death occurs when the cankers completely encircle the twigs or stems. There are ligustrum varieties that are resistant to this disease.

There is no known control for it. The best thing to do, if your shrubs are attacked by this disease, is to pull them out and plant those varieties that are resistant to this disease.

Lettuce Diseases

DOWNEY MILDEW—Generally, the first symptom of downey mildew on lettuce is pale, green to yellow spots—usually angular in shape, which appear on the upper side of affected leaves. These spots may enlarge and join together to affect large areas. On the underside of the spots a white, fluffy fungus produces an abundance of spores capable of infesting other leaves. Under favorable conditions the white fungus growth and spore-lation may occur over both upper and lower surfaces of the spots, especially in the young seedling stage, prior to or at the time of planting. Unfortunately the spores of the fungus are carried by the wind, causing widespread distribution. Spore production and lettuce infestation are greatest when the air temperature is about 50° or 60° F., and the air has been extremely moist for five to seven hours. Rain, heavy dew or fog can provide heavy moisture. As far as we know, there are no varieties that are resistant to all strains of this fungus. The best control is Maneb, a fungicide, considered to be the best for control of downey mildew. Copper compounds cause some damage to the plant. Do not plant two years in succession on the same ground where this disease is prevalent.

LETTUCE MOSAIC—This disease is characterized by the light green to yellow mottling of young plant leaves. In young rosette stage, leaves shown vein clearing and bronzing. The mottling condition disappears in older plants. Older plants are stunted and are dull green to light yellow. The tips of older leaves roll downward and the underside of the plants have protruding leaf stalks, or a ribby appearance. The disease is carried in the seed and is spread in the field by aphids. About the only control measure is to make absolutely sure that you obtain mosaic free seed.

Oleander Bacterial Gall

Bacterial gall of oleander primarily occurs in the Southern half of Texas and is one of the most common disease of Oleanders. It occurs only in this one plant. Certain parts of the shrub may die back, galls or tumors are found on the dying branches. Galls also occur on shoots and flowers and leaves. The bacterial disease causes small swellings to develop on leaf veins, surrounded by yellow tissue. Sticky bacterial ooze comes from affected leaf veins in large quantities. Young shoots have elongated swellings with small knob like projections, and young leaves and seed pods may be distorted and curled. On the older branches, tumors are soft or spongy and rough with small projecting knob like growths; these slowly turn dark with age.

The disease can be controlled by pruning out affected portions. The pruning cut should be made several inches below the disease, and make sure your sterilize the pruning shears after each cut. Dip the shears in formaldehyde, using one part of formaldehyde to 25 parts of water, and destroy the diseased parts that are pruned. Propagate only from healthy plants and avoid purchasing plants that have symptoms of the disease.

Onion Diseases

DAMPENING OFF—Small seedling plants are attacked at or just below the soil line. The tissue shrinks rapidly at that point and the seedlings fall over. Generally, the disease occurs in rough surface spots of various size. There is no specific control measure known. Generally good cultural practices, including frequent cultivation, good drainage and good fertilty discourage dampening off. Seed should be treated prior to planting with Semesan or Arasan dust, according to the manufacturer's directions. Excellent control has been obtained in some cases where the soil, prior to planting, has been fumigated with Methyl Bromide.

BLAST—This disease is characterized by the leaves turning white from the tips downward within a few hours. In milder cases, white spots appear around the breathing pores of the leaf and gradually expand as the leaf dies back from the tip end. The damage continues, if bright sun persists, milder occurrence of cloudy weather may result in the plants returning to fairly normal growth. Looks somewhat like leaf blight. No effective control is known. The condition arises when a period of cloudy, wet weather, high temperature and high relative humidity is followed by one of bright sunshine, high temperature and low relative humidity.

LEAF BLIGHT—This disease is characterized by white spots of various sizes formed on the leaves, with black specks scattered throughout the dead area.

Control—Same as for the Purple Blotch—which is a preventive control. Spray or dust with Maneb or Zineb. Zineb, is the same as Dithane Z-78, and the application of this material should be done at the first sign of the disease. The variety "yellow Spanish" is more susceptible to leaf blight than the sweet Spanish onion.

PURPLE BLOTCH—This disease is characterized by large spots on the leaves becoming purplish. Pink fungus threads the inside of the leaf and often causes dying of the entire leaf surface. Apply preventive sprays or dusts.—using Zineb. Begin at the first sign of the disease and make additional applications as needed. Sprays seem to be more effective than dusts. Be sure and use a spreader-sticker solution. If one is available—

use a teaspoon of liquid detergent to cause the sprays to stick to the leaf, as the surface of the onion is very slick. Another suggestion is to be sure and rotate with resistant crops to this disease.

Pear Diseases

PEAR FIRE BLIGHT—Fire Blight is a very detrimental disease of pear trees, and is noticeable by the sudden die back of the growing twig of the tree, and a dark black discoloration of the dead area. It is very difficult to control. A timely control is essential. If Fire Blight has hit the tree during the growing season, the best recommendation is to prune out twigs and limbs that are affected during the winter. Make all cuts several inches below the visible canker on the affected area. Sterilize cutting instruments after each cut by dipping into a formaldehyde solution— whereby one part of formaldehyde is deposited into 25 parts of water. This is of great importance. Unless sterilization of the cutting instruments is carried out, this particular disease will be spread from one affected area to a healthy segment of the tree. After the twig or limb has been cut out, coat the wound with Bordeaux paste. Heavy pruning and over fertilization of trees causes excessive growth, which is very susceptible to Fire Blight.

An alternate suggestion in the control of Fire Blight is an application during the spring months, especially during the blossoming period, of Phytomycin. Phytomycin is a streptomycin formulation and will do a good job in controlling Fire Blight. This material is essentially a timely application. If you wait too late, it will do no good. Follow the directions on the container of Phytomycin—to the letter—for maximum control of Fire Blight in the spring. Consan 20 is also effective if applied according to directions.

Pecan Rosette

PECAN ROSETTE—This is a nutritional deficiency disease caused by certain soil conditions which make zinc unavailable to the pecan tree. All pecan trees require zinc for growth. Trees showing the first symptoms of zinc deficiency have yellowed tops. The individual leaflet when examined are yellowish and mottled.

Rosette is controlled readily by application of zinc sulfate to the tree, either as a foliage spray or in a dry form as a soil application.

Foliage Spray—Two pounds zinc sulfate (36%) per 100 gallons of water.

1st. Application—after pollination, when tips of nutlet turn brown.
2nd Application—3-4 weeks later.
3rd Application—3-4 weeks later.

Soil Application: Mildly rosetted trees—apply five pounds of zinc sulfate around drip line each year for 2-3 years. Severely rosetted trees —apply 5-10 pounds of zinc sulfate annually until rosette symptoms disappear.

Pecan Scab

PECAN SCAB—This disease, caused by a fungus, is the most destructive disease of pecans in Texas. The fungus invades the young, rapidly growing shoots and leaves, and later the developing nuts from highly scab susceptible varieties fall or fail to develop, resulting in a total nut crop loss. The disease on the leaves occur on the lower leaf surfaces and are characteristically olive brown, somewhat elongated in shape and vary in size from a barely discernible dot to lesions one-fourth or more in diameter. On the nuts, scab lesions appear as small black dots—which are elevated or sunken in older infestations. When infestation is severe, the entire nut surface is black in appearance, development is arrested and the nuts drop prematurely.

Control—Use 1½ pounds of Zineb per 100 gallons of water, *or* two tablespoons per gallon.

Application—Make first application when the first leaves are showing. However, good control can be obtained by combining first spray with insecticide application for control of casebearer. Spray every 21-30 days after first application for maximum production. Do not spray within 45 days of harvest. Thorough coverage of all foliage and branches is a must.

Pepper Diseases

SOUTHERN BLIGHT—This disease is characterized by a stem decay at or below the ground line. The plant soon wilts and dies. Whitish fungus may be seen on the stem during wet weather, small whitish to brownish seed-like fungus bodies may be present.

Remove the wilting plants. Do not allow plant refuse to remain on the soil, and rotate crops. In some instances, the application of three to four ounces of 75% Terraclor per 100 square feet, worked into the top three to 4 inches of the soil will control Southern Blight. Actually, there are three methods for controlling Southern Blight in peppers. One is by using Terraclor by watering it in; two—spraying Terraclor; and three —dusting.

(1) WATERING—Mix three to five pounds of 75% wettable Terraclor to 100 gallons of water, or this would roughly be about 12 tablespoons per five gallons of water and apply one-half pint of this material per plant at time of transplanting. Application should be at the base of the plant and on covering soil. This solution should be agited by thorough mixing before application.

(2) DUSTING—Dust 12 to 16 ounces of 20% Terraclor per 100 square feet over an open V trench—just before setting transplants. Set the plants in the bottom of the trench and then press the walls of the trench against the stems of the young transplants.

CURLY TOP—This disease is characterized by a rolling of the margins of older leaves, pronounced curling of the younger leaves, leaf stems curl sharply downward, plants eventually become yellow and dwarfed. Few, if any, form fruit or produce after infection. This disease is difficult to control; you should practice good management and control all weeds in and around the field. Thicker spacing of plants may help in some areas. Shade plants in the garden, be sure and plant early and use liberal fertilization. This disease is frequently transmitted by the Beet Leaf Hooper, and a control of this insect oftentimes will help to control Curly Top disease in peppers.

To control the Beet Leaf Hooper—Begin application of a 5% Malathion dust when plants are set in the field, and continue up to five days before harvest.

LEAF SPOT—This is characterized by large, light-colored, circular spots with dark borders on the leaves and stems. Oftentimes there is dead tissue and old spots that may become cracked and fall out—leaving large holes. For a control of leaf spot—spray the pepper plant with Zineb or Dithane Z-78, or Captan at weekly intervals or as needed. This is primarily caused by excessive rain.

MOSAIC—This is characterized by stunted plants, crinkled leaves that are mottled with yellow and green areas. Fruits are small and malformed. Destroy all plants showing Mosaic symptoms, also destroy weeds growing in the vicinity that show Mosaic. Keep down infestation of Aphids and be sure and wash your hands thoroughly with soap and water, if you are a cigarette or cigar smoker, before working around pepper plants. Tobacco Mosaic is carried in the tobacco of cigarettes and cigars.

Pyracantha Diseases

BACTERIAL FIRE BLIGHT—Symptoms of this disease appears as follows: The tips of the twigs or small branches die, with black or brown leaves remaining attached. Circular or elongated cankers on branches and stems of the plant, small droplets of orange or yellow bacterial exudate may be seen with hand lens on the underside of the leaf midribs and leaf petioles.

Prune the twigs and limbs during the wintertime, making sure that all cuts are several inches below the visible cankers. In so far as a spray is concerned, the only chemical that might control it would be Phytomycin, which is a Streptomycin compound. The first spray should be applied when the leaves on the new shoots begin to form. Additional sprays should be applied at five to seven day intervals, using a minimum of three sprays. Normally this will bring the malady under control.

Rose Diseases

POWDERY MILDEW—Home growers are advised to check their plantings for signs of the disease. The fungus appears as a white to grayish growth covering the surface of the plant parts, mainly the leaf surface. Dust the plants with 325-mesh sulfur at the first appearance of the disease or spray with wettable sulfur (one and one-half to two level tablespoons to one gallon). Repeat the application if needed.

Folpet has an advantage of being less toxic to plants. Folpet used as a dust or spray may give better control but is probably more expensive. Sulfur or Folpet are available in insecticide-fungicide combination sprays or dusts. Captan and Phaltan also are excellent fungicides.

Some of the more commonly grown plants which should be watched for mildew are violets, chrysanthemums, honeysuckle, phlox, zinnias, live oak, crape myrtle, euonymous and hydrangea.

Unless the disease is controlled, the plants may lose their foliage and thus fail to make normal growth and production.

BLACK SPOT—This disease is characterized by large, roundish, black spots with irregular or frayed margins. The spot may occur on either or both surfaces of the leaves, and frequently develop unnoticed on the soft twigs and branches, and also on the petioles and stipules of the leaves. When severely infested, the leaves may turn yellow and drop off. This weakens plants and makes them more susceptible to die-back, drouth and winter injury. It also results in smaller flowers that are weak in color and fragrance. One of the best preventative treatments is the sulfur-copper dust mixture, applied as for powdery mildew. If the disease becomes established, spraying once a week with Captan, Maneb, Zineb, Phaltan, Folpet, or Consan 20, is effective if care is taken to coat both sides of the leaves. A spray pressure of 150 to 300 pounds is desirable. Sulfur compounds are likely to cause burns in hot weather. Providing a good mulch just before new growth starts in the spring has been helpful in some cases.

DIE BACK—Die Back is a common disease apparent in roses throughout the South, and it is characterized by browning or blackening, and death of the stem—beginning at the old flower and progressing downward. Usually the disease occurs in bushes weakened by Black Spot defoliation, by drouth, or winter injury. Keep plants in healthy, actively growing condition, and by all means control Black Spot by either using dusting sulfur, Captan or Consan 20. Cut off all old flowers. Cut blooms with short stems until bushes become strong and vigorous.

Spinach Diseases

BLUE MOLD—This is a disease characterized by yellowish spots appearing on the upper surface of leaves of the spinach. Spots are covered underneath with a bluish-moldly growth. Later the entire leaf may be killed and the plant often dies from severe infection. In gardens, to control this malady—you should plant on ridges and avoid crowding of the plants. In field production—use Dithane Z-78 dust or a spray of 2 quarts of Nabam, plus 1 pound of Zinc Sulfate in 100 gallons of water. Begin applications at first sign of the disease and apply at weekly to 10 day intervals as needed.

213

CUCUMBER MOSAIC (BLIGHT)—The characteristics of this disease is that the young plants are chlorotic. In other words, the coloring of the leaf has been leached out. The leaves are malformed, wrinkled, rolled inward, or small and feathery. There is no known control measure for this particular malady, the only thing suggested is to plant a variety that is resistant to the cucumber mosaic. Those varieties would be: Virginia, Savoy, Califlay and Early Hybrid #7; they are all resistant to this particular malady.

WHITE RUST—This disease is characterized by white blister-like pustules that occur mostly on the underside of the leaves, surrounding parts of the leaves also turn yellow. For a chemical control—use the same thing as for Blue Mold. In this case, on small patches, one could use the Dithane Z-78 to dust the foliage of the plant. It is also recommended that one should plant in rows instead of a flat bed wherever possible to receive as much drainage as is necessary to prevent this malady.

CURLY TOP—The characteristics of Curly Top in spinach show that the young leaves curl and turn yellow. Plants often die from the center outward, and this disease is spread by leaf hoppers. The best control for this would be to dust the plants periodically with a 5% Malathion dust, or—spray with a 5% Malathion spray. You could use the 25% wettable Malathion powder, mix about four or five tablespoons of this material to a gallon of water and spray the top of the spinach periodically.

Strawberry Diseases

LEAF SPOT—The symptoms of this particular disease are noticed by brown to white spots one-fourth to one-half inch in diameter that have purplish borders on the leaves. The fungus lives in diseased leaves. The malady is not often serious and can be controlled by applying a Bordeaux mixture to the foliage of the plants as soon as new Spring growth appears. Repeat treatment every ten days until the first berries are about one-third grown. Remove and destroy old leaves when making new plantings and after harvest.

BERRY ROT (FUNGI)—This is characteristic of strawberries that are decayed, which vary in color from grey to leathery-brown, and the color depends upon the fungus causing the rot. The disease is worse during rainy periods of the year than the dry season. The fungi that causes this particular malady lives in the soil. Use hay or pine straw, and space your plants six to eight inches apart to prevent shading of berries. *Do not* use nitrogen fertilizers early in the spring as this will aggravate the condition.

VERCILLIUM WILT—This disease of strawberries lives from year to year in the soil. Besides strawberries, many other common crops and several kinds of weeds are also host of this fungus. It is found throughout the United States. The fungus is most active during cool weather. In new plantings—symptoms appear about the time fruit begins to ripen. Outer leaves wilt and dry at the margins and between the veins, and they become dark brown, few if any new leaves develop. New roots that grow from the crown are often very short and have blackened tips, plants appear to be dry and flattened and black sunburned leisons may appear on leaf stalks and runners. Severely affected plants collapse, sometimes abruptly. Less severely affected plants are unproductive. Some of the most susceptible varieties are Lassen, Shasta, Elrillidawn, Dixieland, Klondike and North West. Plants that have some resistance are Marshall, Blakemore, Siletz, Caskill, Sure-Crop and Vermilion.

The best control is to plant a variety that is relatively resistant to this malady. *Do not* plant strawberries on land where tomatoes, peppers, potatoes, cotton, okra, melons, eggplant, apricots, almond, pecan, cherry, avacado, rose or cane fruits are grown.

Vercillium Wilt Fungs has been known to persist in the soil in some states for as long as 10 years. In areas where the wilt is a major problem, you should consider a variety that has some resistance to this disease.

Fumigation of the soil with Methyl Bromide has given good results, but on large extensive acreage the cost is too much to bear. On a small garden plot, the best control measure is to fumigate the soil with Methyl Bromide prior to transplanting the plants.

Sweet Potato Black Rot

Black rot occurs wherever sweet potatoes are grown. Growers are more likely to see damage just before or during harvest. Sweet potatoes that appear sound when stored may become badly affected within a few weeks.

Roundish, almost black spots of different sizes appear on the sweet potatoes. The surface of the diseased spot has a somewhat metallic luster. The tissue just beneath the spot is greenish. When cooked the diseased sweet potato has a very bad taste.

Small black spots often completely girdle underground stems. Frequently the infection extends up the stem to the surface of the soil. Young plants may be killed soon after being set in the field. Infected plants that continue to live rarely produce any sweet potatoes.

The disease fungus is spread long distances by exchange or sale of sweet potato slips used in propagation. In a local field or farm the fungus is spread by insects, farm animals and farm implements. It is also spread by drainage water, wind and discarded diseased roots dumped on fields.

The fungus may live for two or three years on old plant trash in the soil. Infection takes place in the plant bed or in the field throughout the year.

Black rot is controlled by using disease-free seed sweet potatoes, root disinfection, clean plant beds and crop rotation.

Turnip and Mustard Diseases

LEAF SPOT (CERCOSPORELLA)—This disease is characterized by white or greyish spots on the foliage, if severe—the entire leaf may curl and dry up. A fixed copper fungicide spray might be effective; such as Bordeaux Mixture. This disease makes greens unmarketable. However, cool weather seems to help check the disease. Another suggestion is to be sure and rotate the crop.

LEAF SPOT (ALTERNARIA)—This is the same type of fungus that causes leaf spot in cabbage. It is characterized by round, brown to black spots with concentric rings occurring on older leaves. In cauliflower, heads are discolored. Sometimes the disease is serious in the field and may cause heavy losses in storage. If this disease has been prevalent previously, be sure and rotate the mustard or turnip greens with some other crop than those of the cabbage family.

WHITE RUST—This disease is characterized on turnip greens, spinach and mustard greens by white blister-like pustules—which occur mostly on the underside of the leaves. Surrounding parts of leaves turn yellow and crop rotation should prevent primary infestation from the soil. Avoid flooding areas, such as irigation or by watering excessively with a sprinkling hose, and plant in rows instead of flat beds wherever possible to enhance drainage. Dust or spray as for Blue Mold, using Zineb as a dust or spray, and begin the application of this fungicide at the first sign of the disease. Apply at 7 to 10 day intervals as needed.

Tomato Diseases

TOMATO WILT—A highly detrimental disease of tomatoes characterized by the lower leaves turning yellow to brown, and the plant may wilt first on one side only. The entire plant gradually turns yellow or brown, wilts and dies. The disease is most serious during warm weather and usually appears shortly before the first fruits ripen in the spring.

There is no absolute, 100% control. It is best to plant a wilt resistant variety. *However*, here is *an old fashioned remedy*. I would not guarantee it, but it is worth a try. Take four tablespoons of household lye and dissolve into one gallon of water. Pour this mixture around the roots of the affected plant. Try it—no guarantee.

BLOSSOM END ROT—The main symptom of this disease is characterized by dark, sunken, leathery spots appearing on the blossom end of the green fruit. The spots vary in size, sometimes affecting half the fruit. This is a physiological disease caused by fluctuating moisture supply and the lack of available calcium. Based on a soil test, add adequate limestone to deficient soils, use adapted varieties, and adding calcium chloride to the spray or the use of calicum nitrate as a side dressing may be beneficial. As a suggested application medium, mix five pounds of calcium chloride into 100 gallons of water and thoroughly spray the upper portion of the plant.

Maintain (if possible) an even supply of moisture in the soil by adding organic material and by irrigating. Oftentimes, the supplying of excessive amounts of phosphorous will help. Side dress with somethink like a 13-39-0 fertilizer to raise the P_2O_5 content of the soil.

TOBACCO MOSAIC—Leaves crinkled with dark green and yellow spots. Leaves may be curled. Plants may be stunted with reduced yield, especially if infested while small.

Control—Wash hands with laundry soap and water every time after using *tobacco*, before handling plants.

Watermelon Diseases

BLOSSOM-END ROT—What is the cause of blossom-end rot in watermelons? Scientists know the relation of certain factors, particular variety, moisture and calcium, to blossom-end rot, but the complete answer still is a mystery.

VARIETY—Researchers as well as growers have found that long watermelons such as the Charleston Gray variety have more of a tendency to get blossom-end rot than round-type melons, such as the Black Diamond. Since Charleston Gray is now the predominant variety, more blossom-end rot is expected now as compared with a similar year a few years ago when Black Diamond was the principal variety.

MOISTURE—There is a definite relationship between soil moisture and blossom-end rot. The amount of blossom-end rot in any field can be reduced by maintaining uniform moisture throughout the growth and development of the fruit. Alternate periods of high and low soil moisture increases the incidence of blossom-end rot. The amount of blossom-end rot increases or decreases according to the length and severity of the wet and dry periods.

CALCIUM—The Florida Agricultural Experiment Station has reported a direct relationship between the available calcium and blossom-end rot incidence. Florida researchers were able to reduce the amount of blossom-end rot under all types of conditions by increasing the available calcium in the soil or by spraying plants with a calcium chloride solution. Calcium was added to the soil in the form of lime, gypsum or calcium nitrate. Spray the vines the same as recommended for tomatoes —use five pounds of calcium chloride to 100 gallons of water.

Cotton Root Rot of Shade Trees and Shrubs

Cotton root rot is one of the most common plant diseases in the South. Except for the Panhandle and High Plains the disease generally is found throughout the South. It is very common in heavy, alkaline soils. The disease first occurs in south Texas during the last of May, and has spread to north Texas by July. About 80 percent of the wild and cultivated plants are susceptible in varying degrees.

Small shrubs and trees die suddenly after the first symptoms of wilting. Large shrubs and trees may die more slowly. The bark of affected roots is decayed and brownish. Wooly, buff or brownish, fungal strands are on the surface of the damaged roots.

The whole root system decays. Bark is rotted off the harder wood of the root. Roots slip out of the soil with comparatively less pulling effort.

Under moist conditions, with or without affected plants, spore mats sometime appear on the soil surface. These mats are two to twelve inches in diameter, at first snow-white and cottony; later they appear tan and powdery.

The disease fungus generally invades new areas by continued slow growth through the soil from plant to plant. It may live in the soil for many years. The disease fungus is often found as deep in the soil as roots penetrate.

The disease is controlled by the growing of resistant or immune trees and shrubs. Certain cultural practices may help prevent the disease from occurring more often. If recognized in time, an application of save the tree.

Lichens on Ornamentals

Lichens frequently occur on trunks and branches of trees. They are also found in river bottom areas where there is poor air drainage. Lichens are not a disease, however their presence on weakened or dying shade trees leaves many people to mistakenly believe that they are the cause of the trouble. The lichens attach themselves to the dead part or bark of the tree, and each lichen is a combination of a fungus and algae. Plantation Nematode and Root Rot Cure will control the disease and The fungus and algae are each dependent on the other and cannot live separately. Lichens grow equally well on rocks, fence posts, rotting logs, and other objects. A common form of lichen is the greyish-green paper-like growth that occurs on the bark of pecan trees. This irregular shaped growth may be anywhere from almost an inch to several inches across. Its edges are usually lobed and curled upward, they can be controlled by regularly spraying with Bordeaux mixture, fixed copper or copper containing fungicides.

Stem Rot in Ornamentals

There are two primary soil organisms that cause stem rot in ornamentals—namely Rhizoctonia solani and the other one is Sclerotinia. They cause trouble primarily in carnations, poinsettias, chrysanthemums, begonias, African violets, snapdragons, and similar bedding plants, as well as larkspur, calendulas and sweet peas.

Stem rot is also known as "Dampening Off or Wire-Stem," and is probably the most destructive fungus of floral crops. Soft brown rot attacks at the soil level and the plant eventually wilts and dies. The disease occurs in both field and greenhouse soils, and may appear at any time.

It is most serious in the Spring and early Summer when excessive moisture and high temperatures prevail.

Terraclor is effective for treating and controlling this particular fungus.

In reference to Stem Rot—called Rhizoctonia solani, the recommendation is to apply two pounds of 75% wettable Terraclor per 1000 square feet, mixing it thoroughly in the top four inches of soil.

The control for Sclerotinia, which attacks such things as sweet peas and snapdragons, use the 75% wettable Terraclor at the rate of one-fourth pound per 100 square feet and mix thoroughly into the bed in the top four inches of soil, making absolutely certain that you get thorough mixture of this material prior to planting. If applied early enough prior to planting, an application of Medina will suppress the disease.

Sooty Mold Damage to Trees, Shrubs and Flowers

Sooty mold disease occurs in all areas of the South, but it is likely to be more common in areas of high rainfall, such as the Gulf Coast.

The black coating on the surface of leaves or fruit of infected plants is easily rubbed off by the hand. The coating is made up of a web of black, fungus microscopic threads. The black mold is the result of certain fungi living on secretions (honey-dew) from insects. Scale, aphids and immature stages of white fly are mainly involved. Injury to the plant is indirect in that the black mold prevents sunlight from reaching the leaves. Too, the esthetic value of the plant is affected. Usually more of the black mold is on the top part of the leaf than the underside.

The disease is likely to occur on Arborvitae, Azalea, Cape jasmine, Cedar, Cottonwood, Gardenia, Lemon, Ligustrum, Magnolia, Oak, Orange, Peach, Pear, Pecan, Pine and Redbud.

Prevent the mold by controlling the insects which leave secretions on the leaves.

The Greenhouse White Fly is often the insect that causes the mold to form. To control the fly and the mold use 3 tablespoons of Diazinon and one teaspoon of liquid soap to one gallon water. Repeat spray every five to seven days. After the third application use the water hose to wash off fungus.

Fungicides and Their Uses

A fungicide is a toxicant or a poison for a fungi, a chemical or physical agent that kills or inhibits the development of fungus spores of mycelium. It may be an eradicant applied to a plant or plant part, or environment to destroy fungi established in a given area or on a plant. Or, it may be a protectant applied to protect the plant or plant part from infestation. It works by killing or inhibiting the development of fungus spores that may arrive at the infection spot.

The term fungicide, as generally used, includes bactericides, toxicants for bacteria. Since there are a large number of fungicides on the market today, thus it is advisable that a list of them be made, and the uses that they are employed for.

1. ACETIC ACID—present in vinegar, one of the oldest preservatives, and suggested as a soil disinfectant about 20 years ago, particularly for "dampening off" of evergreen seedlings. For a brief period, acetic acid was suggested as a flower spray for Azalea Blight. Since that time, new and more effective fungicides have replaced it.

2. ARASAN—sold under this name for seed treatment, as is Terasan for turf and bulb treatment. Recommended for peanut, corn, beans, peas, beets, carrots, and some of the other vegetable and flower seeds, as well as being mixed with fertilizer for onion smut control.

3. ORTHANE—This product is used basically as a miticide, fungicide, and as an insecticide on fruits, vegetables, and ornamentals. Promising good results for Apple Scab, and Powdery Mildew, it may be injurious to young foliage in emulsible form. It is safer to be used as a wettable powder.

4. BORDEAUX MIXTURE—Made from copper sulfate, lime and water, and forming a membranous coating over plant parts. The first protecive spray, and perhaps the most widely used in the country today.

Although others had previously used the chemicals, the Frenchman Millardet is given the credit of discovering and publicizing the efficiency of Bordeaux mixture. So named because it was used on grapes along the highway to Bordeaux, France. In 1878, Downey Mildew introduced into France from America was threatening the vineyards. Millardet, one of the workers assigned to the problem, noticed in 1882 where grapes near the highway had been treated with a poisonous looking blue mixture of copper and lime to prevent steeling, there was little or now Downey Mildew. A description of the Bordeaux mixture was published in 1885 and remains to this day one of our most efficient and widely used fungicides.

It does have a most conspicuous residue, and is injurious to many plants. Bordeaux mixture is made in varying concentrations. The most normal formula found on the market today is 8-8-100, which means that it contains eight pounds of copper sulfate, eight pounds of dehydrated lime, to 100 gallons of water. Stock solutions are made up for each chemical, the lime solution placed first in the sprayer, diluted to nearly the full amount, and the copper sulfate solution added. However, it is more advisable for a backyard gardener, rather than to try to mix his own, to buy a commercially prepared Bordeaux mixture formula.

5. CAPTAN—A fungicide used primarily for the control of Black Spot and Powdery Mildew on roses. However, it is highly effective on Powdery and Downey Mildew on vegetables and other fungus growth. It has a wide range of adaptability to a number of plants. It is safe to use and comes both in a dust and a wettable powder.

6. CONSAN 20—A new broad spectrum fungicide liquid, easy to apply and recommended to be used for fungus control on plants and in lawns.

7. DITHANE Z-78—A trade name for Zineb, a fungicide used primarily in the control of Pecan Scab on pecan trees.

8. SPERGON—Used as a seed treatment of vegetables, especially legumes and corn, sunflowers, bulb treatment for lilies, root and sprout treatment for sweet potatoes and a spray or dust for cabbage Downey Mildew.

9. SULFUR—The oldest known fungicide, dating back prior to the writing of modern history. Around 150 million pounds are used annually in the United States as a fungicide and an insecticide. Wettable sulfur has agents added for ready mixing with water for use in sprays. Sulfur sprays and dusts are more useful for ornamentals and fruits than they are on vegetables. The are used for the control of Powdery Mildew, Rust, Apple Scab, Brown Rot of stone fruits, and Black Spot. Sulfur, oftentimes, is unsafe to use on many varieties of cucubits, causing stunting and a decrease in yield in squash and melons particularly. Wettable sulfur and sulfur dusts are safer than lime sulfur at high temperatures, but may injure plant at 85° F and foliage at 100° F. On roses there may be some foliage burn above 90°.

10. TERRACLOR—A fungicide with a wide range of adaptation, and is primarily used for the treatment of soil borne fungi, treatment of seed, and in the control of Brown Patch in lawns.

Conversion Table To Be Used For Mixing Insecticides and Fungicides

Since dosage directions are usually given in most charts at 100 gallons of water, it is essential that a breakdown be given so a conversion can be made to mix a smaller amount of spray. Therefore, if you will remember a few measurements listed in this conversion table it will be very simple.

3 teaspoons = 1 tablespoon

2 tablespoons = 1 fluid oz.

16 tablespoons or 8 fluid ozs.
    = 1 cup

16 oz. or 2 cups = 1 pint

2 pints or 4 cups = 1 quart

16 cups, 8 pts. or 4 qts. = 1 gal.

1 acre consists of 43,560 sq. ft.

Chapter 10

Gardener's Questions and Their Answers

These are the most common questions asked, those coming up again and again. Read them all through. Then if you can't find your question—give me a call or drop a note anytime.

Questions and Timely Tips

QUESTION—How do I control Spanish Moss and Ball Moss on trees?

ANSWER—Spanish Moss on trees is detrimental to the growth of a tree, not from the standpoint that it is a parasite, but it does cause damage, as it covers up the foliage of the tree—thereby interfering with its natural transpiration and the use of the leaf. For maximum control of Spanish Moss—spray the tree during the warm season of the year (June or July) using two pounds of Lead of Arsenate to 50 gallons of water. Be sure and get thorough application of this spray. If the spray drips off onto the foliage of the grass, be sure and cut cattle or livestock out from it. The Arsenic would be quite detrimental as it is highly toxic to animals.

QUESTION—I've heard that lye solution is good on roses—how much and when should I apply it?

ANSWER—This is an old "timey" method passed along to me by one of my listeners, whereby the application of lye to shrubs, trees and even garden plants, and roses has a beneficial effect. The recommendation is to use two tablespoons of lye to a gallon of water and apply this gallon of solution around each rose bush. Be sure and keep it off the foliage, but apply it to the soil in the area where the feeder roots are growing. After applied, be sure and water in real good. This application should be made in the spring, preferably in March or April; during the mid-Summer—June or July; and late fall—September or October. This method can also be utilized on shrub trees, as well as pecans. A number of fellows have applied as much as two cans of commercial lye to a grown pecan tree and have received additional benefit from the application thereof. As I said, this information was passed along to me by a listener, and 99% of the people who have used it have found it to be quite successful. If you use it, you do so at your own risk; it is not recommended by some of our agricultural authorities, but from practical experience, it has proven to be quite worthwhile.

QUESTION—I'm bothered with poison ivy or poison oak, is there anything I could take, either orally or by shot to help this condition?

ANSWER—A new preparation manufactured by C. F. Kirk & Company of New York called *AQUA IVY* will do the trick. This is a tablet, a preventive control rather than a cure. A person should start taking Aqua Ivy tablets prior to the poison ivy season in order to build up a resistance to this condition. The formula is not harmful and can be taken over an extended period of time without any harmful effects. These tablets can be purchased from any drug store without a prescription. To help dry up skin irritations, apply Aloe Vera twice to affected area.

QUESTION—Could you give me a good whitewash formula?

ANSWER—For a longer lasting, better looking job, remove old whitewash materials. Use a stiff brush, or wash old material off with water. If a smooth surface is desired, fill rough spots with putty prior to applying the new coat of whitewash. Dampen the area to be finished so whitewash will dry more slowly and set better. Make up only enough mixture for immediate use. Most types deteriorate rapidly. Apply thin and quickly. Allow first coat to dry thoroughly before adding second coat. Apply any one of the four formulas listed below.

Formula #1

Place in a container 31 pounds of unslaked lime, or 42 pounds of hydrated lime (builders lime) and sufficient water to cover it. Allow to stand until thoroughly hydrated or slaked down. Strain mixture and add a peck of salt dissolved in warm water. In another container, mix three pounds of ground rice, one-half pound of Spanish whiting and one pound of clear glue to two and one-half gallons of water. The ground rice should be mixed with the hot water until it becomes jelled. Add the whiting and glue to this jelly. Pour the second solution into the lime while stirring vigorously. Allow to stand for a few days and apply with brush. If it is too thick, add water until it brushes well.

Formula #2

Use a container large enough to hold 62 pounds of quick lime or 80 pounds of hydrated lime (builder's lime) and 15 gallons of water. Allow to stand until thoroughly slaked down. In a second container, stir two and one-half pounds flour into one-half gallon of cold water. Then when thoroughly mixed, add two gallons of boiling water. Dissolve two and one-half pounds salt in two and one-half gallons of water, one pound clear glue in one gallon of water. Mix salt and glue solution and pour the mixture into the lime solution, stirring vigorously while adding. Add sufficient water for it to brush well, strain the solution and use. Rye flour, if obtainable, would be better than ordinary flour.

Formula #3

Mix two and one-half gallons of skim milk with three pints household ammonia in one gallon of water. In separate bath, mix 50 pounds of builders lime in six gallons of water; then add the milk and ammonia mixture to the lime bath, stirring vigorously while adding, and strain. Just before you are ready to use this solution add five pints of formaldehyde in three gallons of water, pouring this into the lime mixture slowly and stirring vigorously. Add water to brush well and use the same day the mixture is completed.

Formula #4

The following recipe for a cement whitewash is used by owners of cold storage warehouses who desire a snowy whitewash that dries quickly, adheres strongly to cement, brick or wood, and does not rub off on clothes.

Slake lime one-half bushel with boiling water; add the water slowly, stirring constantly until a thin paste results. Add one pint of salt to the lime paste; stir thoroughly until all salt is dissolved, add water to bring the whitewash to the proper consistency. Throw a handful of cement in and a teaspoonful of ultramarine blue powder into each pail of whitewash. Add cement and the blue powder just before the wash is used and stir thoroughly, strain, otherwise the whitewash will streak. In formula No. 4 the cement makes the whitewash adhere strongly to any surface, and the bluing counteracts the grayish color of the cement in a white appearance.

QUESTION—What can I use to repel mosquitoes, chiggers and ticks?

ANSWER—There is a compound on the market called "KIK." It is made by Geigy and is available at most drug stores and grocery stores. This material comes in an aerosol spray. It can be applied directly to clothing or to the body without staining of fabric or detrimental effects whatsoever. It also will repel, under most conditions, for as long as six hours.

QUESTION—What can I use to repel dogs and cats from a flower bed?

ANSWER—There are a number of commercial compounds on the market that will do an excellent job of repelling animals such as cats and dogs. SCRAM is one such compound. Mix it according to directions on the container and spray onto the flower and beds. Several dusting compounds are also available that do a good job.

One tried and tested remedy that works fairly well, is to take nicotine sulfate (three-quarters tablespoons per gallon of water) and spray onto the shrubs and flowers. Repeat application of this preparation in about three to four days as the material will break down chemically.

Another suggestion that some of the old timers recommend, that seems to work too, is to apply finely ground *red pepper* around the beds. This seems to discourage dogs and cats.

QUESTION—What can I use to repel armadillos that are rooting up my garden and flower beds?

ANSWER—Sprinkle Spirits of Ammonia onto some old rags and lay them in the path and around where the varmints root up things. When they get a whiff of this material, they will take off for parts unknown and will not return. If they do, just repeat operation.

QUESTION—How can I keep snakes out of my yard?

ANSWER—A lot of folks have written—giving the following suggestions to repel snakes.

(1) Cut up garlic and place around the yard. It seems that a snake cannot stand the garlic odor.

(2) Run geese in your yard. In South Africa, the natives use this method to repel and control snakes.

(3) Spray with Toxaphene—using five pounds to 100 gallons of water. Spray this material over the entire yard. This will be a short term control process as the Toxaphene will break down chemically. After spraying, keep pets and children off the grass for a few days.

QUESTION—Can I control hookworm eggs in my yard by spraying with some chemical?

ANSWER—The answer to this comes from Dr. R. D. Turk of the Veterinary Parasitology Department of A&M College.

Adult females, in the small intestine of the dog, lay thin shelled eggs which pass out and hatch in 24 to 48 hours. In about seven days the small larvae resulting from the hatch of the egg has molted twice and is now infective. This infective larvae usually migrates only a short distance from where the original eggs were deposited and waits for a proper host to come along. In this instance the host is a dog, and the larvae may penetrate the unbroken skin or be taken in through the mouth with contaminated food. All of the larvae that penetrate the skin migrate through the lungs and may take from 30 to 60 days to reach the small intestine. Treatment will remove only those worms that are in the small intestine. For this reason it is usually necessary to re-treat an animal at least two times and occassionally three times at intervals of two to three weeks if the animal is heavily infected.

For your information the infective hookworm larvae is a tough customer. We know of no powder, spray or other chemical that will kill hookworm larvae without injuring vegetation. Boron compounds, salt solutions or toxic gases are used to kill larvae in pens, runs or other enclosures where there is no vegetation.

Unfortunately, the modern well kept, well fertilized and well watered yard with an abundance of shade furnished by well tended shrubbery, forms an almost ideal incubator for the free-living stage of the hookworms. About the only control in this case is to prevent the dog from access to a yard or daily policing of the yard picking up all fecal material within the first 24 hours, thus removing the eggs before they have hatched.

QUESTION—I would like to know if putting house paint on trees will hurt them?

ANSWER—Yes. Do not put house paint on trees as most of our house paints carry a percentage of lead, and lead is toxic to trees.

QUESTION—Is there any compound that can be used to prevent stumps from sprouting back out?

ANSWER—Yes. There are a number of chemicals on the market to-day that can be used to apply to a freshly cut stump that will prevent the stump from resprouting. However, in all instances these materials must be applied to the cut surface shortly after the main tree has been cut. In other words, you cannot wait several weeks after the tree has been cut and then apply the chemical and expect satisfactory results. It must be applied shortly after the main trunk of the tree has been sawed off. This will also apply to the sprouts.

The best compound to use is Ammate—applied to the freshly cut surface of the sprout or the stump which ever it might be. This material will be absorbed into the roots of the tree and will prevent it resprouting. Ammate is not toxic to either animals or humans, but is highly corrosive and should be applied by either using a wooden spoon or a glass container. On large trees—applications of 2,4,5-T mixed with diesel oil to the cut surface of stumps and sprouts will also prevent the brush of stump from resprouting.

QUESTION—It there any product on the market that will kill the sting or the itching sensation caused by a red bug or chigger?

ANSWER—Yes. The main thing of course is to destroy the chigger that is buried into the skin and releasing toxic poisons that cause the irritation. One such product is called "Aloe Vera." This material will not only kill the chigger, it will also relieve the itching sensation from chiggers, wasps and bee stings, as well as ticks—about 5 minutes after it is applied to the affected surface of the skin. It is safe to use on children.

QUESTION—I have a Persimmon tree that is healthy but never bears fruit, could you tell me why?

ANSWER—Persimmons have male trees that produce pollen, and female trees that produce fruit. It is necessary to have at least one tree of each kind to produce the fruit. Fruit trees of some species have perfect flowers, that is—they pollinate themselves. In other words, the tree produces both male and female flowers and are self pollinating. But, such is not the case with Persimmons. Therefore, unless you have another Persimmon tree of a different specie, one that produces the female flower and one male, there will be no fruiting, and there is nothing that can be done to change this situation.

226

QUESTION—When I apply my insecticide in the form of a spray it seems to run off—it doesn't stick like it should. Of course to get control I realize you must get that insecticide to stick to the leaf surface, how can I do it?

ANSWER—One of the simplest ways to cause an insecticide, whether it be in the wettable powder form or the liquid form, but being applied by spray, is the addition of liquid detergents; such as Lux soap. Take about a teaspoonful of this and add to two or three gallons of spray and this will give it the adhering ability to stick to the leaf, thereby getting a better kill. The small amount of liquid detergent is not detrimental to the foliage of the plant in any respect, and will do an excellent job in causing the insecticide to stick.

QUESTION—I have had a tremendous amount of trouble with figs dropping from my trees. Could you give me a formula or answer to prevent this next year?

ANSWER—Anytime fruit drops from a tree it can generally be pin-pointed as one of two problems. Either disease or insects, or it is a soil plant food deficiency. In most cases it is due to the deficiency of phosphorus. An ideal program to follow, in reference to overcoming this malady, is to apply two to three pound of 0-45-0, commonly called triple super phosphate, around the drip line of the tree during the month of October or November. This should be applied evenly spaced around the drip line of the tree, in holes or in furrows dug into the soil, and then cover over.

Next spring, during the month of April, remove all weeds and grass from around the trunk and underneath the tree and apply two to three pounds, depending upon the size of the tree once again, of ammonium sulfate—21% (around the drip line also). The nitrogen, in the 21% is to be used for the growth of new leaves and stems, as well as the growth of the fig itself, and the phosphorus that was applied during the fall months will help to hold the fruit for you.

QUESTION—Can tomatoes be grown successfully in the South in the fall months?

ANSWER—Yes. A number of good gardeners grow a successful tomato crop in the fall months, and it can be done one of two ways.

1. You can cut back the old original stump or stalk of the tomato that was planted, or transplanted, in the spring. Cut back to about an inch or two above the ground line and keep it well watered and mulched. It will sprout out shortly after the main stem of the tomato has been removed, a branch will come out from the old stub or the old root stock, which will grow back and produce a good tomato crop in the fall. This is what is called the second crop from the original root system. Care and a little experience and a little research on your part will prove to you that this method is sound and will work. Keep it well

watered and with tender care and attention to keep insects off of this new growth. Protecting it from excessive sunlight, from the rays of the sun during the hot summertime, is essential.

2. Another sequence to follow is to plant the tomato seed right out in the open field, or in the garden plot. They will germinate and come up, and of course protect them as best possible from the excessive rays of the sun during the hot part of the day, and with care and attention, proper watering and fertility, insect control, you can produce tomatoes successfully during the fall months.

QUESTION—How can I remove stain and fungus growth from Austin Stone or other masonry type buildings?

ANSWER—From a listener of ours, comes the answer that the best chemical to use for removing the mold and weather discoloration from this type structure is Oleic acid. This is used by buiding contractors, expressly for this purpose. Cut the acid with three parts of water to each one part of acid.

As a cautionary measure—this acid is very powerful and will burn metal. It should be mixed carefully in an earthen crock. One should be careful to avoid getting it on hands and face. We have found that the application to the surface of the area to be treated with a fibre milk-can brush, produces excellent results. Be sure to get the concentrated Oleic acid. The cost is very low, as one gallon normally of concentrated Oleic acid generally runs about $1.65 or $1.75. This certainly beats sand blasting, which is much greater in cost.

QUESTION—What is the best policy to follow to determine whether a watermelon is ripe or not?

ANSWER—There are three distinct signs one can generally follow to determine if a watermelon is ripe.

1. If the watermelon is still growing on the vine, check the curl (located at the stem end of the melon), if it is dried and dead, this is almost a positive sign that the watermelon is ripe.
2. Thump it. If it has a dull thumping thud to it, this is a fair assurance that the watermelon is ripe.
3. Lay a broomstraw across the watermelon, if the melon is ripe the broomstraw will vibrate and have a tendency to turn lengthwise toward the long ends.

But, still the only way that one can be assured that it is ripe and suitable for eating, is to cut it.

QUESTION—Do you have any suggestions as to how to keep up with garden tools to keep from losing them in the garden, and also in the lawn and flower beds?

ANSWER—A suggestion I would like to pass along to you comes from R. E. Leigh of Austin, who suggests that you use bright yellow tractor paint, painting a 6-inch band around the handle of each of your garden tools, in fact—all tools. The yellow will contrast vividly with the green of the vegetation and with the drab colors of the soil, and makes it very easy to find the tools and to place them in their proper spots. This also can be used as a mark for identification, it works quite well.

QUESTION—Can roastin' ears be roasted in the shuck?

ANSWER—YES. Here is an excellent recipe sent along once again by R. E. Leigh of Austin. 1. Preheat the oven to 400° F before the corn is cut from the stalk. The reason for this is because the high percentage of the sugar in the ear is converted to starch within the first hour after the corn is cut. 2. Cut off the tip end of each ear and remove only one layer of the outer shuck. Do not remove the silks as they will come off more easily after the corn is baked. 3. Roast 40 minutes in 400° F oven and serve. 4. Shucks and silks should be removed at the table by slipping a sharp knife under both and pull back toward the stem end. Silk will turn loose easily. You might try this, it works quite well.

QUESTION—There have been a number of questions as to the age of various fruit trees and when they should start bearing. In order to give a correct answer in all cases, we are listing a table below which I think will give the answer in so far as those questions are concerned.

As an Example:

VARIETY	YEARS
Apple	4-7
Apricot	4-5
Citrus	3-5
Fig	2-3
Peaches	3-4
Pears	4-6
Plum	4-6

QUESTION—If one should be stung by an Asp, what is the best policy to follow?

ANSWER—From most sources, the best practice to follow is to put an ice pack on the area. *Do not rub it*, but put an ice pack on the sting. If severe symptoms should follow, the best policy is to get in touch with the doctor. An application of Aloe Vera will help to relieve the pain.

QUESTION—Our St. Augustine grass is never green in the winter. Is there a winter grass seed that we can use with our St. Augustine grass, and how would you go about planting it?

ANSWER—St. Augustine grass does turn brown during the winter months due to the cold weather and frost. One can over-seed St. Augustine grass turf with Rye grass. *However, it is not advisable.* The major reason being the Rye grass will be detrimental to the growth of St. Augustine grass next spring. The heavy stem and stalk of the Rye grass will have a tendency to shade the St. Augustine and hold it back during the spring months when it should be coming forth. In addition to that, you have a heavy mass of growth from the Rye grass to contend with for the first several weeks after the St. Augustine grass begins to green up, and this will turn brown and make the lawn unsightly, and this will interfere with the natural growth of St. Augustine grass. Leave your St. Augustine grass as it. Fertilize it in the fall months to enhance its beauty during the winter months.

QUESTION—Are there any poisonous plants around here?

ANSWER—According to a recent report put out by the Department of Health, there may be many shrubs and flowers growing in one's backyard that are masking powerful poisons behind a facade of beauty.

The report stated that recently a group of persons sickened suddenly after broiling steaks over an open fire. A doctor detected symptoms of digitalis poisoning, all denied any connection with digitalis—a powerful heart stimulant. The doctor learned that Oleander limbs had been used to skewer the steaks—thus he had his answer. The Oleander limbs contain a poison that acts as an overdose of digitalis to people who chew them or use them in such manners as described above.

Of all the plants grown in the average American home garden, an expert on plant poisons has counted more than 100 which contain poison, some lethal, others not quite so toxic. Here are a few of the examples of the toxicity of the various commonly known plants.

1. A dime package of Castor Bean Seeds packs a poisonous punch sufficient to kill 5 children.
2. One Tulip bulb contains enough poison to kill a man.
3. Sweet peas, although seldom fatal, are poisonous enough to keep a victim bedridden for weeks with a form of paralysis.
4. A poison in Elephant ears causes painful swelling and itching of mouth, tongue and throat when chewed.
5. The Christmas Rose, all parts of this plant are poisonous, especially the leaves.
6. Deadly Nightshade—the berries of some plants are very poisonous, especially when eaten green.
7. Dogwood—the fruit is slightly poisonous to people who might consume it.
8. Foxglove—the leaves of this plant are particularly toxic.
9. Holly—the leaves and berries of Holly are toxic to a person that consumes them.
10. Jimson weed—all part of this plant are fatal if consumed.
11. Larkspur—the foliage and roots are toxic.
12. Lily of the valley—berries are toxic.
13. Mountain laurel—the young leaves and shoots, if eaten, are fatal to children.
14. Polk weed—roots are toxic.
15. Rhubarb—leaves are toxic.
16. Water Hemlock—the whole plant is toxic, particularly the root.

17. Monk's hood—foliage and root of this plant are toxic.

Admittedly there are few actual deaths attributed to eating poisonous plants, but the potential is always there, and your guess is as good as anyone's as to how much disabling illness is caused by backyard foliage.

If any one of the above plants are known to have been eaten by a youngster or an adult, administer a strong emetic and call a doctor immediately. Prompt action is vitally essential in all plant poisoning cases.

QUESTION—How can I keep cats out of my vegetable garden as they not only tromp the vegetation down, but also cuase damage through fecal material.

ANSWER—One of the safest and best ways to keep a cat out of the garden is to sprinkle some red pepper in the garden where the cat treads and they will not come near it. Red pepper is a good repellent for most animals—ven dogs, and especially cats.

QUESTION—How do you get paint to stick to a newly poured concrete slab?

ANSWER—I suggest that you should use a 5%-10% hydrochloric acid solution. Mop it on using a cotton mop—so as to get even distribution all across the slab. You will notice as you apply the material that bubbles will appear on top of the newly poured concrete slab. Then, take a water hose and wash off thoorughly. Let it air dry, wait several days (I would suggest 5 to 7 days) before you apply your paint, and this should assure you a good smooth painted surface on a concrete slab.

QUESTION—What can I use in the way of a repellent to keep rodents and animals, such as deer and rabbits, from chewing and gnawing on the bark of a newly set fruit tree?

ANSWER—The best preparation available commercially is called "Goodrite ZIP." This material is available in a limited supply in the Houston area, and the recommended procedure is to paint or spray it on. A suggested method would be to take 1 quart and add it to three quarts of water, with a low pressure sprayer spray the stump area of the newly set tree, up to and as high as the rodents or the animals can reach. This works as a repellent, is non-toxic, will not harm the animal or the rodent in any way, but will repel them and keep them away from the newly set tree. Thus giving it a chance to become established and grow to maturity.

QUESTION—Should I or should I not prune citrus trees?

ANSWER—Pruning is the act of removing unwanted branches from horticultural plants. In the case of young citrus trees, the objective of pruning is to give the tree a desirable shape and establish a strong framework of scaffold branches.

In older trees, the objective is to establish a balance between vegetative vigor and fruitfulness, which will enable the tree to produce maximum yields of fruit of desirable sizes at reasonable costs. Other reasons for pruning are to facilitate certain grove operations and to maintain the health of the tree. Pruning of citrus trees, as related to fruit production, is not really so important as it is with apples, peaches and grapes.

In general, on individual trees, or two or three trees such as grown in the Texas Gulf Coast, citrus trees are not to be pruned except those limbs that are near the ground which are letting the fruit touch the ground. Any dead twigs, cankers and so forth should be pruned.

QUESTION—I have moles or gophers in my lawn and garden, what can I do to control them?

ANSWER—Research work that has been done by the Ohio Experiment Station leads us to believe that where there are grub worms present in the soil, moles will generally always be there. In order to alleviate the condition of moles, I would suggest that you use either 40% Chlordane, 10% Heptachlor or 5% Dieldrin—sprinkled over the area in which they are infesting and water in. To get even coverage, mix the insecticide with 10 gallons of water and apply with a sprinkling pot. By handling in this manner a single application of any of these will grub proof the space for several years. By alleviating the grub worm problem you will take care of the mole.

Gophers are a different rodent. The easiest and simplest way to control gophers is to inject a small amount of Methyl Bromide into his run. This can be done with a special rodent gun that can be purchased at your local feed, seed and fertilizer dealers. This works quite well on large agricultural acreage, as well as in the home garden. One word of CAUTION—whenever Methyl Bromide is used—remember—it will kill anything that it comes in contact with, so don't inject this material into the soil near the root system of a tree or shrub as it will kill it. Also gopher baits are highly effective.

QUESTION—How do I keep birds from pecking my strawberries?

ANSWER—Here is a suggestion passed along by one of our listeners. They suggested that you take paper sack bags (sizes No. 6, 8 and No. 12), open by blowing up with air from your mouth, and put tiny pieces of dirt clods, the size of a marble or gravel, to cause a rattle when the wind blows. Tie, with a string about 6 inches long, onto sticks that have been stuck in the ground about 5 feet tall. Hang these throughout your strawberry patch and as the wind blows, the small gravel in the bottom of the bag will rattle and birds will never come near the patch. This is the simplest way to keep birds out of a strawberry patch or berry patch, as well as from pecking tomatoes. Try it and see what happens.

QUESTION—The bark on my Pecan Tree is awfully rough. Is this normal? What can I do to control it?

ANSWER—It is perfectly natural for a pecan tree to develop dry, scaly bark as it grows. This consists of one or more layers of dry periderm tissue, which are formed in the outer part, or cortex, of the live bark. It is there for the protection of the vital cambium of the inner bark against the hot sun, fire, insects, mechanical injury, etc.

Different pecan varieties have somewhat differing bark characteristics because of inherent differences in the many individual periderm sections of which the bark is composed, which affords one means of identifying them. Some varities produce a relatively large amount of dry bark and others, such as Van Deman, produce relatively little. Also, there is a wide difference in the type of bark found near the ground on seedling and on grafted trees, which difference is associated with growth regulating hormones. In a similar manner some trees, such as the bois d'arc, have thorny branches near the ground but no thorns on branches high in the tree.

It is not uncommon for people to think there is something wrong with a pecan tree because it has a scaly bark. This fact is sometimes taken advantage of by fly-by-night tree doctors.

QUESTION—How do I appraise the value of a tree?

ANSWER—How much is your tree worth to you in dollars and cents? Probably you have never estimated its worth. You have appreciated the shade and the added asset of its beauty that it gives to the surroundings.

If your tree is destroyed by unauthorized workmen, or killed in any kind of an accident for which other persons are responsible, you have a legal right to file a claim for damages, but first the tree's value must be determined.

This is a problem unless you know how to figure it. If the tree is damaged or killed by a hurricane, the loss often can be deducted from your income tax. See your tax agent for details. The same method of estimating its value can also be used for this purpose.

A joint committee of National Arborist Association and the National Shade Tree Conference devised a formula by which the monetary value may be estimated.

The formula sets the basic value at $5.00 per square inch of trunk cross section measured at four and one half feet above the ground. Recently this basic value was increased to $6.00.

However, this value is modified by the general desirability of the species for shade and ornamental purposes, and also the physical condition of the tree.

Example: If a shade tree is 12 inches in diameter, then use the mathematical formula used to calculate the area of a circle—.7854 × square of the diameter. The trunk cross section area will be found to be 113.1 squares inches.

If your tree is for shade and ornamental use and is perfect in form and health, its value would be 113.1 × $6.00 or $678.60.

Other Factors: If the tree has brittle branch wood or some undesirable characteristic, it might be regarded as only 60% of the basic value. If in addition, the tree lacks symmetry or is diseased, it might be rated

80% of perfection with respect to physical condition. Then multiply $678.60 by 60% and the result by 80%, which would give you a figure of $325.12, the value of the tree.

Fair application of the foregoing depends upon the judgment of the appraiser in rating the tree as to species, desirability and its physical condition. Perhaps after all, it may be wiser to have a specialist in Horticulture to make the appraisal.

QUESTION—What can I mulch strawberry plants with as a safeguard against root damage from ground freeze during the winter time, and also make sure that I have an ample protection for the berries against the soil when they bear fruit?

ANSWER—Strawberries benefit from mulching with clean hay. Oftentimes pine straw can be used, but in our vicinity prairie grass hay, or any type hay will work quite well. Place a covering over the plants so that it settles to a depth of about 3 inches. If the wind blows strong during the winter time, hold the mulch down with chicken wire.

Put the mulch on strawberries after the first light frost in the fall, but before severe frost begins, applying mulch too early (say in September or October) can do harm to the plant and interfere with the natural setting of fruit the next spring. As this mulch works on into the ground it will decompose, forming organic matter, which is of benefit to the plant itself. Black plastic mulch also proves to be very effective in controlling weeds and grass, conserving moisture plus protecting berries from direct contact with the soil.

QUESTION—What is Medina? Can it be used on all growing plants, trees, shrubs, lawns?

ANSWER—Medina is one of those new products that has made its advent upon the scene in the field of Gardening and Agriculture in recent years and though it's difficult to understand its nature and its workings; nevertheless, it's not difficult to understand the results obtained by using it. Simply stated, Medina is a culture of Soil-Micro-organisms in dormant forms, crystalline form which when applied to the soil in the presence of water become activated and also reactivate those already present in the soil to provide live, vigorous organisms of every known kind to be found in the healthiest of soils. These organisms are placed in an acid media under controlled conditions and are locked up and remain dormant until water is added to the media. The micro-organisms as well as the constituents that are added during the incubation period are properly controlled to produce a uniform balance of the various component parts of Medina. And we all know that the health and well being of all plants that grow in the soil, depend directly upon the functions of micro-organisms that make the plant food nutrients available. Medina is safe to use around all plants, and should be used on all soils. It's the one media that can over a period of time alleviate soil toxicity. The organisms in Medina that when cultured out in the soil attract the sodium and the chloride by breaking it into elementary sodium and the chlorine goes off into chlorine gas. The material is non-toxic whether applied in full strength or diluted form— of course nothing is to be gained by applying it in concentrate because a little goes a long way.

The proper application is to apply Medina in enough water to cover a 1,000 or 1,200 sq. feet broadcast in beds, lawns or vegetable garden. Around shrubs or trees, use 5 tablespoons of Medina to 1 gallon of water and use 1 gallon of this mixture per foot of height of the tree or shrub involved. Medina should be used twice in the spring and again in the fall and a good gardening program and it can be used to water house plants with by mixing 5 tablespoons to 1 gallon of water and watering the plants periodically with it.

Medina is a tool—it is not a cure all and should be used in a good management program; good fertility program and a good insect and disease program. When Medina is used you'll find that the micro-organisms which are cultured out give the soil a better tilth making it work easier. The soil will take in water better and retain it longer for use by the plants and plants on Medina treated soils are healthier, fruit more, mature earlier and produce a much higher quality crop. You'll also find that Medina activates the soil micro-organisms to free up fertilizer elements— Nitrogen, Phosphorus, Potash and Trace Elements and Medina will enhance the quality of the bloom and the fruit of your gardening crops. Results obtained with this product often times are phenomenal and a person has to work with it in order to appreciate the merits of this product. It's not a fast acter—it takes some 21 to 30 days before the cultures are activated and then given proper time and proper sequence; they'll do the job.

QUESTION—What can I use to put around the base of a Christmas tree to keep its foliage green, vital without excessive drying and dropping of the needles?

ANSWER—We have found that in a container of water—say ½ gallon of water in which the stump of the tree is placed when it is cut, add about 5 tablespoons of Medina and 1 teaspoon of Sequestrene Geigy Chelated Iron, the plant will absorb more moisture and stay green longer without excessive drying.

There is a new experimental product on the market that should be available almost immediately called Folicoat that's made available by Sun Oil and you mix this at the ratio of one to 20 and spray the tree before it's erected and this will put a waxy substance over the foliage and keep the needles from drying. This product can also be used on live plants at the same application rates—Azaleas, Gardenias, etc. in the peak of the summer months to cut down on excessive loss by transpiration. This product as this book goes to press is not available, but should be within a very short time.

235

QUESTION—What is Borena and is it good to use on trees?

ANSWER—Borena is a double water soluable, an insecticide non toxic to warm blooded animals but highly toxic to the borers in all types of trees. It features constitutents of Zylone and Zylene which actually are constituents of coal mixed in a double water soluable emulsion and sprayed directly onto the tree without dilution. It will penetrate to where the borer is located and kill it at its source. This product as stated is non-toxic and safe to use and should not be diluted to get maximum benefit.

QUESTION—Is there any product that can be used in the vegetable garden to control weeds and grass without affecting the plants that are growing?

ANSWER—For years we've blistered our hands pulling weeds out of gardens and flower beds and fighting with ineffectual results, but now a bright day has dawned for the gardener because there is a chemical compound known as Dacthal that can do the job highly effectively and with effect upon the existing plants. Dacthal is an Agricultural Product manufactured by Diamond Alkali but is available in some products made in the nursery field and available for the home gardener. This product has been cleared for over 30 different vegetables and a large number of flowers when applied according to the manufacturers' directions. It's safe to use.

QUESTION—Is there any product that can be used in an existing stand of grass that will control crab grass?

ANSWER—For years Gardeners have been waiting for a way to control crab-grass and especially in stands of San Augustine and Bermuda Grass, but now they have a herbicide that will do the job. That herbicide is called Symazine. It's a product of Geigy generally available in some formulated products mixed with fertilizer so that when you put the fertilizer out, the symazine will penetrate the soil and then be taken up by the seedling root systems of crab grass and will kill it before it reaches over 2 inches high. The major important factor about using this crab-grass killer is to make sure that you apply it early enough in the winter months so that it penetrates the soil into the seed and root zone before the seedling sprouts. This should be done probably in February.

QUESTION—Will aluminum foil repel aphids?

ANSWER—According to some experimental work done at Beltsville, Md. at the U.S.D.A. Agricultural Research Service, Aluminum Foil when placed as a mulch around the base of plants did repel aphids. In fact, it proved so feasible that one Aluminum foil manufacturer is going into production of a soil foil. The scientists are not sure as to what causes the aphids to be repelled, but undoubtedly it has something to do with metallics or the effect of the magnetic field being exerted through the aluminum foil being felt by the aphids. Nevertheless in the future, rather than applying insecticides to plants, you may apply aluminum foil to the row in which they grow and the foil in turn will reflect the sun's rays back into the leaves aiding the plants in the photosynthesis process plus at the same time repelling aphids and perhaps other insects.

QUESTION—What is agaskarising?

ANSWER—Agaskarising is a term which means that you give the plant electrified water. Wherever a growing part is given such a mannel of electrified water, its growth is in most instances increased. This is more than just irrigation which is watering the roots only—the water is electrified by taking it into an earthen ware container and placing that container on a rubber mat and then dipping one end of a high tension cable into the water while the other end is hooked onto the ignition of a motor car and the engine runs for one minute. One should make very careful that the wire leading from the plug over the fender is insulated so that the spark or the electrical charge does not transmit to the car body instead of to the water as it is supposed to be done. In doing this, they say that the water somehow, someway enhances the productivity of the plants as much as 20% in growth and yield.

QUESTION—What good are earthworms in soil?

ANSWER—For years we have come to believe that earth worms' primary purpose in the soil is soil aeration so that the water can percolate and air can enter. But now, from a research station in New Zealand, scientists reveal that earthworms emit as yet an unidentified substance which does stimulate the growth of plants. The effect of the compounds as yet unidentified that are secreted by the earthworms serves as a stimulating compound to the plant. The higher the concentration, the faster the plant grows. So, as to what these substances are we do not know, but they must be growth hormones in a fashion that are taken up by the root system to stimulate the plant. Now, remember if your garden or flower beds are void of earth worms, the quickest and fastest way to get an infestation of these wonderful creatures of nature is to apply Medina and add plenty of organic matter and you'll have earthworms galore.

QUESTION—I've heard that there is a new way of starting rose cuttings by freezing the cuttings—is this true?

ANSWER—An old gardener recently told me that the quickest way to start a rose cutting is by freezing it. Here is the technique—take an 8 to 10 inch scion from a cane of a rose that you want to propagate making sure that it has 3 or 4 thorns on it. Remove all foliage from the cutting and place this in the freezer of the refrigerator or your deep freeze and leave until it's frozen thoroughly. This may take from 30 minutes to 1 hour. Then, take the cutting and place in the flower bed where you want it to grow. Rather than planting it upright, place it laterally in a trench in the soil and cover over with a light fill of sandy loam soil. It will perhaps be better if you will do this during the early spring months when the flush of growth is bringing forth most of our plants with green foliage. The old gardener told me that from each thorn would come the sprouts for the new rose and you'll have a much healthier, faster growing rose by using this technique than any other. Remember, leave the new rose in place for at least one year before you attempt to move it and he says this is the simplest, easiest way to start a rose from a cutting.

Index

W

watermelon diseases 217
white grub 189
white marked tussock moth 189
white wash formula 223, 224
walking stick 188
walnut caterpillar 188
wasps 188, 189, 191, 192
weed control 236

wettable powder 195
white fly 156
wireworms 189, 190

Y

yellow flesh peaches 63
yew podocarpus 94

Z

zineb 204, 208